Calvinism versus Democracy

*Timothy Dwight and the Origins of
American Evangelical Orthodoxy*

Calvinism
versus
Democracy

Timothy Dwight and the Origins of
American Evangelical Orthodoxy

BY

STEPHEN E. BERK

ARCHON BOOKS
1974

Library of Congress Cataloging in Publication Data

Berk, Stephen E.
  Calvinism versus democracy.

  Bibliography: p.
    1. Dwight, Timothy, 1752-1817. 2. Calvinism—
United States. 3. Evangelicalism—United States. I.
Title.
BX7260.D84B47   285'.8'0924[B]   73-20053
  ISBN 0-208-01419-5

©1974 by Stephen E. Berk
First published 1974 as an Archon Book,
an imprint of The Shoe String Press, Inc.,
Hamden, Connecticut 06514

Printed in the United States of America

Contents

Preface

In the early years of the American republic, democracy was not yet a national ideal. Many citizens, and particularly those who had been reared in Puritan New England, felt uncomfortable with popular self-government and a pluralistic society. When a movement for democracy crystallized around the person and ideas of Thomas Jefferson, conservative reaction occurred largely in the old strongholds of Calvinism. The American Calvinist tradition, which flourished in Massachusetts and Connecticut, was rooted in a somber view of human nature. Puritans believed that without the gift of God's mercy, man can only behave sinfully. The doctrine of innate human depravity led them to place severe restrictions on conduct in order to control the indulgence of sensual appetites. With the Bible as their guide, magistrates and ministers cooperated as guardians of the public morals. Without such paternal supervision, New Englanders believed their communities would fly to pieces. Common, lustful people viii

needed the stern, benevolent guidance of a well-educated, refined element. American Puritans supported a traditionally deferential society not unlike some of the Old World aristocracies. The gentry of New England served throughout the colonial period as legal custodians of a distinct way of life. Leading families in the commonwealths of Massachusetts and Connecticut shared responsibility for governing and educating the people. They were charged with the preservation of a godly order, based on popular subordination and adherence to a strict moral code.

Other American colonies also developed ruling gentries and deferential standards. But New England clung to its aristocratic arrangements as circumstances were breaking them down elsewhere. To be sure, economic opportunity and the ideology of the Revolution had levelling effects in the Puritan commonwealths, as they had in Pennsylvania and Virginia. But the Calvinistic social orders generated a much stronger resistance to democratization and its accompanying institutional pluralism. This study examines that resistance and its lasting ramifications in American culture.

Timothy Dwight, a latter-day Puritan minister and educator was a major architect of post-Revolutionary American conservatism. Ardently committed to existent New England institutions, he devised new means for preserving them. Dwight epitomized the New England Calvinist mind in an era of institutional transition. The Congregational gentry of Connecticut, to whose opinions he gave voice, were by and large members of the Federalist Party. As followers of Hamilton and Adams, they were far more concerned with keeping order than encouraging liberty. They were appalled at the ungodly democratic revolution in France, and their principal fear was that a similar upheaval would erupt in the United States, should Jefferson and his party come to power.

Dwight and the other Calvinist ministers based much of their world view on scriptural prophecy. They were particularly affected by the final book of the New Testament, a wholly prophetic document full of vivid and provocative imagery. Written in the name of the Apostle John, this book has alternately been called Revelation, The Book of Revelation, the Revelation of John, and the Apocalypse. Together with prophecies in the Old Testament Books of Daniel and Isaiah, it undergirded New Englanders conception of their place in the divine scheme of history. Since their migration in the 1630's, Puritans had viewed themselves as the planters of God's new Zion.

The Apocalypse figuratively delineated all the great events leading up to the millennium, or return of Christ. In the 1730's and '40's when a languishing Puritanism revived itself in the Great Awakening, New England Calvinists began to see their homeland as the place in which world renewal, and the reign of Christ on earth would commence. The Great Awakening spread beyond New England into the middle and southern colonies. One of its most lasting effects was a growing popularity of the idea that America was the harbinger of the millennium. The nationalism of the American Revolution strengthened many Christians' belief that their new Protestant country was destined to save the world. But New England Calvinists saw the skeptical philosophy and liberalism of the Enlightenment as a serious impediment to their redemptive mission. These impious European aberrations had to be checked before the millennium would arrive. Calvinists believed that social orders not founded on the principles of original sin and the redemption of Christ could only be in league with the devil. Millennial prophecy interprets history as a continuous war between God's faithful and the followers of satanic delusion. New England conservatives like Timothy Dwight placed their quarrel with pluralism and liberal democracy in this context.

As president of Yale College, Dwight was head of Connecticut's ecclesiastical establishment. As such, he took it upon himself to organize a crusade against what he and others considered a French-inspired conspiracy against God. To arrest democratic change, he resorted to evangelization. Revivalism had revitalized orthodoxy in the Great Awakening, but the spiritual descendents of that religious upsurge had largely fallen prey to ecclesiastical formalism. A generation of Congregational schoolmen had arisen to codify the strict Calvinist doctrines which had grown out of the Awakening. Pedantic logicians preached distilled formulas while passively waiting for God to intervene and revive the hearts of their congregations. The reasons behind the failure of these ministers are complex and receive scrupulous consideration in chapter four. In short, the Puritan heirs of the Awakening had fallen behind developments of their era. Americans were becoming more cosmopolitan and self-reliant, and any attempt to save the New England way had to reckon with such changes. The influence of the Puritan clergy had declined appreciably, and if they were to arouse their parishioners to the dangers of innovation, they had to adjust their theology to a more secular climate. Dwight met the challenge by discarding the supernaturalism of the Great Awakening and formulating a revised practical Calvinism. The content of his system is the subject of chapters five and six.

The Second Great Awakening, an evangelical movement which began at Dwight's Yale, was the outgrowth of his enterprising approach to religion. Unlike the earlier Awakening, it was not a spontaneous upwelling of faith, but a calculated endeavor, planned and executed by conservative evangelicals. As the acknowledged leader of this Protestant counter-reformation, Dwight did much

to set its tone and pace. His immediate concern was the
fate of a privileged Federalist-Congregational establishment in Connecticut. The Federalist Party, however, and
the aristocratic order it represented, eventually gave way
to the more open society of the Jeffersonians. If Dwight's
work applied only to an outmoded Puritan order, then it
would have died with Connecticut's religious establishment. But in his war for orthodoxy, he conceived of a
union of evangelical denominations. He called for interdenominational organizations to suppress vice and propagate "True Religion" throughout the nation. His disciples put this plan into effect in the "benevolent"
movement. Gearing Dwight's moral activism to a set of
new institutions, they succeeded in reestablishing an
orthodox creed for America. In the new orthodoxy, voluntary associations and persuasion replaced coercive ecclesiastical establishments. In this way, Dwight's goal of a
national evangelical faith was virtually accomplished.

Revivalists of the Second Great Awakening expanded
Dwight's promotional techniques to develop a standard
of morality for the United States. As the new orthodoxy
merged with practices which became known as "the American way of life," a self-righteous nationalism and a hostility
to alternative values became commonplace. Every nation
has its biases, and reformed Christianity is hardly responsible for our own. Moreover, evangelical Protestantism has
contributed many positive ideals to American culture. Its
abiding interest in humanitarian reform and a soul-
searching pursuit of moral perfection have bequeathed
a unique national capacity for self-criticism. Evangelicals
of diverse sects have frequently been inspired by Christian
conscience to fight against iniquity. The antislavery movement, for example, was carried on largely by evangelical
activists.

But while many evangelicals became involved in humanitarian reform movements, nineteenth century Protestantism developed an essentially conservative, middle class

outlook. Particularly after the Civil War, evangelical spokesmen grew increasingly attached to vested interests, as were orthodox New Englanders of Dwight's time. Today, growing numbers of evangelicals are critical of ethnocentrism and social complacency in their churches. They are moving to extricate orthodox Protestant Christianity from its connection with the competitive, individualistic shibboleths of American culture, and to restore a Gospel of mutual aid and compassion for the downtrodden.

The fusion of evangelical Protestantism with American cultural values really began to take shape in the Second Great Awakening. The pages which follow examine the emergence of a conservative American evangelical consensus in that early nineteenth century movement and the significant role of one man, Timothy Dwight, in its formation.

*   *   *   *

The author wrote this work from the point of view of a non-Christian. However, after having submitted it for publication, he experienced conversion to evangelical Christianity, the culmination of a long search for inner peace. While remaining critical of certain human failings in American revivalistic Protestantism, the author wishes here to affirm its overall spiritual basis. The Awakening which Timothy Dwight led was an honest, though sometimes overheated, Christian response to growing secularism. Orthodoxy's problems have stemmed not from the practices of evangelism and scriptural morality, but from an overly close connection with narrow cutural norms.

ACKNOWLEDGMENTS

This work was inspired by Sidney Earl Mead, with whom I had the honor of studying at the University of Iowa. He is one of the kindest and most compassionate people I have ever known. Since Professor Mead had written his 1942 monograph on Nathaniel Taylor, he felt that further research was needed on the origins of New School orthodoxy and the benevolent movement. He guided me toward an examination of Timothy Dwight, the major influence on Taylor. In looking at Dwight's career, it becomes possible to probe the early development of many lasting themes in Protestant American culture.

I have been influenced by the finely hewn thinking of Stow Persons, who also supervised my doctoral dissertation. He expounded his thesis on American gentility, its foundation in the colonial period, and gradual decline in the nineteenth century in a brilliant series of lectures at Iowa during the late 1960's. Recently, he has published an exhaustive work on this subject.

In helping me gather materials for research, the staffs of Yale's Sterling and Beinecke libraries were most alert and conscientious, I am particularly grateful to Ms. Judith Schiff of the Sterling manuscript division.

While I was at Yale during the 1969-70 academic year, and thus separated from my Iowa advisers, Professor Sydney Ahlstrom took time from his busy schedule to provide me with wise direction and criticism.

I am also indebted to Messrs. Robert Ferm, Gaspare Saladino, and John Herbert Giltner for giving me permission to incorporate material from their unpublished dissertations into my study.

The scholars of the Association for the Study of Connecticut History took an interest in my work while it was in thesis form and publicized it in their newsletter. Thanks are especially due to Freeman W. Meyer of Central Connecticut State College, who selected me to present a paper, "Calvinism Versus Democracy," at an Association meeting in November, 1972. He and other members have offered me much encouragement.

The final manuscript was typed by Dee Cerillo. Her husband, my colleague, Augustus Cerillo, Jr., shares an interest in American Religious History. Both Cerillos have been very helpful to me in my work.

The index was prepared by Anna Marie and Everett Gordon Hager, and I appreciate their efforts for this work.

Finally, I would like to express my deepest appreciation to my wife, Betsy Joan. She trekked with me from Boston to Iowa, and subsequently back to Connecticut, where she taught school in a New Haven suburb so that I could devote a full year exclusively to research and writing. Again, she was willing to pull up roots and journey to Long Beach, California, in 1970. Her abiding confidence in my creative ability has been a source of strength.

PART I
Religion and Social Control

CHAPTER I

The Emergence of Contention

American colonial history is largely a record of England's failure to transplant traditional institutions to a hostile environment. Availability of land and economic opportunity gradually levelled society and eroded aristocratic domination. The Revolutionary War was a watershed, separating two antagonistic social ideals. On the one side was the authoritarian commonwealth, with a clear distinction between rulers and ruled, or magistrates and freemen. On the other emerged the novel concept of popular sovereignty. American conditions had precipitated a change from representative aristocracy to representative democracy, the new form requiring many decades of growth, and not achieving maturity until the Jacksonian period.[1]

While denominational pluralism and social fluidity were facts of life in eighteenth-century America, many colonists were uncomfortable with institutional democratization. People are generally reticent to exchange familiar ways

for new and untried ones. Such cultural inertia gains
strength from the aversion of ruling interests to relinquish
their privileges. A parochial citizenry feeling secure in
tradition combines with upper classes desirous of retaining
power to serve together as guardians of the established
order.

A slow erosion of the older culture does occur, however,
as its forms lose relevance in a changing mode of life.
The Revolution concluded a century of gradually widening interests between Mother Country and colonies.
Americans, whose provincial legislatures had become
important governing bodies, responsive to their immediate
needs, balked at England's reassertion of parliamentary
authority in the 1760s. Revolutionary spokesmen rationalized their position with the theory of popular sovereignty
in a representative government. Formulating a political
concept suited to American conditions, they rejected the
contrary ideal of parliamentary sovereignty, which
threatened to curtail their long practiced political and
economic freedom.[2]

Independence set America loose from the fetters of
imperial control and was hence a boon to economic
growth. As wartime commerce and manufactures grew,
new entrepreneurs rose to prominence.[3] Gradually political leadership ceased to be the private preserve of small
groups of notables. The increasing dispersal of wealth
was creating a situation in which aristocratic interests
could no longer monopolize power.

As American society grew open and expansive, religious
institutions suited to a stratified system lost relevance.
Ecclesiastical establishments had functioned as the religious counterpart to political aristocracy. Traditional
state religions placed authority in the hands of minister
and magistrate, who ruled paternalistically over a docile
populace. But in revolutionary America, individuals often
felt stifled by close oligarchical supervision.

In New England, religious dissenters, many of whom were prosperous merchants and independent farmers, resented the exclusive rule of Congregationalism. Dissenters were second-class citizens, holding their privilege of worship from the established church. A self-perpetuating caste of Congregational leaders dominated every aspect of life, from economic enterprise to the educational process. As other sects gained prominence, their opposition to Congregational hegemony grew in intensity. In order to institutionalize *de facto* self determination, American revolutionaries had seized sovereignty from Parliament. After the war, democratic insurgents in old Puritan regions championed much the same cause. A factionalized society existed, and liberals sought to legalize dynamic pluralism by providing equal access to government for everyone. Their goal was to replace Congregational control with a new order of many denominational interests in equilibrium.

Connecticut became the center of confrontation between latter day Puritans and democratic insurgents.[4] Out of this battle came an elaborate apology for the traditional faith and culture of New England. Its chief architect was Timothy Dwight, Congregational minister and president of Yale College from 1795 to 1817. A resourceful defender of the faith, Dwight differed from most orthodox ministers in his preoccupation with social issues. His explicitly social theology added a new dimension to American Prottestantism which profoundly affected later generations. Though conceived in defense of a faltering, antidemocratic establishment, the evangelical system of Timothy Dwight had a practical flexibility which enabled it to transcend the provincial bounds of Puritan Connecticut. The specific content of Dwight's theology, its divergence from traditional orthodoxy, and its concrete relationship to an emerging American civilization are topics for subsequent examination. Suffice it to say here that the unique charac-

ter of Dwight's defense provided orthodoxy with a fresh
approach, adjustable to the needs of democratic pluralism. Prior to any consideration of Dwight and his cause,
it is important to outline the gradually lethal effects of
social change on Connecticut's Puritan institutions.[5] Thus
we may understand the course of events which led to the
Armageddon, at which Dwight believed he stood in 1795.

Puritanism, based as it was in the Calvinist conception
of the human condition, took a dim view of man's ability
to govern himself. Worldly pride, and selfishness were
inescapable characteristics of unregenerate humanity.
Moreover, the individual could do little to overcome his
sinful desires. Without the mediatorial agency of Christ,
and the resultant free gift of grace, it was impossible to
be virtuous. Only the saint was equipped to repress his
passions, and even he needed constant supervision, lest
he backslide. In Puritan society, the civil and ecclesiastical
arms of government cooperated to restrain all inhabitants
from temptation. Without such overarching authority,
passion would prevail and the social order would disin-
tegrate.

While New England Puritans often wrote and spoke of
liberty, they certainly intended no democratic or equalitarian meaning of the term. They referred to the liberty of
godly societies to follow divine commandments. John
Winthrop distinguished this "civil or federal" liberty
from the liberty which was "inconsistent or incompatible
with authority," condemning the latter as mere license.[6]
In the 1760s, the liberal Puritan Jonathan Mayhew justified resistance to the crown in terms of the Puritan concept of liberty. Disobedience to authority which violated
the strictures of God was both "lawful and glorious."[7]
Even the American Revolution could be supported as a
cause in keeping with Puritan liberty. If England's rulers
had failed to keep their covenant with God, if they were
interfering with regular, divinely-constituted govern-

ment in Massachusetts, then resistance was a God-given right. Puritan patriots did not, therefore, embrace the Revolution as a democratic movement. They merely regarded it as scrupulous resistance to unlawful authority. Puritans always expressed a deep aversion to democracy. In the seventeenth century, the influential clergyman John Cotton condemned it as a species of mob rule, taking pains to show that Massachusetts was an aristocracy, even though the people chose their own governors.[8] And in the Revolutionary epoch, orthodox ministers like Timothy Dwight, who wholeheartedly endorsed the American cause, opposed democracy as destructive of social order and contrary to the moral government of God. The ideal of popular self-government was disrespectful of established authority, setting the impassioned children to rule over the wise fathers. It would subvert public agencies for the constraint of brutish appetites and would dissolve social bonds in an orgy of self-indulgence. As a vehement enemy of democracy, Dwight felt a duty to defend the aristocratic institution of Puritan New England. By the late eighteenth century, however, the governmental structure which men like Dwight sought to preserve had deteriorated from authoritative guardian of the social covenant to a mere instrument for perpetuating the rule of one faction over a society which had splintered into numerous contending interests. As such, it had ceased to inspire the reverential obedience of a united community. Its legitimacy had been tainted by secularization and years of religious controversy.

Seventeenth-century Puritans had geared every aspect of their commonwealth to effect conversion. Consequently they considered sumptuary legislation necessary to curb the lusts of natural man and prepare him to receive grace.[9] Civil and ecclesiastical officials worked together to control acquisitive behavior. But the cetrifugal lure of land, and the open field for commercial enterprise were forces which defied arrest. Such disintegrative tendencies preyed upon New England from the beginning; almost two centuries passed before the heirs of Puritan ecclesiasticism were forced to acknowledge their failure to contain a relentlessly expansive society within a crumbling old fortress.

Eighteenth-century Connecticut witnessed continual exertion of Congregational church and state, the "Standing Order," to reassert its eroding authority. Enactment of the Saybrook Platform; repression of the Great Awakening; the New Light campaign against heresy; and finally the orthodox crusade against infidelity and democracy— all these reactions to change illustrate a Puritan obsession with the need to impose strict doctrinal and behavioral controls.

The rising commercial spirit in early eighteenth-century Connecticut generated a passion for land. Many backsliding farmers, seeking economic advancement, moved into outlying regions, beyond the pale of magisterial oversight. Often full-scale migrations occurred, and new settlements arose.[10] But since heresy posed an ever-present threat to community well being, the isolated parish provided no assurance that it would not stray from orthodoxy.

To insure religious uniformity, the Congregational leadership of Connecticut enacted the Saybrook Platform in 1708. The new arrangement expunged congregational autonomy, and centralized authority in a set of ministerial councils called consociations. Thereby, the sole democratic factor in the Puritan Commonwealth was eliminated. In the early years of New England, magistrates and *ad hoc* synods operated as custodians of orthodoxy. But since these powers had lost much of their effectiveness in a more dispersed and less homogeneous society, the Standing Order resorted to increased ecclesiasticism. Maria L. Greene, in her history of Connecticut religious development, notes that the Saybrook Platform "replaced the sympathetic help and advisory assistance of neighboring churches by organized associations and by the authority of councils." Such "rigid formalism in religion" actually helped destroy the very piety it was supposed to stimulate.[11] As the lure of wealth increased, vital religion declined into ritual, and the churches slowly lost their hold on society despite their frequent efforts to affirm spiritual leadership. But ecclesiasticism was a singularly ineffective means of recalling wayfaring fortune seekers to their eternal concerns. Piety returned on a broad scale only when prophetic figures arose to answer spiritual and psychological needs which orthodoxy had ceased to fulfill.

The Great Awakening grew out of social and religious conflict with civil and ecclesiastical authority and served to exacerbate existent disharmony among the various elements of society. Such party strife undermined the prescribed function of church and state, completing the transformation of these structures into the mere spoils of factional officeseeking. Richard Bushman's study of social change in eighteenth-century Connecticut finds the origin of the Great Awakening in economic conflict. A merchant aristocracy, in the older sections of the colony, had come to dominate the provincial government. When entrepreneurs in developing regions began to seek legislative accommodations, the controlling mercantile faction sought to inhibit these competitors by resorting to sumptuary regulations. As a result, the newer merchants often found themselves in conflict with vested authorities. In order to pursue their interests, they often had to disobey governmental restrictions on speculation and economic expansion. In Puritan theory however, Connecticut was an organic commonwealth, and its political leaders represented the common good. Disobedience to their will was sinful, since it stemmed from placing one's private interests above the wise prescriptions of God's ordained

authorities. Hence, many new merchants suffered pangs
of guilt and remorse as they contradicted government
proscription. Bushman has found that the Great Awakening was most pervasive in areas of the colony where opposition to legislative policy was strongest.[12]

In viewing the essence of religion as subjective, rather
than organizational, evangelicals of the 1740s drew a
sharper distinction than did traditional Puritans between
moralistic behavior and divine illumination. Religion
became more privatized, leaving individuals free, at least
in a psychological sense, to go their entrepreneurial way
without disabling fear of thereby compromising their
chances for salvation. Ministers thundering strict Calvinist decrees that an omnipotent God has arbitrarily predestined an elect few to receive Christ, drew cathartic
reponses from Guilt-ridden parishioners. For if God is
the sole author of spirituality, then every human being,
no matter how sinful, may hope for eternal life. The convert's anxiety over worldliness became expunged by a
sense of dependence on, faith in, and love for a merciful
God.

New Light revivalism, with its stress on the personal
elements in religion, became a greatly disruptive force
within the ecclesiastical establishment. Many historians
have chronicled the bitter confrontations between evangelical pietism and rationalistic moralism in eighteenth-
century New England.[13] The Great Awakening split
Puritanism into four antagonistic factions. On Connecticut's evangelical side were New Light Congregationalists,
who sought to control the Standing Order. In addition,
however, were Baptists and Separatists, who shared the
evangelical fervor of the Awakening, but who stalwartly
rejected ecclesiasticism. While in the minority, these
groups were more consistent in their pietism than were
the New Light contestants for domination of the establishment. They understood the contradiction between political
and administrative concerns, and spontaneous experience.

Consequently, as one historian has pointed out, New England's Baptist and Separatist churches enjoyed revivals throughout the eighteenth century, while Congregationalists, embroiled in doctrinal controversy, failed to maintain the subjective piety of the Awakening.[14] New Light establishmentarians developed an elaborate theology to defend the Great Awakening against its detractors, and to gain the offensive in their fight for orthodox supremacy. Referring to themselves as New Divinity men, or Consistent Calvinists, these ministers became increasingly involved in polemical controversy and ecclesiastical in-fighting, much to the detriment of their parishioners.

Their opponents were the Arminians and Old Calvinists, who had opposed the revivals excessively emotional exercises in self-delusion. Both of these groups perceived religion in more moralistic and less evangelical terms. The Old Calvinists were the heirs of traditional New England Puritanism. While holding, in good Calvinist fashion, that God is the sole author of grace, they also claimed, as did their seventeenth-century forebears, that unregenerate man can do much to prepare his heart for spirituality. Hence, they accentuate the religious ordinances known as the Means of Grace. In their view, God requires fallen man to hear the Word, pray for forgiveness, study the scripture, and endeavor to lead a moral life. In this way, one prepares his heart to receive the Holy Spirit. Old Calvinists disclaimed any necessary connection between preparation and salvation; but they also maintained that God usually santifies hearts that have been adequately prepared. Hence, distrusting the emotional subjectivity of conversion experiences, they preferred to place their faith in a God who prescribes rational requirements for religion.[15]

Arminians held much the same objection to revivalism as the Old Calvinists. They too viewed religion in terms of adherence to scriptually imposed duties. But they went

further in their moralism than the Old Calvinists, drawing a closer connection between attendance to the means
of grace and regeneration of the heart. Consistent Calvinists accused Arminians of blatantly preaching justification through works, the cardinal heresy to all Protestants.
Moreover, they accused the Old Calvinists of tending in
the same direction. Both antirevivalist factions denied this
claim, asserting that God does not save sinners because
they attend to means, but those who receive divine mercy
have usually been scrupulous in their religious obser-
vances.

If Consistent Calvinism was the most supernaturalist
position among eighteenth-century Puritans, Arminianism was the most man-centered. While New Divinity men
stressed the sinner's total dependence on God, Arminians
preached a more self-reliant and moralistic theology. Adjusting to the temper of a secularizing if not complacent
society, they enjoyed their chief appeal in the relatively
cosmopolitan Boston area. Connecticut's evangelicals
faced no direct threat from the Arminians. Their ecclesiastical battle was primarily with the Old Calvinists. But
because the Arminian camp contained the most aggressive
opponents of the Awakening, some of whom were prolific
writers, Connecticut's New Divinity men often engaged
them in debate. Regarding Arminians as dangerous here-
tics, and Old Calvinists as covert Arminians, they fought
a long, bitter dispute which involved the Congregational
clergy throughout New England.

The Great Awakening was a movement involving most
of the American colonies. Awakeners held millennialist
pretensions, regarding their critics as serious impediments
to worldwide evangelization. Thus, New Divinity men in
Connecticut never restricted themselves to purely local
matters, nor did their counterparts in Massachusetts or
the middle colonies. Evangelical Protestantism has always
evinced cosmic designs, and the first American movement

was certainly no exception. It set the pattern for later awakenings, all of which have been intentionally national and ultimately international in scope.

Because the Great Awakening began as a spontaneous popular movement involving challenge to authority, it is tempting to the historian to interpret this religious phenomenon as a harbinger of populistic democracy. One writer, Alan Heimert, has even gone so far as to say that Consistent Calvinism was an early expression of Jeffersonian-style democracy. Heimert stresses the fervor with which New Light ministers appealed to the hearts of common people. He also lays heavy emphasis on the ideal of "Christian Union," which grew out of the Awakening, viewing it as an initial expression of a tolerant denominational pluralism. On the other hand, he views the Arminians and Old Calvinists as defenders of an aristocratic establishment, disdainful of the mass appeal and broad participation in the revivals. But consideration of post-Awakening developments in Connecticut reveals this thesis to be entirely without foundation. If New Light ministers spoke of Christian union, they meant not denominational or doctrinal pluralism, but the uniform consent of all nations to a single Calvinistic interpretation of Gospel truth. Although revivalism once again made conversion the basis of church membership, and regeneration strictly an affair between man and God, this development in no way led Congregational Awakeners to espouse any doctrine of religion by popular consent. On the contrary, they continued to regard coercive establishments as a neccessary means for promoting the faith and expunging heresy. Their immediate task, as they saw it, was to gain control of existing establishments.[17]

The intent to establish a new orthodoxy engendered the New Light campaign to take over Connecticut's Standing

Order. Old Calvinists, holding a similar commitment to
religious orthodoxy, sought to suppress revivalism. Enjoying control of the consociations, the colonial legislature, and educational system, they made strong efforts
to counteract their evangelical opponents. Legislation
against itinerant preaching, and consociational maneuvering to keep evangelical ministers out of pulpits were
among the measures used to curtail the ecclesiastical impact of the Awakening. But the New Lights made steady
progress in their campaign for orthodoxy. Yale's President
Clap was a pivotal figure in the prolonged battle. During
the Awakening, he had been an ardent opponent of experimental religion, doing his utmost to arrest its influence within the student body. But as the fires of the Awakening died down and New Light revivalism crystallized
into New Divinity doctrine, Clap's position began to
change. He had feared the ecclesiastical chaos, and disrespect for established authority which had characterized
the Great Awakening at its height. But since New Lights
had come to support the Saybrook system, and since they
were rapidly gaining power within the Standing Order,
Clap began to feel less threatened by their presence. In
1750, when New Lights succeeded in getting the law against
itineracy revoked, Clap joined their ranks. Together with
Joseph Bellamy, an energetic ecclesiastical politician and
major advocate of the New Divinity, Clap conducted a
war on "heresy." Imposing a test for religious orthodoxy
in the college, Clap used this instrument to remove Old
Lights from the Yale Corporation.

By the 1760s, New Lights had gained control of the
Connecticut legislature, and New Divinity men had become dominant in the consociations. In no sense were
these heirs of the Awakening any more tolerant of religious
dissent than their predecessors. While they had opposed
the old orthodoxy, their goal had merely been to construct
a new one. Bellamy epitomized the new establishment in

his stalwart opposition to Separatism. The Separatists had played an active role in the Great Awakening, but, like the Baptists, they deplored ecclesiastical establishments. Revivalistic emphasis on the individual relationship with God grew out of, and justified opposition to, the authoritarian church and state sanctioned at Saybrook. As such, continued growth of the evangelical impulse demanded at least the autonomy of congregations. Early New Lights had joined with Separatists and Baptists in arguing for such independence. But fusion of the New Divinity with centralized orthodoxy undercut its pietistic basis.[18]

The lure of ecclesiastical power set evangelical ministers on the highway to priestly rationalism. Their faith became less spontaneous and subjective, and more abstract and doctrinal. The personal element all but vanished from the new orthodoxy, as its adherents sought to consolidate their power by campaigning against all forms of religious dissent. Vilifying their Old Calvinist opponents as converts to Arminian moralism, New Divinity men fought doggedly to keep them out of pastorates.[19] In this manner, they undermined their millennial intentions by drowning revivalistic fervor in a sea of factional dispute.

By the time of the Revolutionary War, evangelical religion in Connecticut had reached a low ebb. The tumultuous secular changes of that period indicate a preoccupation with nonreligious matters. The Standing Order had become largely a New Divinity stronghold which granted grudging toleration to opposing sects. While resisting Old Calvinist involvement in the establishment, the new orthodoxy gave customary permission to Episcopalians, Baptists, Separatists, and other groups of Christians to support their own churches. But in no sense did this situation approximate democratic pluralism, for New Divinity advocates held supremacy both in secular and religious spheres.

Ezra Stiles, who succeeded Clap as president of Yale,

was the only figure in high office to espouse a somewhat heterodox ecclesiastical position. Sympathizing with the declining Old Calvinist party, he expressed the sentiments of an enlightened liberal. Stiles believed that no one sect possessed a monopoly on doctrinal truth; hence he saw the need for a tolerant society, allowing a diversity of religious opinion. Out of the interaction of numerous interpretations of divinity would ultimately flow true religion.[20] Not unlike the belief of Justice Holmes in a free trade of ideas, the ecumenism of Stiles corresponded to the theory of liberal democracy. He had opposed the Old Lights' suppression of revivalism, and he similarly disliked the evangelicals' war on heresy. In fact, having a distaste for the generally coercive orthodoxy of consociations,[21] he upheld the right to congregational independence in the choosing of ministers. The liberality of President Stiles was a more truly catholic ideal than that of the New Divinity. Their concept of catholicity consisted in worldwide adherence to their own doctrines. But Stiles was a unique personality in Connecticut Congregationalism. After the Revolution, under the leadership of his successor, Timothy Dwight, orthodoxy was to make its most strenuous attack on democratic pluralism.

Dwight was born in 1752 and grew to maturity during the period of New Light ascendancy. Graduating from Yale in the class of 1769, he attended that school a few years after Clap had made it a repository of New Light sentiment. As a ministerial candidate, Dwight absorbed the prevailing faith of the Great Awakening. He was a grandson of Jonathan Edwards, the greatest luminary of that movement. While serving as a tutor at Yale, he studied theology with his uncle, Jonathan Edwards the younger.[22] The second Edwards, a dogmatic, uninspiring champion of the New Divinity occupied a pulpit in New Haven from

1768 until 1795. Dwight's tutelage with him was probably brief and informal. His early biographers neglect to mention it, and one writer presumes that Dwight prepared himself for the ministry.[23] Nevertheless, the young scholar began his career as a firm advocate of Consistent Calvinism. Edwards preached the sermon at his ordination.

In the post-Revolutionary years, New Divinity men stood as victorious exemplars of Connecticut orthodoxy. But the religious establishment which they had fought so long to control was about to undergo its greatest challenge. The new subversion came not so much from the moralistic Old Calvinists or Arminians but from far more radical forces. Secular democracy, with its pluralistic tolerance of deism, skepticism, and Unitarianism, was now the serpent in Eden. The Puritan order's struggle for survival under the adroit leadership of Timothy Dwight, forms the heart of this study.

CHAPTER II

The New American Jerusalem

The elaborate efforts of Timothy Dwight and other members of the orthodox establishment generated an aggressive evangelical counterreformation known as the Second Great Awakening. Full comprehension of the Calvinist response to democratization demands examination of the millennial world view. The apocalyptic interpretation of history provided a strong rationale for both defense of the Standing Order and the unabated growth of evangelical religion during the first half of the nineteenth century.

Reformation theology had revived the long dormant notion of a militant church contending for the ultimate establishment of Christ's Kingdom on earth.[1] Based in the Old Testament prophecies of Daniel and Isaiah, and in the Revelation of John, millenial doctrine envisioned a world gradually made tranquil, free and holy by diffusion of Gospel Truth. The Book of Revelation, or Apocalypse, transforms Hebrew messianism into the second coming of Christ and allegorically depicts the providential cataclysms of history, which are to prepare mankind for this great event. The figurative language of the Apocalypse made conflicting interpretations inevitable, and while the Medieval Church accepted the Augustinian exegesis, Reformers of the sixteenth century posited an entirely new one. For Augustine, who lived in a time of social upheaval and disintegration, the world could never be redeemed. As the realm of Satan, it would only grow more evil, suffering final destruction when Christ descends to carry off his converted saints to the City of God. The Reformation introduced a progressive version of millennialism, in which Christians would battle and slowly overcome the machinations of the devil on earth. A militant church contending for the faith, subduing God's enemies, and thereby gradually restoring the world to its prelapsarian state, became the eschatological perspective of Protestantism.

Reformed theologians viewed their break with Rome as a most crucial cosmological event, for they believed the Medieval Church to have been a diabolical conspiracy for the idolatrous enslavement of mankind. The Reformation had liberated God's children from the dark ages of Babylonian captivity, enabling them to reclaim the evangelizing mission of the apostles. Satan was still active, but apocalyptic prophesy gave Protestants confidence in their eventual triumph. The convert viewed himself and his church as the sanctified means of God's predestined victory. The Holy Spirit would animate the whole of humanity in Christian love. With Satan conquered and bound in hell the world would be rid of war, pestilence, and famine. Such millennial bliss would last a thousand years, after which God would again unchain the devil, allowing him to permeate the earth with strife and discord. At length, the forces of darkness would meet the soldiers of Christianity in a great battle. This final convulsion would presage the end of the world, when Christ would descend and

execute the Last Judgment. The Son of God would sepa-
ate the faithful from the unrepentant, whom He would
banish to the realm of everlasting misery. All temporal
dominions would then be consumed in fire, and the redeemed would be drawn into the eternal happiness of
heaven.

Colonial and early national America were almost exclusively Protestant. The continent served as a new Eden,
where diverse sectarian heirs of the Reformation could
pursue the cause of Christ by creating pious earthly communities. Puritan New England had furthered this ideal,
and, on a more expansive plane, the revivals of the Great
Awakening had also aimed at Christian brotherhood as
the means for bringing on the millennium. Following a
period of dormancy which accompanied the demise of the
Puritan covenant, the millennial faith resurged with great
vitality as the creed of evangelical Calvinism. Heimert,
while dangerously misconstruing the meaning of Christian
union, furnishes a valuable insight into the relationship
between the religion of the Great Awakening and the
genesis of American nationalism. He argues that inter-
colonial cooperation among revivalists and their primary
concern with forging bonds of love among all Americans
was an important factor in unifying the colonies. Heimert
views the millennialism of the evangelicals as of paramount importance to their faith, and it is clear that theologians of the Awakening, such as Jonathan Edwards,
Joseph Bellamy, and Samuel Hopkins ardently believed
in the millennial portent of their work.[2]
   The Revolutionary experience fired an American belief
in the nation's special mission to reclaim the world for
Christian freedom and brotherhood. God seemed to have
showered the bounty of Paradise on the virtuous republic.

Successful resistance to the arms of a corrupt empire would set the United States on her millennial course. The New England clergy, firmly devoted to the national cause,[3] considered their country a special recipient of Heaven's blessing; and a young Connecticut minister was moved to praise America in sermon and verse.

Shortly after independence was declared, Timothy Dwight, then in his tutorship, was appointed to deliver a valedictory address at Yale's summer commencement. In his discourse, the twenty-four year old patriot proclaimed the redemptive mission of his native land. Giving voice to the major themes of American nationalism, he saw the United States as both a new Eden and a latter-day Zion.[4] The paradisaical characterization of America was common to Christian and non-Christian spokesmen alike. Freethinking Jeffersonians and Transcendentalists would praise the salutary effects of the American environment.[5] Moreover, it had been natural since the earliest years of colonization to perceive the untrammeled continent in this manner.[6] Dwight therefore echoed a universal sentiment of his countrymen when he declared that this luxuriant Eden is indeed "the favorite land of heaven."[7]

The young orator seems to have known that this idea was not original, for he proceeded to reveal the crux of his message in a more novel interpretation of American destiny. Rapidly concluding his remarks on environmental salubrity, he stressed that "the fairest part of the scene is yet to be unfolded." The most important advantages of the new nation were not so much natural, as social and political. Confidently, Dwight predicted that superior manners and morals of Americans would endow "the grestest empire the hand of time ever raised up to view."[8] The United States was to be the liberator of enslaved peoples from tyranny and superstition. Not leaving the ways of accomplishing this holy task to the imagination of his audience, he went on to recommend a course of action for a benevolent empire.

The Spanish inhabitants of the South and West extremities were "as vicious, luxurious, mean-spirited, and contemptible a race of beings as any that ever blackened the pages of infamy." So long as these miserable creatures languished under the cruelty of a "tyrannous government . . . rendered ten times more horrible by the infernal dominion of an abandoned priesthood," they would remain the mere "refuse of mankind." Dwight's solution to this problem reveals the double-pronged tactics of his millennialism. He called for revival of Spanish Americans "to the native human dignity by the beneficient influence of just laws and rational freedom." But should these degraded beings be so audacious as to resist their Protestant benefactors, they must be "entirely exterminated."

Worldwide freedom and happiness, he continued, could only occur under uniform principles of government. One body of "truth" must animate humanity, for pluralistic empires had been ". . . the parents of endless contest, slaughter, and desolation."[9] The new American empire was to unify many nations under a single political and religious system. While Dwight envisioned a vast realm of freedom and enlightenment, his conception of liberty and knowledge was akin to the Puritan ideal that each individual be free to receive instruction in a single set of beliefs. A monistic world view, based on Calvinism, would unify the subjects of this last great empire.

Tapping the patriotism of the Yale graduates, many of whom were about to enter the Continental Army, Dwight explicitly welded his aggressive millennialism to a popular historical perspective of the time. Recalling the cyclical view of history, he said, "It is very common and a just remark that the progress of liberty, of science, and of empire has been with that of the sun, from east to west, since the beginning of time." Each successive empire, he went on, was more glorious than the preceding one. Hence, in America, "the progress of temporal things towards perfection will undoubtedly be finished." Citing American advancement in human rights and the diffusion of learning through every class of people, he concluded that "this continent will be the principal seat of the new, that peculiar kingdom, which shall be given to the Saints of the Most High." For the remainder of his address, he exhorted the young men to perform their various temporal occupations so as best to promote the glory of God and their country.[10]

This first publication of the future Yale president clearly portrayed the duality of American millennialism. On the one hand, the millennium would be, as Samuel Hopkins stated, an era of brotherly cohesion, profuse knowledge, and prosperity. But such a joyous state of affairs was not to come about through peaceful persuasion. Evil was ubiquitous and had to be forcefully suppressed. Thus Dwight would call for "extermination," if necessary, to convert the world to the one true faith. Righteous battle for the Lord was an essential ingredient in this millennialist cauldron, and military imagery often spiced the evangelical sermon.[11] Beneath the cosmic optimism and praise for America's free and just society in Dwight's rhetoric lay a narrow interpretation of freedom and justice. Dwight's faith in his country as the embodiment of these ideals would last only so long as his kind of order continued to hold sway.

During the Revolution and immediately afterward, he retained his belief in the sanctity of American institutions. But it was unlikely at this time that he should turn a critical eye on his own nation. His energies, like those of his fellow citizens, were concentrated on the war, and later internal disputes which would so provoke his ire were still submerged in a spirit of patriotic unity.

Dwight's subsequent works of the Revolutionary epoch

elaborated his belief that God had chosen Americans to
establish His Kingdom on earth. In 1777, while serving as
army chaplain, he preached a sermon in celebration of
the decisive American victory at Saratoga. His words had
a ring of Zionism reminiscent of his early Puritan forebears. Only Palestine, he said, had enjoyed such "extraordinary interpositions of Providence" as Americans were
receiving in their battle for independence. Although such
blessings were tokens of God's approval of the United
States, Dwight admonished his countrymen that the
national covenant enjoined obedience to the Creator;
failure to keep His commandments would call forth
divine wrath. "Nothing obstructs the deliverance of
America, but the crimes of its inhabitants." Only, therefore, if Americans lived up to their holy commission, would
they retain their millennial agency. Only on these terms
would ". . . independence and happiness [be] fixed upon
the most lasting foundations; and that Kingdom of the
Redeemer . . . highly exalted and durably established
on the ruins of the Kingdom of Satan." It was, then, quite
possible for the nation to fall from grace, and such was
the apostasy which Dwight would spend the better part
of his life resisting.[12]

Scholars who have analyzed the poetic efforts of
Timothy Dwight have found his verse banal and thoroughly derivative. Poetry writing was incidental to
Dwight's career and certainly of far less importance than
his accomplishments as pedagogue and religious leader.
Nevertheless, his verse bears significance as a barometer
of his feelings. In the Puritan idiom, he wrote preeminent-
ly for didactic purposes.[13] But the moral lessons of his
poetry were often purer manifestations of emotion than
were those of his more rationally argued sermons. Poetic
expression possessed a certain kinship with the evangeli-

cal religion of the affections. In his introduction to *Green-field Hill*, he noted the utility of verse as a means of enlightening many "who would scarcely look at logical discussion." Like revival preaching, it would touch the heart and would "by most readers . . . be more deeply felt and lastingly remembered" than other forms of instruction.[14] Poetry was then a supplementary implement in Dwight's store of techniques for persuading his compatriots to correct beliefs.

One of his earliest narratives was entitled *America: or a Poem on the Settlement of the British Colonies; Addressed to the Friends of Freedom and their Country.* Written before Dwight's ordination,[15] its theme is millennial nationalism based in provincial ancestor worship. The New England patriarchs had given freedom and order to a savage continent wrapped for eons in the gloom of ignorance. Subduing the aboriginal forests, they had introduced virtuous cultivation and had taught their children and many of the turbulent natives the moral value of the Protestant work ethic.

But as Satan was ever-present, his seductive influence early threatened this tranquil pastoral scene. After depicting the bloodthirstiness of depraved Indian marauders, Dwight proceeds to the diabolic schemes of "Romish" Frenchmen to undo the godly community of British colonists. In Reformation terms, the French and Indian Wars were not only part of a great struggle for empire between the two chief powers of the western world. The Protestant mind perceived this conflict as an aspect of the cosmic war between saints and the papal antichrist. But Generals Wolfe and Amherst, God's instruments for furthering His holy Kingdom, destroyed the infernal foe and returned the American continent to the dominion of piety. Now America was free to fulfill her predestined role as a new Zion.

At this point, Dwight prophesies a holy war to be fol-

lowed by a reign of peace, and universal material progress,
spearheaded by a pious America. "Through earth's wide
realms thy glory shall extend, and savage nation at thy
sceptre bend."[16] Following the millennium would come
the familiar Day of Judgement with the final dispensa-
tions of Christ. In this piece, Dwight says little of the last
great battle, choosing instead to concentrate on a lesser
war (probably the American Revolution). Dominated by
the issues of his time, he tended to adjust divine prophecy
to his preoccupation with the national cause.

This propensity more thoroughly dominates his next
major poetic effort, *The Conquest of Canaan*. A tiresome,
verbose attempt at Miltonic biblical epic, this piece, published in 1785, compares Joshua's victory over the heathen,
and Israelite entry into the promised land, with the sub-
stance of the American Revolution. Joshua is a brave,
humble leader, whose sole purpose is to carry out the revealed will of God. Dwight's generally implicit comparison of the Hebrew chieftain to General Washington
provoked criticism from British reviewers, whose occupa-
tion thus incurred his lifelong enmity.[17] London was
still the literary capital of the United States, and Pope,
Goldsmith and other English writers were the models for
American poetry of this period.[18] The hostile reception
of *The Conquest of Canaan* was therefore a severe blow to
the aspiring young bard. Dwight, however, must have had
some misgivings about his presumptuous comparison of
Joshua to Washington, and Israel to America, for he dis-
avowed this intent in a letter to his friend Noah Webster.
"The essential parts" of the poem, he claimed, "were finished before the war began."[19] But research has uncovered
Dwight's continual revisions of the epic throughout the
war period. Analysts of Dwight's poetry have found *The
Conquest* to be a collection of American heroes and cultural values cloaked in biblical garb.[20]

Despite his vehement denial of the reviewers' allegations, Dwight confided to Webster his belief in "a considerable resemblance between the cause of the Israelites, and that of the Americans." He in fact had dedicated *The Conquest* to Washington, and after the General's death, he would compare him to Moses. But in the eulogy of the first President, he would be careful to distinguish between national leaders under God's direct inspiration, and those who are only His pious human vehicles. Although this essential difference exists, we can, he would maintain, still discover similar qualities in the two kinds of moral agents.[21]

The parallel attributes in Dwight's Moses and Washington strongly suggest virtues he had seen in Joshua. All three were faithful servants of God; like the Calvinist Deity, they were stern and just, yet compassionate. Carrying righteous vengeance to God's enemies, they acknowledged their own utter dependence on Providence. Each of these paternal figures inspired the reverential obedience of his people. With God, they walked above petty discord. They were arbiters of their nations' quarrels; and their wise judgments carried the force of law. Dwight portrayed these patriarchal figures as human images of the Creator.

In Book Ten of *The Conquest of Canaan,* America is explicitly presented as the new, millennial Israel. Near the end of the ninth book, when Joshua is grief-stricken by the death of a comrade-in-arms, God appears to him with the consoling reminder that He has predestined all events for the ultimate good of the universe. The Most High then sends an angel to reveal the entire scope of human history before the eyes of the Israelite commander. First is depicted the tranquillity of the Promised Land. An account of ancient Israel ensues, replete with God's destruction of the backslidden nation. Following years of strife and complete disregard of moral obligation, fallen mankind once again becomes the object of divine mercy. Christ arrives bearing His gospel to universalize the promise of salvation. But sinners spurn the Redeemer and again call forth the wrath of God. While evil continues to plague the world, converted messengers of Christ slowly restore the temporal creation to holiness.

The vision's peak comes with the advent of the millennium, when a new western people shall be chosen to conclude the extension of virtue throughout humanity. A description of the new Eden follows, together with the concept of a last great empire based on freedom, truth, and virtue. Like ancient Israel, this redemptive nation would be born in righteous battle. "See mighty Justice lift his awful reign! Behold new Joshuas sway thy realms again!"[22]

In spite of Dwight's premonitions, the War for Independence was essentially a secular matter. Absorption of Americans in material concerns left them little energy for the pursuit of holiness. Dwight's Connecticut, during the war years, experienced the initial phases of economic revolution. Extensive privateering and the lucrative business of supplying a needful army were rapidly creating a powerful commercial class.[23] Historians have often noted the parallels between capitalist growth and the liberalization of religion.[24] Throughout the eighteenth century, Boston had witnessed the rise of Arminianism in a society increasingly dominated by prosperous merchants.[25] Connecticut, although it too had early experienced worldly disruption, was slower to secularize. Not until the Revolutionary era did the new state begin to lose its agrarian provincialism and enter a period of development which would, by 1800, establish it as "an integral part of regional, national, and international economies."[26] More frequent intercourse with neighboring states and with the world during this time opened the once homogeneous community to the influx of cosmopolitanism. Both the French and Indian, and the Revolutionary Wars spurred commercial agriculture and the shipping trade in Connecticut, thus encouraging a more acquisitive way of life. In his *Travels in New England and New York*, written after the turn of the century, Dwight mentions a marked rise in irreligion which had accompanied the two wars. He was not alone in his detection of widespread deism and skepticism. In 1780, during the height of a war-related economic boom, the General Association of Congregational Churches in Connecticut passed a resolution enjoining all pastors to lead their congregations in fasting, prayer, and repentance for the "awful Judgment of the Most High" on a "stupid and backsliding generation."[27] Edmund Morgan offers another explanation for religious decline in Revolutionary Connecticut. The New Divinity clergy, preaching doctrinal Calvinism in all its metaphysical obscurity, had alienated many parishioners and precipitated a wave of anticlericalism during the late 1760s and early '70s. Consistent Calvinist ministers were strict disciplinarians, often assuming dictatorial powers over their congregations. Several parishioners, feeling little sympathy with the rigors of high Calvinist dogma, left their churches. Attacks on the clergy, and on Yale College as the garden of New Divinity theology, became commonplace in Connecticut newspapers. "Anticlericalism did not necessarily lead to deism, but it furnished an atmosphere in which deism could grow as it never had before."[28] Morgan has documented the contiguous rise of deistic and anticlerical sentiments in the postwar years.[29] Wartime confusion and the plunder of many Congregational churches by an invading British Army also contributed to religious decline.[30] For all these reasons, Calvinistic orthodoxy was on the defensive in late eighteenth-century Connecticut.[31]

By the 1790s, liberal religion and "Infidel Philosophy"

had even wormed their way into Yale, the hitherto bastion
of orthodoxy. Lyman Beecher, Dwight's protégé, and one
of the most important figures of the Second Great Awakening, remarked on the popularity of French freethinking
with the students of the time.[32] For Dwight, the prevalence of such irreverence severely damaged the millennial
hope of the young republic. In the above-mentioned
Travels account, he attributes the growth of infidelity to
atheistic French influence during the Revolution and
exposure to British skepticism during the previous
American war.

Decline of Calvinist piety provoked Dwight to write
his most controversial piece, an anonymous poetic diatribe
entitled *The Triumph of Infidelity*.[33] As minister of a
rural parish at Greenfield Hill, he poured forth his venom
on evil sowers of disharmony among God's chosen people.
Far more impassioned and consequently less rational
than his later recollections of the causes for religious
lanquor, this narrative attributes conscious satanic
agency to everyone from the Old Calvinist minister to the
French-inspired skeptic. The main culprit is Charles
Chauncy, a Boston Arminian who had published an
unsigned discourse on universal salvation shortly before
his death, and thereby thrown open the gates for the
devil's entry into the American Eden. The poem in fact
is cast as an account by Satan himself of his means for
corrupting a once pious and happy continent. Dwight
dedicated the work to the French deist, Voltaire, whom he
considered a major infernal accomplice of the times. Like
The Conquest of Canaan, this epic is highly digressive.
It begins with Satan's arrival in America to subvert existent
"freedom, peace, and virtue," but becomes sidetracked in
explanation of the cosmic battle since the time of Con-
stantine.

Of prime significance are the disastrous social and

political consequences Dwight believed would flow from the propagation of Infidel ideas. In a footnote he maintains that "the same principles, which support or destroy Christianity, alike support or destroy political order and government."[34] To Dwight's mind, the turmoil of the Confederation period was occasioned by a popular and licentious infidelity. Since Puritanism commanded respectful submission to constituted authority, rebellion, except against tyrants, was a serious crime. And certainly refusal to acquiesce in the lawful rulings of virtuous New England magistrates was a most frightful act of disobedience.

Before he was called to Greenfield in 1783, Dwight had resided for some five years at the family farm in Northampton, Massachusetts. The oldest of thirteen children, he had become head of his household and executor of a sizeable estate after the unexpected death of his father in 1777. The inflation and general instability if the post-Revolutionary years had played havoc with Dwight's finances. Western Massachusetts was embroiled at this time in an extended debtor-creditor conflict which culminated in Shays' Rebellion of 1786. It became impossible for Dwight and other members of the gentry to collect their debts, and the young clergyman was forced to liquidate much of his real estate at a substantial loss.[35] It is not, therefore, difficult to comprehend his enduring opposition to all change which might adversely affect vested property interests. Probably to recoup his losses, Dwight became active in state politics. An early eulogist mentions his exertion of "influence in the country meetings of Hampshire in favor of law and order, then threatened with subversion."[36] His son Sereno, in a memoir, describes Dwight's brief participation in regional government as well as in the Massachusetts state legislature. The account states that at the Northampton County Conven-

tion, "in connection with a few individuals, [Dwight]
met and resisted that spirit of disorganization and licentiousness which was then unhappily prevalent in many
parts of the county . . . ."[37]

In *The Triumph of Infidelity*, Dwight was therefore
presenting a prophetic explanation for the kind of social
unrest he had experienced in Northampton. Essentially,
he argued that the popularity of European irreligion and
Chauncy's universalism among the people had removed
their fear of eternal punishment. Riotous misconduct
resulted as individuals refused to obey the law and ceased
to heed the warnings of their clergymen. Liberal and Old
Calvinist ministers, in their fashionable worldliness and
dilute moralism, failed to steer their congregations away
from perdition. Only the hell-fire preacher of evangelical
doctrine could pierce the soul and bring convictions of
sin, repentance, and faith. But Dwight acknowledged and
lamented that misguided parishioners were indeed de-
serting their New Divinity pastors.

Although dismayed at the downward trend of orthodox
piety, he was not about to consign America over to the
devil. For all its vitriolic negativism, *The Triumph* was
essentially a summons to battle, the opening bugle call
of Dwight's lifelong crusade for "the faith once delivered
to the saints." Prophecy had warned that Christians would
have to contend with enemies every step of the way to the
millennium. As Satan's emissaries had succeeded in infil-
trating Zion, a sustained flanking action was necessary.
On a local plane, defense of orthodoxy entailed an energetic campaign to preserve the Standing Order. This
goal naturally appealed to the Puritan gentry, whose control the governing structure served to perpetuate. A ruling
familial aristocracy joined with the privileged clergy of
the Congregational establishment in the interest of retaining the status quo.

CHAPTER III

Connecticut's Standing Order:
Vanguard to the Millennium

The electoral process in early national Connecticut was superficially democratic, but its effect was to secure the uninterrupted control of one small group of notables. Balloting in the town meetings was open, and carried on under supervision of the Standing Order's representatives. Congregational clergymen played an important part in the election ritual, while pastors of dissenting denominations suffered formal exclusion. Well-known ministers of the established church gave election sermons, in which they usually instructed voters to retain "tried and true" officeholders. The entire functional apparatus of the government was geared to this purpose. Names of incumbents were always read first in the balloting process, and any freeman who withheld his votes so as to support opposition candidates, at the bottom of the list, would receive the uniform disapproval of community poten-

tates. A Connecticut historian has commented that officeholders viewed their positions as "freeholds." They considered persons opposed to their reelection "dangerous
innovators, trying to subvert the constitution, law and
order."[1] An English traveller, who published an account
of his experiences in the United States of the early nineteenth century, described Connecticut's government as
"altogether unfit for imitation." His major criticism
was that such a system acted "to keep in power the party
which has from the first possessed it."[2]

Connecticut's ruling interest consisted of the state's
wealthiest and most influential men. By 1800 many of
them had diversified and strengthened their economic
preeminence by investing heavily in an expanding network of banks. During the Federalist era, Connecticut
saw a rapid proliferation of banking and insurance com-
panies, all controlled by the same men.[3] They were almost
exclusively scions of old Congregational families, most
of whom had relatives among the clergy. Huntingtons,
Hillhouses, Goodriches, Baldwins, Wolcotts, Trumbulls,
Daggetts, and Dwights were all closely aligned either by
blood or marriage to ministers of the establishment. Timothy Dwight himself shared the directorship of Hartford's Eagle Bank with his prominent younger brother
Theodore, Roger M. Sherman, Simeon Baldwin, and
James Hillhouse. These economic leaders also represented
the state in Congress, as well as in the Connecticut Council
and Assembly, the state's respective upper and lower
houses. The legislature controlled the judiciary, holding
appointive power over all the local judgeships. Hence,
the Congregational gentry were able to keep these important offices filled with their own representatives.
Functioning as a supreme court of errors, the council was
the most powerful governing body. Concilar Assistants,
who deliberated in secrecy, prided themselves on their

independence of "prejudicial" popular influence. Individuals who acceded to this pinnacle of aristocratic control were all men of established wealth and prestige, who had spent many years in lower offices under scrutiny of their compeers. If their ideas were unorthodox, they stood little chance of ascending the ladder of power.

The established clergy provided their secular counterparts with priestly sanctification. Based in Puritan social theory and reinforced by the Saybrook Platform, the authority of the orthodox pastorate as guardian of public order and morality remained formally intact throughout the eighteenth century. The feuds of the Great Awakening had been, for the most part, internecine, with Congregational New Lights making no attempt to destroy existent ecclesiastical arrangements. By the 1790s, the established clergy were reduced to apologists for a privileged leadership which was coming under increased criticism from excluded minorities.[4]

In 1791, Dwight preached the election sermon. He proclaimed his loyalty to Puritan traditionalism by heaping praise on Connecticut's long line of "virtuous rulers."[5] To his conservative mind, order and prosperity had been the direct result of the authorities' unwavering support of Congregational schools and churches. Throughout his career, Dwight would cling stolidly to the concept of religious establishments as the only means of securing public morality. Responding to the dissenters' objections to privilege, he cited the law permitting support of other denominations. But neither he nor his Congregational colleagues ever acknowledged that the requirement of filing certificates of dissent with officials of the established church was humiliating. Nor did it seem unfair that the legislature perpetuated orthodox control of the Connecticut educational system, from Yale College to the parish grammar schools.[6]

In a sermon delivered in 1795, and circulated by the state's leading newspaper, *The Connecticut Courant,* Dwight further elaborated his devotion to the Standing Order. The Council was seeking to appropriate land and money for the building of schools and meetinghouses in the state's newly settled areas. Dissenters objected to the bill because it would place the lion's share in Congregational hands.[7] Dwight argued that the tax would secure ". . . the Western territory to the perpetual support of Knowledge and Virtue." Such legislation was in keeping with his millennial desire to spread New England orthodoxy across the nation. He could not comprehend how any religious individual could oppose such a measure. The law gave sober dissenters the right to support their own churches; thus it seemed obvious that critics must be selfish reprobates merely seeking to avoid taxation. Some of these men were probably opposed "even to the existence of virtue in our land." If given their way, they would bring about "complete disorganization . . . to our ancient system of order and peace, and a state of gross and wild licentiousness to a state of rational liberty." Like his Calvinist forebears, Dwight saw "rational liberty" in terms of respect for established authority.[8]

While he never realized it, Dwight was upholding the particular will of the Congregational gentry, and not the universal interest of the commonwealth. He strongly disapproved of political parties and electioneering, but he refused to see that his "tried and approved" rulers represented only one, albeit the dominant party. Never admitting that he and his friends were campaigning for a party, he lashed out at the "lax morals" of dissenters whom he judged greedy of suffrages and offices. In Puritan theory, it was sinfully insubordinate to question the motives of ordained authorities. Under their rule, Connecticut had been "orderly, prosperous, and happy." Dwight concluded that society's best interest "requires that such men be continued in office, until we are assured of the qualifications of their successors."

The Puritan minister was here articulating an anachronistic political theory which a recent historian, David H. Fischer, has labelled "Old Federalism."[9] Adherents to this ideal could never appreciate the existence of a plurality of interests. An established church and a government of paternal aristocrats, or "natural leaders," were the best means of supervising and restraining unruly multitudes. A society of diverse elements competing for power under the dominion of popular constituencies was unthinkable to these conservatives. Such a polity would quickly dissolve in convulsive disorder. Puritan social theory was a modified form of a more general aristocratic conservatism which had roots in medieval Europe.

Of the two national parties, Federalism expressed greater kinship with New England authoritarian ideals. Although Jefferson spoke of an aristocracy of talent, he also favored decentralized, minimal government and a society of yeomen as the best means to inhibit despotism and insure democracy.[10] Hamilton, on the other hand, advocated governmental paternalism and the leadership of commercial wealth.[11] Both he and John Adams were also more concerned with stable order as the necessary condition for progress and happiness, than with popular rule and equalitarianism. The Yankee Adams possessed a Calvinistic dread of passion unleashed. Like the Puritan founders of New England, he stressed the need for political checks and balances to curb insatiable human ambitions. More than Hamilton, he genuinely feared the unbridled rule of one intrenched interest. A lower house would prevent the upper one from usurping aristocratic powers, and the latter structure would serve to check mob rule. Although Adams was less kindly disposed to aristocracy than Hamilton, both Federalist leaders saw a necessity for strong, prophylactic government.[12]

Where the second President preferred "a well-regulated commonwealth" to control society, the financial expert sought an "energetic" state, which would encourage economic development, while securing the necessary order. Both principles appealed to Connecticut's Standing Order. A dominant merchant class had strongly supported replacement of the loosely structured Confederation with the more centralized system of the Federal Constitution. This new polity would guarantee the stable economic and social preconditions for material advancement. Federal assumption of the public debt and provision of an armed force to suppress domestic insurrections like Shays' Rebellion would serve the needs of the business community, as would Hamilton's active support for expanding commerce and manufactures.[13] While Hamilton's economic nationalism aided Connecticut's enterprising gentry, the Puritanical aspects of Adams' ideology corresponded to their social values and to the morality of the orthodox clergy. Like other "Old Federalists," the Massachusetts statesman regretted the divisive effects of factionalism. As late as 1813, in the serenity of retirement, he wrote a letter to Jefferson in which he blamed "parties and factions" for lack of progress in the "science of government."[14]

Adams put the New England Calvinist stamp on his Federalism in viewing the Bible as the cement of society. Scriptural morality, he felt, must be the basis for any effective and prosperous government. Federalists as a whole were more apt to regard religion as a means of social control than an affair of the private conscience. Their hostile reaction to the French Revolution was cast largely in moralistic terms. Calvinistic New Englanders, with their abiding fear of uncontained desire, were horrified at the French abandonment of their tradional order. Adams and other Federalists believed that France had established atheism. Belief in a God who enjoins popular subordination to ruling authority was the basis of social virtue. To Adams and his fellow conservatives, God was no equalitarian. The Almighty worked to curtail selfish passion by establishing distinct social classes. It was the duty of the educated, genteel element to rule equitably and to impart knowledge to "the lower class of people. . . ." Thereby, they would inspire humble deference to authority and "a general emulation . . . which causes good humour, sociability, good manners, and good morals to be general." The levelling imperatives of democracy only served to destroy social harmony by introducing factional rivalry, electioneering, and a general disrespect for authority. The disastrous consequence had been clearly demonstrated in France. The deferential Old Federalism of John Adams paralleled the sentiments of Timothy Dwight and most of New England's Puritan gentry.[15]

Fischer, however, distinguishes between the aristocratic paternalism of Old Federalist conservatism and the more partisan attitudes of younger members of the governing caste. The older Congregational gentry saw themselves as natural rulers, to whom the people owed respectful deference. Superior education and lengthy experience, they believed, had bred them for leadership. Disdainful of office-seekers, who pandered to the prejudices of the unenlightened majority, they remained temperamentally indisposed to engage in partisan politics. Younger conservatives, however, realized the only way to attain power was to acknowledge popular sovereignty and openly court the favor of their constituents. These men developed a Federalist party machine, employing tactics of mass per-

suasion to perpetuate institutions which would insure
their control. They labored to convince the people that
Connecticut's prosperity depended on continuation of
the Federalist-Congregational Standing Order.[16]

Inclusion of Dwight in Fischer's list of Old Federalists
is not entirely accurate, for he served as the most prolific
agitator for the establishment. Fischer mentions that
younger Federalists turned to evangelical Christianity to
foster loyalty to the Standing Order. It was Dwight who
originated this movement. He and his followers promoted
orthodox revivals and "religious education" to convince
people that existent institutions were sacrosanct. Fischer's
young Federalists joined with Dwight in assailing the sin
of "party spirit," while acting at the same time to further
their own partisan interest. As these conservatives defined
the term "party," it applied only to their democratic adversaries. Traditional monolithic ideals were still rhetorically
useful. Puritan Federalists truly believed and set out to
persuade the citizens of Connecticut that only the Standing
Order favored the general welfare, and not that of a particular faction.

In the 1780s, when the exigencies of war had receded
and the class conflict of the Confederation period was
disrupting the social order, Timothy Dwight published
his first extended apology for Connecticut traditionalism.
Greenfield Hill reflects a growing provincial view of the
American millennial destiny. The poem localized the pastoral Eden motif within the Connecticut countryside. Here
in Dwight's own tranquil pastorate, competent, industrious yeomen enjoy prosperity. As with Crevecoeur's
farmer, the source of felicity is freedom from the bondage
of the European peasant. Because they work for themselves and their own kin, they have incentive to the Pro-

testant ethic, foundation of the good society both for Dwight and Crevecoeur.[17]

The Puritan forefathers had bequeathed this middle-class utopia. They had established "The noblest institutions man has seen, Since time began." Throughout the narrative, Dwight contrasts the freedom and prosperity of this New England locale with the oppression, degradation and disharmony of the Old World. As in *The Triumph of Infidelity*, he blames liberal philosophy for much of Europe's discontent. But while he always exalted the "middling" condition, and a generally equal distribution of property, he stalwartly resisted the democratic pluralism of the middle classes. His advocacy of material self-improvement contradicted his attachment to a static, deferential society. Economic mobility was an appealing characteristic of America, but the social levelling which accompanied fluid circumstances threatened to dislodge sanctioned authority. Hence, Dwight attempted to reconcile individualistic enterprise with reverence for tradition. To his mind, the Standing Order was responsible for suffusing practical knowledge and harmonious prosperity among the whole Connecticut citizenry. The New England way encouraged worldly success, but tempered ambition, greed, and conflict by imposing the stern hand of godly authority. Dwight always stressed the crucial value of the overall environment in imparting Christian virtue and social happiness. The nurturing school and church inculcate "steady habits," teaching respect for the Puritan way. Consequently, the people are disposed to retain godly (Congregational) rulers in office, men whose function is to preserve, not to innovate. Only the institutional restraints of a Calvinist order would protect New Englanders from the temptations of pride, avarice, sloth and iniquity that had gained dominion across the Atlantic. The genius of the system, as Dwight saw it, was in its

balance of liberty with order. It allowed every individual
"to take his portion of the common good. . . ." It prevented any one class from monopolizing the wealth and
subjecting others to servitude. The Standing Order was
not in Dwight's eyes a ruling class or interest, but the
guardian of freedom. Its Christian influence had, for example, abolished the degraded condition of the black
slave, introducing him to opportunity. Dwight compared
Negro slavery to feudalism and blamed the European slave
traders for defiling the American Eden with this source of
moral degeneracy. Christian brotherhood naturally
emanates from a society of freedom and equality, where
"no haughty owner drives the humble swain." The virtuous Connecticut citizenry, in removing the slave's
shackles had lifted him from poverty, ignorance, and vice,
by giving him incentives to work and self-advancement.
What clearer proof could exist that the Connecticut of
Greenfield Hill was God's chosen order?[18]

The zenith of Dwight's parochialism was his millennial
belief that Connecticut's institutions would eventually
revivify the world. But the Calvinist mission of redemption
hinged on adherence to the faith and way of life of the
fathers. In a time when rising anticlericalism threatened
to undercut the preeminent influence of the parish minister, Dwight sought to rekindle the reverence of the flock
for their loving paternal shepherds. A section of *Greenfield Hill* entitled "The Clergyman's Advice to the Villagers" depicts a minister on his deathbed surrounded by
faithful parishioners. Concerned not for himself, but for
the welfare of his community, the dying man implores
his followers to retain the hallowed institutions which
have bequeathed orderly happiness. As key administra-
tor of the varied means of grace, the clergyman has been
the linchpin of cohesive social virtue. And these religious
ordinances—household prayer, Bible study, public
worship—must be preserved if prosperity is to continue.[19]

Conservatism is also the theme of a venerable farmer's "advice to the villagers." Reaffirming the value of the Puritan ethic, the farmer lauds middle class "competence," and recommends continued industry, prudence, and moderation. A dominant motif of this section, and the foundation for Dwight's overall approach to religious life, is a Christian paternalism. The home and school, like the church and government, are instruments of nurture. Each benevolent authority guides the individual by rewarding virtue and punishing sin, thereby instilling good habits. Human institutions should all be miniature replicas of divine government, and the pious subject must obey each authority whom God has placed over him.[20]

In the conclusion of *Greenfield Hill,* Dwight stresses that America's millennial glory is occasioned by her splendid isolation from European corruption. This observation was an exercise in hopeful thinking, for Dwight was always acutely sensitive to European, and particularly French, influence. Such fears had produced *The Triumph of Infidelity,* and they conditioned his defense of New England culture in *Greenfield Hill.* His 1785 *Epistle to Colonel Humphreys,* a poem composed for a fellow "Connecticut Wit" embarking on a trip to the Old World, was similarly apprehensive. The dominant image is "that foul harlot Europe" seducing the fair "Columbian" youth. Bred in an environment which shielded him from temptation, the impressionable young man arrives in Europe, where a phantasmagoria of sensuality assails his virtue.[21] Like the rural Americans of a century later, who feared their progeny would fall prey to the sins of the city, Dwight pictured a modern Babylon tempting the innocent to every species of vice. In many of his poems he contrasted a direful Europe with an idealized America viewed as New England writ large. While painfully aware that his country was not entirely cast in the Puritan mold, he hoped it soon would be. Persistently, he blamed foreign

intruders for preventing America from fulfilling its Zionistic mission. In 1799, with Humphreys still abroad, he
would inform his friend: "The last year has been healthy
here. In truth, if *you quarrelsome Europeans,* would leave
us alone, we seem hardly to want additions to our prosperity."[22] The bantering tone of this remark belies a
deeper malaise. By this time, Dwight would be the key
figure in an accelerating Calvinist movement against
democracy. His goal was to reverse the liberal course of
the United States by restoring it to the faith of the Puritan
covenant. The Connecticut Standing Order was to be the
germ of this renewal.

In the late 1780s, Dwight published three articles aimed
at reforming national morals. Appealing to the patriotic
impulse, he recalled that the Revolutionary years had seen
"a spirit of union and virtuous exertion spread like light-
ning throughout all the colonies. . . ." By the war's end,
America had reached "a point of elevation for future progress in glory and happiness, unknown to any nation
before them [sic] on the face of the earth."[23] But during
the ensuing Confederation period, discord and contempt
for authority had erupted and threatened to tear the nation apart. The major cause of such strife was neglect of
religion. Dwight observed that while primitive Christians
had gone to great pains to procure knowledge of God,
modern ones neglect their Bibles at a time when printing
has rendered them universally available.[24] Selfishness
and infidelity could be cured if Americans would again
join their exertions, as they had during the Revolution.
Dwight outlined a program for uniting to overcome religious apathy in a 1788 "Address to the Ministers of the
Gospel of Every Denomination in the United States."[25]
Printed in the nationally circulated *American Museum,*
this article is of crucial significance. Not only did it set
forth the underlying conservatism of Dwight's mission,
but also it expounded a new practical approach to reli-

gion greatly dissimilar from the doctrinal logic of Consistent Calvinism. Unlike his brethren in the New Divinity, Dwight was willing to bend doctrine considerably to serve a practical purpose. Perceiving liberalization as a threat to institutions like the Standing Order, he began to use religion as the means for maintaining traditional forms of social control. In his "Address," he sought to call the attention of evangelical ministers to the prevalence of a wide variety of vices in America. Sabbath-breaking, drunkenness, and journalistic slander were three practices which he deemed destructive of moral order. Dwight argued in general terms that these sins produced idleness, poverty, and a spirit of contentiousness. Appalled at the unruliness of a pluralist society, he was the first notable individual to recommend interdenominational cooperation to promote temperance and observance of the Sabbath. An effective orthodox campaign to "suppress vice" would actually foster popular subordination to authority. It would reinstitute respect for established ministries and governing powers, while discouraging the criticism of a democratic opposition. Equating aristocratic systems like that of Connecticut with godliness, and pluralistic freedom with sinful disharmony, he began to construct a promotional Christianity to buttress the old order. Ultimately this social approach to religion would take hold among conservative New England evangelicals and flower into a mass movement, the Second Great Awakening. Dwight devoted much of his work to devising ways to use religion for social control. His students and followers would take up his cause to develop a powerful set of national institutions known as benevolent societies. These agencies would be the chief organs of evangelical conservatism in Antebellum America.

Motives, habits, influence, and example were key elements in Dwight's conception of religion. Piety was the effect of environmental conditioning and not simply a personal experience. God works through human moral agents acting in combination. Such ideas were at variance with the legacy of the Great Awakening. Consistent Calvinists, when not expounding abstruse metaphysical doctrine, concentrated on the dynamics of conversion. While they fully supported revivalism, their dogmatic hyper-Calvinism often disabled their evangelical efforts. They stressed the absolute sovereignty of God in imparting grace to a predestined elect. As man, in his fallen condition was totally depraved, the unrenewed individual was incapable of doing anything with a pure heart. Regenerative grace was a free gift wholly unmerited by the sinner. Only the Holy Spirit, working inscrutably, could bring faith, repentance, and virtue. The unregenerate could do nothing on their own to obtain grace.

New Divinity preachers gave these doctrines foremost importance in their sermons and theological systems. Because they so devalued human agency, they logically de-emphasized the instituted means of grace. Although they stressed prayer, public worship, and the reading of Scripture as necessary for salvation, they also claimed no causal connection between attendance to duties and the experience of regeneration. Such complete supernaturalism offered the sinner little encouragement to do anything on his own behalf. It contrasted sharply with Dwight's confident assertion that God would not fail to bless those who labor in his cause. Though loyal allies in their firm support of New England traditionalism, the Consistent Calvinists posed a severe problem for Dwight's evangelical activism.

PART II
Theology and Change

CHAPTER IV

Metaphysical Inability

Timothy Dwight always considered himself a New Divinity man, a faithful exponent of the Gospel according to his grandfather Jonathan Edwards. Because he wished to unite orthodoxy against liberal religion and infidelity, he never explicitly renounced the Calvinism of the Great Awakening. But, while he retained the revivalistic basis of the Edwardian faith, he reinterpreted its doctrines in such a way as to alter its message drastically. To comprehend Dwight's motives in doing so, it is necessary to examine the development of Consistent Calvinism.

Few would question the statement that in the history of American Calvinism, Jonathan Edwards was the greatest luminary. The uniqueness of Edwards lay in his fusion of remarkable intellectual virtuosity with poetic vision. Generally such heightened development of head and heart do not occur in the same individual. The dissecting, categorizing intellect tends to dampen subjective perception. Even in Edwards, the two modes of cognition did not occur simultaneously. An examination of his life and works reveals two distinct periods, the one dominated by intensely personal experience, the other by a rational objectivity.

The revivals in which Edwards participated, those which touched off the Great Awakening in New England, were a spontaneous occurrence which caught the North-ampton divine by surprise. Edwards, however, was an extremely effective evangelical preacher. He was able to stir his congregation to spiritual awareness largely because he himself had attained a deep level of religious experience. In his "Personal Narrative," he had poignantly recorded the long and anguished journey of his soul. The high Calvinist doctrine he so effectually dramatized in the pulpit, had not been for him the product of scholastic reasoning. Edwards' sermons and earlier tracts were the direct outgrowth of his inner transformation. Serious illness had "[shaken him] over the pit of hell." A deep sense of guilt had produced "inward struggles and conflicts and selfreflections." Overwhelmed with the burden of sin, he had begun to pursue salvation wholeheartedly. But a crippling perception of his own depravity made his efforts seem futile. At the point of near despair, he had begun to feel his dependence on God for mercy. Deeply aware that he could not subdue his inclination to sin, he derived new peace and joy from the doctrine of absolute divine sovereignty. The omnipotent, vengeful Deity, who so often terrified persons not sharing Edwards's level of spirituality "very often appeared exceedingly pleasant, bright, and sweet" to him.[1]

It was this profound feeling for the Calvinist God which informed Edwards's revivals and early writings. Momentous inner experience affecting his entire being gave him the distinctive approach to religion which he would call "experimental." In the midst of the Awakening, Edwards wrote his most subjective, pietistic works: the *Narrative of Surprising Conversions, A Divine and Supernatural Light, Religious Affections.* These writings flow from Edwards's immersion in a mounting wave of religious excitement. During this period of his life he played an exclusively evangelical role. Hence his words were concrete and dramatic. His paramount concern was the experience of conversion, and he devoted his labors single-mindedly to that object. He preached to arouse a contrite and abject sense of dependence on God, and he wrote by and large on the "affections" of spiritual regeneration. After the liquid energy of the Awakening had cooled and begun to harden into a set of doctrines, however, Edwards's works became more abstract and rationalistic. Polemical controversy between revivalist ministers and their opponents contributed significantly to the demise of the Awakening. Upon leaving his Northampton pulpit following a dispute with some of his parishioners, Edwards immured himself in the frontier outpost of Stockbridge, Massachusetts. With the New Light-Old Light battle raging, he devoted himself to a scholarly vindication of Calvinist principles. Though outgrowths of his earlier experience, such works as *Freedom of the Will, The Doctrine of Original Sin Defended,* and *The Nature of True Virtue* have a pronounced scholastic flavor. These theological disquisitions ushered from a remote, cloistered existence, out of touch with the strivings and yearnings of the average parishioner. Edwards had turned his attention toward the small body of clergymen who composed the Arminian threat to experimental religion. *Freedom of the Will* and *Original Sin* were highly intellectual treaties constructed for the purpose of general apology. In *The Nature of True Virtue,* Edwards expanded his subjective conception of the religious affections into a broad and abstract aesthetic theory. Emotional "love to Christ" and "joy in Christ" became a rationalized "consent and union with being in general." Typical of the more copious and deductive reasoning in this later work is the following syllogism:

> The *first* object of virtuous benevolence is *Being,* simply considered; and if Being *simply* considered be its object, then Being *in general* is its object; and the thing it has an ultimate propensity to is the highest good of Being in general. . . .[2]

Theological wrangling with his Old Calvinist and liberal adversaries had given the later Edwards a more metaphysical, and less evangelical turn of mind. *Freedom of the Will* was a treatise entirely bound up in the concatenations of polemic divinity. Responding to a worldly, self-confident Arminianism, Edwards sought to reconcile Calvinist necessitarianism with the empirical temper of the Enlightenment. Following John Locke, he viewed man primarily as a reactor to external stimuli. Consistent with the Newtonian cosmology, he argued that every effect must have a cause. The act of will is determined by the "strongest motive," or a desire for the greatest apparent good. Without the aid of the Holy Spirit, the mind is propelled only by carnal motives. Freedom of the will meant for Edwards that the unregenerate were at liberty to respond to worldly desires, the objects of sin. Nothing impeded their sinful acts, which to them were the greatest apparent good. They were not, however, free in the sense of possessing the power of self-determination. Because no energy is self-generating, the actions of the human will must be determined by something outside itself. And while the natural will is propelled by material motives, the restored soul is guided by spiritual ones. Strictly speaking,

Edwards' system was one of moral, but not physical necessity. While natural ability or inability arises from natural causes, moral actions are the products of outside motives which impinge on the passive will, causing it to choose or refuse. Though physically capable of loving God and his neighbor, the sinner lacks the motives, and hence the moral inclination to do so. Furthermore, he will not choose piety until God furnishes holy motives to his heart. Nevertheless, because he desires and chooses sin as the greatest apparent good, he sins freely, and thus does God hold him accountable for his actions and subject to eternal damnation.[3]

Edwards's opponents agreed with him that God alone is the author of regeneration, but they viewed motives in terms of regularly operating religious ordinances, or secondary "means of grace." To Edwards, the ability of sinners to respond piously to the commandments of Scripture without a prior infusion of the Holy Spirit implied a self-determining will. But the question of self-determination was not the underlying issue. The area of disagreement lay in how God imparts holy motives to sinners. While Arminians and Old Calvinists believed that God operates through human agencies, Edwards maintained a "complete supernaturalism." Since God infuses pious motives directly, only the saint can respond to scriptural dictates as the greatest apparent good. Edwards's opponents regarded this notion as incapacitating. To them it drew determinism out to such an extreme that the sinner's "will not" actually becomes "cannot," for he is unable to draw any sustenance from religion until God inscrutably chooses to impart spiritual motives to him.

Edwards's *Freedom of the Will* was an outgrowth of his own vital experience of divine sovereignty and human dependence. But it did not record the experience itself. It involved only the intellect, distilling lifeless doctrine from prior, first hand awareness. As such, it bore only the

most formal relationship to the Awakening. It was as an
architect's blueprint to an occupied home. Theology
could not begin to convey the spirit of the revivals. In its
dissection and objectification of experience, it could not
engender the feelings necessary for conversion.

   His disciples carried the process of intellectualization
further in erecting the New Divinity. Although these ministers were united in their espousal of Edwardian Calvinism, their approach to religion tended to fall in two
categories. They all viewed their doctrines and preaching
as evangelical, but only a part of their number were effective revivalists. These evangelicals of the New Divinity
followed in the path of the earlier Edwards. They subordinated metaphysics to a simple gospel of immediate
repentance and faith in God's mercy. The others were
primarily metaphysicians, drawing their style of address
from the later Edwards. The New Divinity metaphysicals
tended to expound a form of scholasticism rather than experimental piety from the pulpit. Consistent Calvinists
never acknowledged any important differences within
their school, and to be sure, the distinction I have drawn
was more the product of temperament than of any specific
theological disagreement. Nevertheless the division of
New Divinity men into two groups had devastating implications for the future of revivalism. Metaphysicals
drew on the systematizing tendencies of Calvinism to divorce doctrine from its basis in experience. Retreating into
their studies, they tended to let abstract thinking take
control of their lives and sap their spiritual vitality. *Freedom of the Will,* with its pronouncement of moral inability hung like a black cloud over their preaching.

The fatal consequence of substituting Calvinist theology for the evangelical gospel is most clearly demonstrated in the career of Samuel Hopkins. One of Edwards's earliest disciples, Hopkins was the progenitor of the metaphysical New Divinity. He was probably the most adept logician among Edwards's disciples, but his penchant for syllogistic reasoning left his pulpit discourse cold and distant. A man of great moral courage, he was one of the first clergymen in America to condemn the slave trade. He did so in the latter part of his career, while occupying a parish in Newport, Rhode Island, the main center of that infamous practice. In attacking slavery, he risked the animosity of the most powerful elements in the city. Despite his exemplary life, however, he failed to inspire the young people in his congregation. Writing in the 1850s, a minister who had spent his youth in Newport recalled Hopkins as an "exceedingly dry and abstract" preacher who drove much of his congregation into other churches. Dominated by the aged, Hopkins's congregation took on a grave, solemn appearance.[4]

Hopkins's problems as a minister came largely from his penchant for intellectualization. Under his heavy hand, the religion of the affections became a bloodless system of doctrines. Theology served as a point of departure, rather than the result of pietistic experience. As such it served to crowd out subjective piety in Hopkins's own experience as well as that of his congregation. Throughout his career he continually recorded his failure to attain a lasting, experimental sense of God. In 1743, while a young minister in Great Barrington, Massachusetts, he lamented the ineffectiveness of his preaching. "I have for some time," wrote Hopkins, "been much discouraged about preaching, and feel inclined to leave off—am filled with doubts about my own good estate."[5] In 1754, he expressed deep anguish over his lack of success.

This day finishes eleven years since I was ordained in the
work of the ministry. How poorly it has been spent, God
knows! Have reason to be greatly ashamed. Kept a secret
fast. God only knows my misery.[6]

Hopkins gave vent to these feelings at a time when the
Great Awakening was still fresh in the minds of New
Englanders, and the disrupting events of war and revolution had yet to disturb the Calvinistic faith. He occupied
a rural parish, distant from the seductive worldliness of
Boston and Newport. Great Barrington is in Western
Massachusetts, close to the area where revivalism had been
most pervasive. Yet this minister had been unable to lead
his listeners to Christ.

In his old age, when his personal piety and talents as a
theologian were widely recognized, Hopkins continued
to doubt his worthiness. Believing himself a failure as a
man of God, he reflected that private devotion had been
his only well of strong spiritual feeling. Because he had
never been a successful revivalist, he concluded that his
"religion was not genuine." He saw his whole life
". . . stained with . . . an awful degree of moral depravity and pollution. . . ." Since, in his own estimation,
he had none of the "righteousness or moral goodness"
which might gain the favor of God, he concluded that
only the mercy of Christ could save him from eternal
misery.[7] These were pious Calvinist sentiments, but they
encompassed only the negative pole of experimental religion. The positive and most vital aspect lay in an up-
lifting conversion experience. Hopkins's error was in
allowing the theocentrism of Edwards's *Freedom of the
Will* to overwhelm his preaching. He dwelled so exclusively on the doctrine of God's sovereignty and human
depravity, which produced convictions of sin, that he
tended to ignore those which would elevate the sinner to
joy in Christ. He often lamented that "few persons appear

to have been awakened or converted by my preaching."
The reason lay in his relentless emphasis on the doctrine
of moral inability. With his logician's mind, he doggedly
argued that "the unregenerate can do nothing to procure
the influence of the Holy Spirit." Moreover, he made this
pronouncement in a manner which later ministers would
regard as "too highly charged with metaphysical discussion to be readily appreciated by the common mind."[8]

In scholarly withdrawal, Hopkins formulated a system
which carried the high Calvinism of Edwards to its logical
if inhuman extreme. From Edwardian metaphysics, he
deduced a number of corollaries, which, by rendering the
sinner wholly impotent, could only arrest the conversion
process. Because holiness only follows a radical change
of heart wrought entirely by God, the sinner does nothing
morally good prior to regeneration.

While Hopkins never went so far as to advise sinners
not to use the means of grace, he placed formidable
obstructions in their path to salvation. Since God is absolute sovereign, no connection can possibly exist between
attendance to means and the infusion of grace. As if this
proposition were not sufficiently discouraging, Hopkins
reasoned that "the awakened, convinced sinner, who has
taken a great deal of pains in the use of means" appears
"more guilty and vile in God's sight, than if he had never
attained this conviction and knowledge. . . ." For now
the individual is no longer ignorant of his spiritual state
and the divine plan of redemption.[9] As grotesque as this
doctrine appears, it is merely a rational application of
Edwardian complete supernaturalism. If the unregenerate
can only sin, then even their labors to attain piety are
wholly depraved, for they usher from a bad heart, and
hence self-love. Hopkins tried to mitigate the effect of
such unsavory pronouncements by inferring that after all,
the omnipotent Creator might as easily confer grace on
the most hardened reprobate as on one who was not so

sinful.[10] But the dismal implications of Hopkins's message were inescapable. Attendance at public worship,
study of scripture, engagement in prayer, were duties required of all believers; but as vehicles of grace they were
fruitless. What was left for the aspiring convert but to go
through the motions of faith mechanically while helplessly
waiting for miraculous divine intervention?

Edwards had maintained that God's Spirit operates in
conjunction with His Word, opening the hearts of sinners
to receive Truth.[11] But Hopkins, probably as a consequence of his own evangelical failure, entirely separated
Word from Spirit, preaching from regeneration. He held
that "men are not regenerated . . . by light or the word
of God." The Spirit changes the heart prior to any effect
of the Word. Worship and other religious duties aid in
sanctifying the elect, but the Work of the Spirit is distinctly separate from these ordinances.

Hopkins's unequivocal theocentrism logically extended
the Edwardian principle of absolute divine sovereignty.
The inherent difficulty in Consistent Calvinism lay in its
reduction of human powers to such insignificance that any
attempt to reintroduce the actions of men came in conflict
with the sovereignty of God. In the works of Edwards, this
problem smoldered. In the Hopkinsian system, it burst
into flame. The wrath of God ploughs through his works,
leveling everything in its path. Out of love to the Creator,
man should indeed be willing to suffer eternal damnation.

The scholastic abstractions of Samuel Hopkins were
not the idiosyncratic output of one Calvinist mind. Not
only did large numbers of metaphysical systematizers
come to occupy New England pulpits but many came to
espouse doctrines which they called Hopkinsian. Before
further considering the metaphysical style, it is illuminating to contrast it with the evangelical orientation.

If Hopkins was the first New Divinity metaphysical, the Connecticut revivalist Joseph Bellamy was the father of the evangelical line. In temperament, he could not have been more opposite from his withdrawn, self-effacing colleague. Writing for Sprague's *Annals of the American Pulpit*, a mid-nineteenth-century evangelical described Bellamy as a commanding figure who "did not need to be told what was his position either in the church or in the world."[12] While Hopkins and other metaphysicians would progressively alienate themselves from their parishes and from the religious currents of their times, Bellamy was far from the detached intellectual. In his day, he played a role similar to the one Timothy Dwight would play a few decades later. Scholar, teacher, and evangelical defender of the faith, he possessed many of the future Yale president's attributes and sources of appeal. His most noted work, *True Religion Delineated*, served a similar purpose in the mid-eighteenth century to that of Dwight's *Theology Explained and Defended* in the early nineteenth. Both works were timely apologies for evangelical Calvinism. Sprague notes that Bellamy "adapted himself with great felicity to the state of his times. . . ." As was the case with Dwight, an overriding goal of winning converts gave him practical flexibility. Unlike Hopkins, he subordinated doctrine to practice, giving foremost attention to extension of the faith. As a result, he was regarded as "undoubtedly the most powerful preacher of his day, or of any other day." He knew how to be dramatic and compelling in the pulpit. With his explosive style of preaching, not only could he arouse a deep sense of sin, but also a heartfelt repentance and faith in God's mercy. In short, Bellamy was completely attuned to the whole process of conversion.[13]

Both Bellamy and Dwight occupied positions of esteem as authoritative spokesmen for Connecticut orthodoxy in their respective eras. The consequent "love of dominion" and "dogmatical manner" attributed to Bellamy was also characteristic of Dwight. But the dogmatism of both men was firmly anchored to practical evangelization.

Like every Consistent Calvinist, Bellamy never wavered from the belief that means in themselves could not produce conversion.[14] But he succeeded in adapting the mortifying principles of strict Calvinism to the service of revivals. Like Edwards, he employed the means of grace as an integral part of the experimental process. Reliance on such instruments of conversion forms the heart of the evangelical approach as distinguished from the metaphysical New Divinity. The use of means was a potent device for breaking down resistance to grace. It humbled the sinner before God, making him feel his dependent and precarious state.[15] This conception of religious ordinance actually compromised the sovereignty of God and enhanced human powers to some extent. But for Bellamy, evangelical concerns necessitated some relaxation of divine omnipotence.

The practice of revivalism inevitably led Bellamy into doctrinal contradictions which forfeited the consistency of his Calvinism. One important doctrine was that saving grace must be irresistable. For if God is absolute sovereign, then no merely human inclination can possibly resist His Spirit. When God chooses to have mercy on a sinner, He will prevail, no matter how callous the unregenerate heart. Bellamy fully agreed that ". . . those influences of the Spirit . . . sufficient to awaken, convince, and humble the sinner, and recover him to God, must be irresistable and supernatural."[16] While this doctrine was a theological necessity, it presented the practicing minister with a thorny problem. If, like Hopkins, he subordinated evangelical to metaphysical preaching, he would avoid the risk of contradiction. But if, like Bellamy, he took an active part in the process of conversion, he was apt to empower the creature at the expense of the Creator. Bellamy had no trouble with irresistable grace while writing impersonal disquisition. When directly addressing prospective converts, however, he felt compelled to thrust the doctrine aside. After dramatizing the contingent state of apostate humanity he concluded with a ringing evangelical appeal to "see your entire dependence on sovereign mercy for salvation; and be looking diligently lest you fail of the grace of God by resisting the Holy Spirit. . . ."[17] Bellamy realized that individuals need some incentive to strive for salvation. For if the doings of the unregenerate were to no avail, what would be the use of making any effort? Hence the evangelical minister contradicted his Calvinist premises by warning his parishioners that inattendance to their eternal concerns would lessen their chances of salvation. Earlier in the same sermon, he had exhorted sinners to consider their most pressing self-interest. Religious devotions were a matter of utmost "expediency" and would be of inestimable personal "advantage." These arguments appealed to the very attributes of self-love that Bellamy and all Consistent Calvinists decried as infinitely evil in God's sight. In the more logical system of Hopkins, the elect would naturally come to use the means of grace, as a result of love to God, and not out of any self-interest. And to exhort sinners who were not of the elect to use the means for their own good was inconsistent and absurd. Bellamy, in his evangelistic fervor, had violated the principle of divine sovereignty and sacrificed holy love on the altar of utility. But such theological compromise was far more likely to produce converts than was the benumbing absolutism of Samuel Hopkins.

Bellamy had lived with Edwards at the time of the Awakening and imbibed the revivalistic theology of his teacher. But unlike Edwards, he spent his whole career as a public figure. Hopkins, on the other hand, spent the major portion of his time in scholarly retreat. In general, the New Divinity metaphysicals followed his example, working from study to pulpit. The more evangelical Consistent Calvinists formulated their sermons out of closer contact with their parishioners' spiritual needs.

New Divinity metaphysicals often completely lost touch with their congregations as they constructed their elaborate systems and descended into the labyrinth of polemical controversy. John Smalley illustrates this group's tendency to bury experimental pietism beneath an avalanche of scholastic dogma. Born in 1734, Smalley was a member of the second generation of New Lights. With no real memory of the Awakening, he went even further than Hopkins in separating theology from revivalistic practice. He had no qualms about his lack of success as an evangelical preacher. In fact, he deplored what he considered the excesses of revivalism. To his sober mind, the evangelism of a George Whitefield was too much an affair of the passions, contributing to popular self-deception. A member of Connecticut's Standing Order, Smalley reacted strongly against the insubordinate pietism of Separatists and other anti-etablishment sects. His brand of Consistent Calvinism was an institutionalized dogma, completely devoid of experimental vitality. Significantly, he ascribed his true conversion to a reading of Edwards on the will. Smalley spent some fourteen hours a day in his study, where he labored over the metaphysics of Consistent Calvinism. In the pulpit, he was a graceless figure "with his manuscript before him [reading] as doggedly as most of his contemporaries."[18]

Jonathan Edwards the younger was another Calvinist metaphysician, influential among his colleagues, but out of touch with his flock. One parishioner criticized him for spending too much time writing polemics against

Charles Chauncy's universalism and not enough in "studying how he may win his people to Christ."[19] As minister of the White Haven Society, Edwards was for a time a major figure in Connecticut's ecclesiastical establishment. But during the eventful 1780s, he suffered growing alienation from his congregation. Dissatisfied families abandoned his church in such numbers that by 1795 it had become financially destitute. At length, the remaining members felt constrained to dismiss their ill-fated minister and dissolve the church. Many of the deserters had gone over to the local Episcopal and Old Light churches, where discipline was less rigid, preaching less abstruse, and doctrine less harsh in its appraisal of human nature.[20]

The metaphysicals steadfastly refrained from even the slightest compromise with the growing humanitarianism of the times. Years of dispute with Old Calvinists and Arminians had led them to logical extremes in their defense of the Edwardian system. The peculiar doctrines of Samuel Hopkins and his followers were the ultimate creation of isolated intellects, spinning fine webs of metaphysics in a vacuum. So great was their obsession with an absolutely sovereign God and totally depraved humanity, that they obliterated all agencies of religious nurture. Harriet Beecher Stowe has compared Consistent Calvinism to a rungless ladder with piety at the top. The only way of ascent was by a miraculous intervention of the Holy Spirit. Ironically, those ministers who most strenuously defended experimental religion were often the least capable of producing it. Their metaphysical preaching usually had quite the opposite effect. But they were complete supernaturalists, who placed little faith in human instrumentation.[21]

New Divinity evangelicals followed Bellamy in accentuating the positive elements in Calvinism. Theoretically, they ascribed no greater powers to man than did the metaphysicals, but they confidently adapted their preaching to produce conversions. They differed with their scholastic brethren in their conception of the minister's role. Like the revivalists of the Great Awakening, and the evangelicals of the nineteenth century, they thought of themselves as winners of souls to Christ. Metaphysicals tended to regard their office in traditional pedagogical terms. As they saw it, their role was to explain the true Gospel and to distinguish it from heretical perversions. In viewing the minister as teacher, they hardly differed from the Old Calvinists and Arminians. But their high Calvinist principles led them into a problem which never troubled their opponents. Because they insisted on the futility of all human endeavor to obtain grace, they tended to undercut the efficacy of their pastoral function. In Old Calvinist and Arminian systems, grace was the culmination of a long and assiduous observance of constituted religious exercises. God caused his Spirit regularly to sanctify these ordinances, so that sincere devotion would probably not fail to produce holiness. Parishioners of New Divinity metaphysicals, however, had to wait for a sudden, mysterious rain of sovereign grace before the words of their ministers could enliven their hearts.

Among the evangelical New Divinity were some ministers with Hopkinsian sentiments. But these clergymen departed from Hopkins in assessment of their purpose. In the pulpit, they subordinated theology to revivalistic concerns. Stephen West, and Hopkins's son-in-law, Samuel Spring, were representative of this position. A minister acquainted with West commented that he refrained from preaching metaphysics. "A Hopkinsian would understand the bearing of some of his language as leading to that system, but the common hearers would recognize nothing beyond a general view of the Gospel plan of salvation."[22]

In like manner, Spring "avoided the rash expressions which some others employed, viz: that we ought to be willing to be damned . . . for the glory of God; and he urged men with great earnestness to seek salvation."[23]

Next to Bellamy, Nathan Strong was possibly the most evangelical preacher among the New Divinity. Graduating with Timothy Dwight in the Yale class of 1769, Strong went on to become an eminently successful revivalist. Along with Dwight, he was an early leader of the Second Great Awakening. An 1847 commentator provided this revealing anecdote of Strong:

> During a time of revival, Dr. Edwards being at Hartford with Dr. Strong, said to him with much emotion, "why do the influences of the Holy Spirit attend your preaching so much more than mine; when our congregations are so much alike, and we preach the same system of truth?" Said Dr. Strong—"The reason is that *you* present Gospel truth as a proposition to be proved, and go on to prove it; whereas *I* endeavor to exhibit it as something already admitted and to impress it upon the heart and conscience."[24]

This statement underlines the essential differences between the styles of New Divinity metaphysicals and evangelicals.

By the turn of the century, Consistent Calvinism was in a tenuous position. Liberal religion and outright skepticism were on the upsurge as the nation became more secular. Massachusetts was on the brink of Unitarian schism, and Connecticut's establishment was beseiged by dissenters seeking equal status in a pluralistic society. Men like Dwight and Strong saw the need for uniting orthodoxy in a new revivalistic campaign, but the hard-line metaphysicals bridled at the thought of such humanly contrived religion. The metaphysical New Divinity was a sizeable stumbling block for it had become extremely influential among New England Calvinists.

In the early years of the nineteenth century, Nathanael

Emmons was the leading exponent of New Divinity metaphysics. Born in 1745, he grew up in the climate of theological controversy between Old and New Light factions
of the Great Awakening. As a divinity student of John
Smalley, he received a highly intellectualized Calvinism.
His own system, however, became an unstable compound
of metaphysical dogma and experimental activism. The
crusty Puritan, who reigned fifty years over an isolated
parish in Franklin, Massachusetts, had an almost com-
pulsive need to portray Calvinism in its most severe, self-
denying light.[25] Yet, at the same time, he felt a deep
concern for the welfare of his parishioners and sought to
lead them to evangelical faith. The key to his practically
unworkable scheme of evangelical hyper-Calvinism lay
in his agonizing confrontation with personal tragedy.

Emmons married in 1775, and his wife bore him two
children. But within three years, tuberculosis and dysen-
tery had carried off his entire family. Overwhelmed with
grief, Emmons at first felt a strong sense of rebellion
"against the government of God." After much anguish, he
came to realize the fleeting quality of life, and the vanity
of placing one's faith in temporal wishes. The young
clergyman could only surmount his despair through
resignation to the designs of an omnipotent Deity, who
governs all things for the greatest good of the universe.[26]

Because his own peace and piety stemmed from radical
self-abasement, he stressed the exclusiveness of divine
agency in his preaching. Only, he believed, if sinners
would come to feel their utter dependence on God, would
they have a true sense of Gospel holiness. Emmons resembled Hopkins in his complete rejection of self-reliance.
He often preached the moral inability of the unregenerate
to do anything but sin, and he expressed the Hopkinsian
belief that sinners only grow more guilty in attending the
means of grace.

The Edwardian doctrine of the will formed the center
of Emmons's system. From the distinction between moral
and natural inability, he deduced a theology in which
active choice was the basis of holiness. Rejecting the
Hopkinsian view that the individual is passive in regeneration, he believed this concept would incapacitate the
preacher in exhorting sinners to repent and believe.[27]
When Emmons himself had submitted to divine government, he had done so in an act of will, or a "free, voluntary
exercise" of love to God. In his estimation, the older
Edwardian concept that benevolence flowed from infusion
of a "taste, habit, or principle" was erroneous because it
was "totally inactive and involuntary in nature."[28] Hence
the sinner actively makes himself a new heart in response
to his minister's exhortations. Emmons preached for conversions, but at the same time, he told his listeners that
they were morally unable to repent. They could only
make effective use of means when God independently provided them with grace.[29] Emmons's doctrine of active regeneration enabled him to preach evangelically, and he
was sometimes successful in bringing about revivals.[30] His
pastorate was well removed from the commercial centers
of New England. A long established agrarian community,
Franklin withstood the liberal trends of Boston, and remained "emphatically a Puritan parish." But a substantial emigration did occur during Emmons's time,[31]
probably composed of restive young men bound for the
more varied life of the city. The existence of a new England farmer was difficult and often unrewarding. The
soil was rocky and parsimonious in its yield to backbreak-
ing labor. A religion of self-denial and total dependence
on a God who controlled all the elements harmonized well
with conditions in rural New England. Hence, Emmons's
overall success as a preacher is not difficult to fathom.

But while his congregation was large, the rigors of his

theology detracted from his popularity among a younger, more worldly generation. They derived no solace from knowledge of their natural ability to love God, if all their efforts to do so were in vain. To nineteenth-century evangelicals, freedom of the will was coming to mean freedom to choose between alternatives. The mere power of choosing implied no human liberty, if the sinner could not choose holiness without divine intervention, and if God had restricted the choice of virtue to a predestined elect. Harriet Beecher Stowe, who grew up during the evangelical shift toward self-reliance, regarded Emmons's system as "a skillful engine of torture [calculated] to produce all the mental anguish of the most perfect sense of helplessness with the most torturing sense of responsibility."[32]

Horace Mann, the great educational reformer, spent his childhood in Franklin. Every Sabbath, "the awful tale of woe and wrath" had preyed upon his youthful sensibilities. Reminiscence of early religious practice did not for him evoke the security of Christ's paternal love, but the gloom and anguish of inescapable depravity and damnation.

> Often, on going to bed at night, did the objects of the day and the faces of my friends give place to a vision of the awful throne, the inexorable judge, and the hapless myriads, among whom I often seemed to see those whom I loved best; and there I wept and sobbed until Nature found that repose in exhaustion whose genuine reality she should have found in freedom from care and the spontaneous happiness of childhood.

Mann eventually rebelled against Consistent Calvinism. He moved to Boston and joined William Ellery Channing's Unitarian congregation. But his formative impressions had permanently scarred his religious sensibilities. He

always found it difficult to love God, for when he medi-
tated on Christ's benevolence "the grim old Calvinist
spectre" would return to plague him.[33]

Apostasy from the Puritan faith was becoming a widespread phenomenon. As the Unitarian controversy erupted,
Emmons managed to keep heresy out of his parish, but all
around him schism was rampant. While recognizing the
threat to orthodoxy's survival, Emmons and his Hopkinsian allies looked askance at the idea of a contrived evangelical campaign. Revivals were solely the work of
Providence. Nevertheless Hopkinsians did establish the
Massachusetts Missionary Society in 1799 with Emmons
as its first president. To aid in propagating the Gospel
according to Emmons and Hopkins, the Society published
a magazine. A perusal of its contents over its brief tenure
of existence (1803-08) reveals a doctrinaire and rigidly
sectarian Calvinism. Much of the publication was devoted
to defaming Methodism, Baptism, and every other system
of divinity—Calvinist or Arminian, Trinitarian or Unitarian—which did not concur exactly with Consistent
Calvinism.[34]

This periodical was published to advance experimental
piety, but paradoxically it pulled the rug out from under
the feet of every reader who sought to comply with its
wishes. When a subscriber asked what duties he might perform "in order to acquire an experimental knowledge of
salvation," the editors replied that a natural man "has
neither will nor power to perform holy exercises. . . ."
Moreover "his very best sacrifices are bad and abominable
in the sight of God. . . ."[35] In keeping with strict Calvinist principle, the *Massachusetts Missionary Magazine*
continually described the effects of piety and exhorted its
readers to become holy; but at the same time it denigrated
all means for the nurture of piety. Man's natural ability
and moral impotence to repent and be virtuous and the

dire consequences of this situation are portrayed in many articles. One headed "A Word to the Profane: Don't Be Damn'd," concludes with the following bit of hortatory discouragement: *"May God incline your heart to listen to this friendly warning, or that which was intended for your benefit will aggravate your condemnation."*[36] Unfortunately the evangelicals among the Hopkinsians did not exert appreciable influence on the magazine, for it exhibited all the most incapacitating doctrines to its readership. Sinners were informed, as above, that without prior divine intervention they must grow more sinful in striving for grace.

Some articles written by Emmons or his followers fused the sinners' moral inability with his "voluntary exercises" in regeneration. In the Emmons interpretation, the returning sinner resembles a marionette, highly active, but totally dependent at every moment on the wire-pulling Deity. Otherwise, the magazine's theology was strictly Hopkinsian, for in the systems of Emmons and Hopkins, the only significant difference lay in the concept of activity or passivity in regeneration. Hence Emmons and his students, and the Hopkinsians formed one unified school of Consistent Calvinism. Their entirely theocentric universe tended to drain all human content from religion and make God appear tyrannical.

One reader objected that the arbitrary Calvinist Creator violated Christian belief in God as loving "father of his great family." Dogmatically, the editors replied that anyone who did not fully accept their system was compromising God's sovereignty, and to oppose omnipotence was an act of "unreasonableness and wickedness." Why sovereignty must be so unequivocal as to reduce man to utter helplessness is never explained. But any objection to this severe doctrine "if allowed to operate, would tear the Almighty from the throne of the Universe as effectually as atheism itself."[37] Theoretically, the system was logical, for it rendered God independent of all human action, but practically, it was unreasonable. Many found grave injustice in a system which so disabled man and yet placed full responsibility for sin on his shoulders. It was no encouragement to sincere individuals to have their religious efforts disclaimed as abominable and their paternalistic conception of the Creator denounced as atheistic.

The Hopkinsians were indeed so wrapped up in absolute sovereignty that they failed to relate their system to the spiritual needs of human beings. At a time of increasing democracy and self-reliant enterprise, Consistent Calvinism was beginning to appear a theology of anti-human, monarchic despotism. Indulgence in worldly affairs had ceased to provoke the feelings of remorse which had characterized the piety of an earlier epoch. After the Declaration of Independence, the principles of self-determination gradually became ingrained in the American conscience. As the nation had asserted its intrinsic right to mold its own destiny, many religious denominations so rejected the authoritarianism of established creeds. In economic, political, and religious life, many citizens began to object strenuously to aristocratic privilege. Consistent Calvinism seemed at odds with the emerging concept of the free individual. The doctrine of absolute sovereignty seemed despotic, and the predestined elect seemed unfairly privileged. Moreover, a theology which so disparaged human effort was out of step with a burgeoning entrepreneurial democracy, with its *quid pro quo* ethic. Lyman Beecher, a prime mover in the Second Great Awakening, saw the practical need of reconstituting orthodoxy on a more humane basis. During the Unitarian controversy, he accepted a Boston pastorate in order to

aid the embattled Calvinists. "When I first came to Boston," he later recalled, "nobody seemed to have an idea
that there was anything but what God had locked up and
frozen for all eternity. The bottom of accountability had
fallen out. My first business was to put it in again."[38]
Beecher drew his militant evangelical activism from his
teacher, Timothy Dwight.

New England Federalists turned increasingly toward
evangelical religion as an instrument for refurbishing
established values and institutions. Dwight was the
leader of this movement. Politically and theologically, he
resorted to democratic methods to further orthodox goals.
As theologican for the Second Great Awakening his purpose was to enhance man's capacity to promote the cause
of Christ on earth and turn back the satanic forces of
liberal democracy. With intent to arrest what he considered
moral degeneration, Dwight revised a theology which had
expunged human exertion beneath the withering power
of an Absolute Sovereign.

With Jeffersonian democracy and growing anti-Calvin-
ist sentiments challenging New England Puritanism, this
pragmatic conservative deplored the intractable posture
of Hopkinsian preaching. In an 1805 letter to an English
minister, he wrote:

> I am not a Hopkinsian . . . Their Systems I know, but do
> not believe; I think some of them in danger of injuring
> seriously, the faith once delivered to the Saints. It is now a
> doctrine, rife in Massachusetts, that nothing can be said
> to Sinners from the desk. Yet many things are to be said to
> them in Scripture. This seems to be complete proof to a
> Divine that such things are to be said to sinners.[39]

Dwight feared that with liberalism and infidelity threatening, Consistent Calvinist dogmatizing could only aggravate a dangerous situation. He detected the need to employ

many forms of persuasion to restore the Puritan faith to preeminence. Like Joseph Bellamy, he did not feel constrained from preaching for conversions. He was, in many respects an heir to the evangelical strand of Edwardian Calvinism. But his methods of winning souls were more diverse and flexible than those of the New Divinity. While never admitting his departure from Consistent Calvinism, he constructed a new moderate evangelical theology which served as rationale for the humanly contrived revivalism of the Second Great Awakening.

CHAPTER V

Calvinism Humanized

With the single goal of preserving and extending the Standing Order, Dwight worked at Yale to adjust Calvinism to prevailing conditions. Having been trained in the New Divinity, he always retained a strong bond of sympathy with the Edwardians. But he was also grievously aware that his pious brethren were losing their popular following, and that new measures were necessary if orthodoxy was to survive.

Dwight remained loyal to the religion of the affections. He objected vehemently to the purely moral preaching of Old Calvinists and Arminians. In theory, he held to the Reformation doctrine which denied saving power to any merely human action. Because the more liberal theologies had rationalized the pursuit of virtue to the point of obscuring the vital change of heart, Dwight regarded them as unscriptural. But his own extensive campaign for conversions modified his Calvinist principles and drove him appreciably toward liberal moralism. The New Divinity would not admit moderate Calvinism as a tenable position. If the sinner could act righteously on his own behalf, then he must not be wholly apostate; grace must not be completely free; and justification must come partially through works. In other words, if the use of means was effectual in procuring grace, then the Arminian system must be true. But every Calvinist regarded Arminianism as heresy, and Dwight was certainly no exception. His reliance on means, however, gave his theology such a dangerously Arminian tinge that his students, Nathaniel Taylor and Lyman Beecher, needed only to make minor modifications to place conversion within the grasp of every aspirant.

Unlike Hopkins or Emmons, Dwight did not approach theology in a metaphysical way. Neither was he exclusively the revival preacher, though he was very much the evangelical. His means for defending and propagating orthodoxy were primarily pedagogical.[1] While at Greenfield, he had established a thriving academy which imparted Christian knowledge to children of both sexes. "Religious education" was for Dwight the mainspring of virtue and hence the primary means of grace. Refusing to confine God's gracious influence within the bounds of instantaneous conversion, he viewed the overall environment as instrumental in regeneration.

In 1795, the year of his appointment to the Yale presidency, Dwight was asked to deliver the election sermon. His discourse suggests the key elements in his theology. Its title, *The True Means of Establishing Public Happiness,* bears crucial significance. Dwight regarded the schools and churches of the Congregational establishment as agencies for promoting virtue among the Connecticut

populace. Far from an anachronous vestige of aristocracy,
the Standing Order guaranteed the right of every citizen,
as stated in the Declaration of Independence, to pursue
happiness. Seeking to marry Connecticut institutions to
American revolutionary ideals, Dwight stressed the human sources and social consequences of piety. His conservative intentions thereby drew him away from New Divinity
supernaturalism and toward an institutional theology.
In Edwardian fashion, he maintained that conduct is
based in the good or evil direction of the will. But he went
on to argue that two natural means, "Religious Education"
and "Public Worship," most effectively channel the will
in a virtuous direction. The general thrust of his argument
was that traditional institutions ought to be continued,
for they are the source of all blessings.[2]

Social and political conservatism underlay all of
Dwight's works and activities. During the first decade of
the nineteenth century, when Jeffersonian democrats were
challenging Connecticut's paternalism, Dwight composed his *Travels*. By and large, this four-volume work was
cast as a defense of the Standing Order. The glowing de-
scriptions of Connecticut society echoed the sentiment of
Greenfield Hill. Inhabitants of the Connecticut valley
were in Dwight's eyes the most sober, orderly, and productive in the nation. The reason was of course the Con-
gregationally controlled system of public education and
worship. In a section of the *Travels* devoted exclusively
to a "Vindication of the Establishment of the Public
Worship of God by Law," he responded to dissenters,
who were campaigning for disestablishment. Again he
tried to harmonize the old order with the new. Aware
that his opponents based their argument on the Federal
Constitution's support for religious freedom, he invoked
the Preamble to that document in defense of the Standing
Order. Religion, by making people moral, was of crucial
importance for promoting the general welfare. Only

where regular worship rendered people obedient to God's government did morality prevail. Where support of religious institutions was not enforced by law, church attendance and piety declined. To prove his point Dwight marshalled empirical evidence. Of course, the observations he recorded were filtered through a parochial mind. In Rhode Island and New York, religious pluralism had been fully institutionalized. Contributions to churches existed on a purely voluntary basis. Dwight condemned this system because it failed to assure the churches' financial support. The ministry ceased to be a powerful opinion-molding element, and became dependent on the "fluctuating feelings of parishioners." Dwight feared the decline of ministerial influence in a society ruled by the popular will. In Connecticut, compulsory support of the clergy rendered them independent of the people. They functioned as an arm of the paternal governing structure. In the more democratic states, they were compelled to survive on their own and were thus no more privileged than lawyers, tradesmen, or artisans. Pluralism also threatened the continued viability of orthodoxy. In Dwight's estimation, the complete separation of church and state would encourage immorality by giving license to every form of heresy, irreligion, and infidelity. Puritan and Federalist that he was, Dwight believed that strong government supervision was needed to suppress such destructive aberrations. Again paraphrasing the Federal Constitution, he declared that ". . . the first great concern of the people of New England is to secure the blessings of their Kingdom [of Christ] to themselves and their posterity." To Dwight's mind, the diffusion of Puritan orthodoxy best accomplished this national goal. Since Connecticut institutions were best accommodated to the dissemination of virtue, they were most harmonious with Constitutional dicta.[3]

The idea of a Christian environment, based on subordination to paternal authority, was the cornerstone of Dwight's religion. He advanced not only the Gospel, but the overall pattern of Puritan culture as most conducive to godliness. In the older settlements of New England "every child is carried to the church from the cradle to the grave." Each township is a cohesive community under the fatherly care of minister and elders. Public opinion is united and social norms remain constant. Planned settlements provide their inhabitants with easy access to education and public worship. "Scattered plantations," however, like those of the South and hinterlands, are "subject to many serious disadvantages." Dwight remarked that "neither schools, nor churches can without difficulty be either built by the planters, or supported." He concluded that lack of close personal contact engenders "social insulation," which in turn gives rise to a coarse-grained ignorance.[4]

Puritan institutions served as important instruments of social control. In Connecticut, the ruling gentry continued to benefit from a type of social organization which perpetuated "steady habits." As their spokesman, the Yale president deplored the turbulence of more fluid societies. He noted that "idlers and rovers" disrupt the newer settlements. Often engaging in shady speculative ventures, they exhibit "ignorant and licentious" conduct. Dwight looked forward to the permeation of traditional New England culture into these pockets of disorder. This phenomenon was already occurring in New York, Maine, and Vermont. The Second Great Awakening would see the Connecticut establishment increase its missionary efforts in the back country.[2]

In defending Connecticut Puritanism, Dwight relied heavily on a new, empirical method of apology. During the eighteenth century, a number of moderate Calvinist and Arminian thinkers in England attempted to show that Christianity is more reasonable than enlightened deism and skepticism. Their purpose was to harmonize Protestant theology with the new learning of the scientific revolution, and thereby demolish their opponents' grounds for attack. These supernatural rationalists[6] held that man can discover basic principles of religion by using his natural faculties or senses. Scriptural revelation does not contradict, but supports the principles of natural religion. By simply perceiving and reflecting on the works of the Creation, man can discern the existence and attributes of God. Revelation, however, is necessary to enhance limited human capacity. Rational Christians of England and America reaffirmed the orthodox contention that original sin had much diminished man's natural powers. But they resorted to empirical means of proving inherent depravity, as well as the entire Christian scheme of salvation. In rational and empirical terms, these theologians of the Enlightenment cited historical evidence of Christian doctrine. They argued that Christ had exactly fulfilled Old Testament Messianic prophecy, and his miracles, attested to by hundreds of witnesses, had proved him to be the Son of God.

Supernatural rationalism was not a particular creed, but a method of Christian apologetics. As such, both Calvinists and Arminians made use of it. Rational Calvinists, however, were invariably moderates, deeply colored by Arminianism. They could not, like Edwards, be complete supernaturalists, because their style of divinity enhanced the position of natural religion. Edwards had made profound but limited use of Newton and Locke. Sense perception had been the framework for experimental religion, but Edwardian grace was much too subjective and cataclysmic to fit the mechanistic universe. The arbitrary,

mysterious God of Consistent Calvinism was out of joint
with uniform laws of matter and motion. Newtonian
theory implied a God who works through secondary
means, in which His constituted agencies invariably produce the same results. Application of this system to Christianity demanded that religious institutions function in
much the same rational fashion. Deists rejected the Christian scheme because they construed its miraculous content
to violate Newtonian law. But the supernatural rationalists held that God carries out his scriptural plan not
directly, but through regular operation of secondary agencies, or human religious institutions.

Prior to Dwight, New England evangelicals were not
supernatural rationalists. Since Consistent Calvinism
eschewed natural religious endeavors, the rational attack
on infidelity had come largely from liberal moralists. But
supernatural rationalism served Dwight well in his design to resuscitate Calvinism and establish an orthodox
environment. As an evangelical, he stressed conversion,
but his method of divinity bore greater resemblance to
that of Arminians than to metaphysical Consistent Calvinist systems.

Dwight's use of supernatural rationalism had the effect
of humanizing his orthodoxy. Throughout his theology,
he carefully grounded each doctrine in the circumstances
of life. His system was not one of abstract reasoning conceived in isolation from the daily currents of existence.
It was preached in a collection of sermons specifically
designed to influence the students at Yale. To counter the
growth of heresy and skepticism on campus, Dwight put
into practice the pedagogical skills he deemed so important as a means of furthering piety. His lectures were
terse and conversational, calculated to persuade the

young men that orthodoxy was relevant to their lives. The entire series of didactic sermons took him four years to deliver. Thus, each succeeding class received exhaustive nurture in orthodox theology.

Dwight was a masterful orator. As a youth, he had ruined his eyes in a quixotic, but typically Puritan attempt to master all knowledge. Consequently, he had been forced to perfect his oral and extemporaneous skills. Difficulty with his eyes plagued him throughout his adult life. Probably suffering from glaucoma, he was never able to read or write for an extended period of time. In his correspondence, he often complained of this problem, and the few letters he penned were abbreviated and to the point. For the most part, he employed students to transcribe his thoughts, the most famous of whom was Nathaniel Taylor. Dwight's poor vision may be one explanation for his public, gregarious style of life. Perhaps with better eyes he might have been a cloistered metaphysician.[7]

Beginning with the existence and attributes of God, Dwight's sermons on theology were designed to show that orthodoxy was reasonable and singularly beneficial to mankind. Basic to his defense of Calvinism was the refutation of opposing viewpoints. In establishing a First Cause, he had only to confute atheistical objections. His empirical method of proving supernatural causation sets the pattern of his argument. He maintained that observing the effect of temporal creation leads us to conclude that it has a primary cause, a Creator. It is as natural to arrive at this conclusion as it is to infer man's presence from the existence of buildings. After demonstrating God's existence in the manner of Locke and Berkeley, to whom he refers,[8] he proceeded to consider the creation as a reflection of the divine character.

Dwight's goal was to make orthodoxy an appealing system by proving it most useful in giving man happiness. He sought to harmonize Calvinism with the humanistic and utilitarian values of middle class America. Like the deists, he viewed God as a Supreme Architect, who has benevolently contrived the smoothly running mechanism of the universe. While the deists, however, theorized that God, once having set the universe in motion, retreated from the scene, Dwight balanced reason with revelation. Experience informs us that God is benevolent, for he has constructed a beautiful and useful world, and Scripture reinforces this observation by telling us that the "highest blessedness" is in "communicating good."[9] In this opening sermon, Dwight introduced the technique of supernatural rationalism, which would pervade his theology. Because God created man, we are immediately dependent on him for our continued welfare. When we unite with Him in doing good, we help to further His glory. If, however, we oppose Him, we must fear His wrath. The Calvinistic orientation of Dwight's system is modified here, by a rational presentation which gave Reformed doctrines a concrete, humanitarian flavor.

Considering atheistical objections, he continued the utilitarian argument from design. The universe is a perfect adaptation of "means" to "ends." Similarly every organism displays a "union of parts in a smoothly functioning whole." It was absurd to suppose that such an elaborately contrived order could be the product of mere chance. Dwight found atheism so irrational that he attributed it to an "indisposition of the heart to acknowledge the existence of the Creator." In this case, common sense proved not only the existence of God, but of moral depravity. That intelligent beings could violate their own reason to espouse atheism, was clear proof that they hated or dreaded God in their hearts.[10]

Dwight agreed with the Edwardians that virtue and sin are based in the heart; like them he saw the regenerate heart as the source of pious volitions. His crucial divergence with Consistent Calvinism lay in how "the taste or relish of the mind" might be altered. He believed that religious training can influence the mind by holding out natural motives to virtue. The concept of natural motivation formed the heart of Dwight's evangelical theology. Essentially it was simply a broader conceptualization of the means of grace. Motives arise not, directly from God, as the Edwardians believed, but from nurture; and when properly instilled, they generate virtuous habits. Influence, motives, and habits were three interrelated aspects of Dwight's system. They functioned together as the means by which religion and a virtuous society are advanced and perpetuated.[11]

The atheistic world view can only impart evil motives, for it places mankind entirely under the dominion of chance or fate. Dwight believed, as did most of his contemporaries, that only faith in a God who rewards virtue and punishes sin can make man morally responsible. For concrete evidence that widespread atheism effaces morality New England Federalists like Dwight cited the French Revolution. In his judgment, atheism and other forms of infidelity had been directly responsible for three million deaths in France during a ten-year period. The atheistic conception of death as an eternal sleep had removed fear of future punishment for wrongdoing, and hence powerful motives to virtuous conduct.[12]

Like Edwards and Hopkins, Dwight conceived of Christian virtue as voluntary love and disinterested benevolence to being in general. But he saw such love in relation to its humane results. In a sermon entitled "Utility the Foundation of Virtue," he asserted that "voluntary usefulness" or "the spirit of doing good" is the only cause of happiness. And human happiness founded in utility is the end for which God created the world; it coincides with His glory.[13] This loving, paternal Deity, who seeks no greater end than the contentment of His rational creation was a far cry from the wrathful Edwardian Sovereign. The primacy of Dwight's social concerns led him to stress outward utility, rather than an inner feeling of piety as the culmination of religious experience. His characteristic emphasis on the practical effects of conversion pushed his theology beyond pietistic New Divinity formulae, causing him to make use of moralistic systems.

William Paley, the influential Anglican theologican of the late eighteenth century, constructed an elaborate system of Christian apologetics within the framework of utilitarianism. Together with other British conservatives, he engaged in ideological combat with French liberalism. Like Edmund Burke, Paley defended the institutional status quo in terms of its beneficient utility.[14] In many respects, he was Dwight's English counterpart. Both theologians were spokesmen for the ecclesiastical branch of a deferential society; and both responded to change by formulating timely apologies for traditional beliefs. Dwight borrowed heavily from Paley's utilitarianism, but he reworked it to fit his own Calvinistic premises. Paley, after all, was a High Churchman, and hence an Arminian, who owed no allegiance to the pietism of Jonathan Edwards. Dwight was cautious in his use of Paley. Utilitarianism made Calvinist doctrines relevant to the immediate concerns of New Englanders, but its overuse ran the risk of distorting the Puritan faith.

Dwight used Paley's *Moral Philosophy* as a text for his senior class. He found it necessary to catalogue the flaws, as well as the strengths of the British theologian's system

in a series of lectures. While the president of Yale broke
with the Edwardian principle that unsanctified moral
exertions are fruitless, he still regarded man as frail and
dependent. His utilitarianism was therefore more super-
naturally oriented than Paley's.[15]

Though Dwight ascribed less power to man than did
the Anglican, his conception of benevolence involved
little of the self-abasement demanded by the New Divinity. He stressed not the divine cause, but the human consequences of holiness. "Virtue is good," he said, "only
because it produces pleasure, or diminishes pain." Similarly, he condemned wickedness not because it is an
infinite sin against an infinite God, but because of its
"tendency to produce misery." Emphasis on action more
than feeling, and reliance on the human resources of
virtue were central to Dwight's religion. Removing orthodoxy from the Edwardian closet, he set it once more
in a social context. But he knew that to increase the appeal
of Calvinism by thus humanizing it threatened its pietistic basis. Consequently, he was always warding off the
luring embrace of Paley's moralism. He did so by asserting that virtue does not consist in the act alone. It "is the
love of doing good" serving as "an operative principle
whenever it has an object to act upon."[16]

In expounding theology to his students, Dwight sought
to fit each doctrine into an overall divine plan for universal felicity. Thereby, he gave the old dogmas a captivating attractiveness. His instructive technique combined
theory with practice, for in explaining the means by which
God accomplishes His ends, Dwight was at the same time
making use of them. Reinterpreting each traditional doctrine, he considered its concrete evidence, its immediate
human effects, and its relationship to God's benevolent

design. Unlike the Edwardians, Dwight was always careful to draw heartening implications from Calvinist doctrine. He agreed, for example, that God must be omnipotent, for only such a Creator can inspire the faithful with confidence that they will be delivered from evil. On the other hand, to discourage complacency he warned his students, "How terrible an enemy to obstinate and impenitent sinners is an omnipotent God." His purpose in voicing this sentiment was wholly evangelical. Earlier in the same sermon, he had reminded his audience that "the Kingdom of God is a kingdom of means," and the Almighty harbors no "favouritism," or prejudice toward any being. An omnipotent God motivates humanity to fear and love Him. He upholds the faithful, even though they cannot refrain from sinning. "Every righteous man" may expect "a final deliverance from his enemies, sorrows, and sins; from death and the grave; from future pollution; from eternal woe." What stronger motives to piety can exist?[17]

Even God's decrees of predestination which so mortified the parishioners of New Divinity metaphysicals, lost their frightful aura in Dwight's evangelical theology. To reconcile human freedom with divine foreknowledge, he assumed a finite agent at perfect liberty "while at the same time no being [knows] at all in what manner he would act until his actions [already] existed." Then he supposed the agent, "without any change in his powers or circumstances in any other respect, to have all his action foreknown by God or some other being." "I ask," said Dwight, "whether they would be at all less free, in consequence of being thus foreknown." In short, God's "foreknowledge has not the remotest influence on the agent, or his action."[18] The purpose of such reasoning was to give prospective converts greater powers in their use of means. Such relegation of God's supervision to the background of immediate human events served aptly as a rationale for religious activism.

Dwight further altered predestinarian Calvinism by rejecting the traditional concept of an inscrutably chosen elect. Thus was he able to impart new vitality to the General Atonement.[19] Bellamy had asserted Christ's sacrifice for all mankind, but he had also clung to the doctrine of predestined election. The General Atonement argued in these terms had lost much of its evangelical impact. By unequivocally dispensing with the Limited Atonement, Dwight was able to provide greater incentive to strive for salvation. In this way he strengthened the agency of Christ as Savior, preparing the way for a humane evangelism based more in the Cross of the Redeemer than the wrath of a vindictive God.

Divine sovereignty also became a rational, humane doctrine in Dwight's enlightened system. Because God stands outside time, his omniscience comprehending all history, it is unnecessary for him to intervene directly. The natural works of His creation are deliberately calculated to accomplish His ends. The sovereignty of God functions smoothly, operating perpetually in all events of the temporal realm. Therefore, saving grace is not so much a supernatural intrusion as the regular effect of a virtuous environment. Again Dwight was revising Consistent Calvinism to buttress Puritan institutions. He asserted that God exercises sovereignty in conferring salvation by placing individuals in circumstances suitable or unsuitable to the growth of piety.[20] New Englanders are principal recipients of divine favor since they enjoy knowledge of the Gospel, and excellent means for its dissemination. Dwight often rebuked his students for their inattention to these most useful blessings of Providence. The inevitable conclusion he drew from belief in his society's peculiar virtue was that orthodox New Englanders had a duty to illuminate regions of moral darkness.[21] This sense of redemptive mission fired the imagination of many a Yale student. Lyman Beecher, for example, who was to be a major architect of the forthcoming evangelical counter-reformation, drew his inspiration from President Dwight. So too did Nathaniel Taylor, Jeremiah Evarts and a great many other religious activists of the Second Great Awakening.

In Dwight's system of modified Calvinism, the individual possessed the faculties to profit from a religious environment, but he was also dependent on God's revealed Word. Those who disregard Scripture must lead a depraved existence. And when an entire nation opposes the will of God, it must suffer the tyranny of uncontrolled passion. Dwight never tired of illustrating the abject failure of pure rationalism with the French upheaval.[22] But he also drew on more immediate sources to prove man's innate depravity and consequent need of divine guidance.

Departing from the Edwardians, he asserted that, "A preacher should not lean toward metaphysical preaching." While it was sometimes necessary to deal with "abstruse subjects," it should be done in an instructive manner. "Illustrations and comparisons should be drawn . . . from such things as are intelligible to all capacities."[23] Dwight cited vices familiar to all his students; and catalogued their deleterious effects. His method was to show how the practice of one vice inevitably leads to indulgence in others. The race track, for example, is not only a place of gambling. "Fraud and falsehood [are] practiced; perjuries, oaths, curses, and blasphemies uttered; drunkenness and sloth are indulged; battles are fought and the universal prostitution of morals is accomplished." Dwight provided numerous variations on the theme of man's corruption, including a Parisian statistical survey for the year 1803, revealing a significant degree (for that time) of crime, divorce, suicide, illegitimate births, prostitution, and the like. Not only therefore did he expound the metaphysical doctrine of human depravity, but he also portrayed its grim consequences in daily experience, thereby making it real to his students.[24]

The Fall of Adam had so corrupted man, that even after the Christian plan of salvation had been introduced inveterate sinners had rejected and perverted its content. Dwight lost no occasion to warn the Yale students against the train of evil seducers who would lead them astray. With the plight of orthodoxy constantly on his mind, he lashed out at infidel philosophers, religious dissenters, and the "Romish hierarchy." His deep prejudice against Catholicism was echoed among the evangelicals affected by his Protestant militancy. Beecher would later play on fears of a Catholic menace in the West to goad his countrymen to evangelization.[25] Samuel F. B. Morse, another Dwight student, would not only invent the telegraph, but also lead an hysterical anti-Catholic movement.[26] Dwight's opinion of Catholicism was typical of many Protestant millennialists. Rome was the beast, the whore of Babylon. It was full of corrupted "wealth, power, splendour, and sensuality."[27] With their ideological roots in the Reformation, Americans had always distrusted the Catholic Church. But anti-Catholicism did not become an important issue until the second quarter of the nineteenth century when Catholic immigrants began to arrive en masse. At that time militant evangelicals, many of whom had been schooled in the apocalyptic orthodoxy of Timothy Dwight, led the nativist upsurge.

But neither did all Protestant ministers escape the wrath of the Yale president. Liberals, with "their latitudinarian doctrines and loose lives [also] exercised a malignant influence on their fellow men, and contributed in serious degree to the depravation of the human character."[28] Only Calvinist societies like Holland, Switzerland, and of course Connecticut, had effectively curbed the passions of depravity. Repeatedly Dwight extolled the virtues of his immediate environment while warning that ungodly systems endangered its prosperity. Inevitably he influenced a number of young men to believe that the Standing Order was the fountain of all happiness, that its religion must be defended against an army of corruptors, and disseminated throughout the nation.

He inspired such commitment by resourceful use of the means of grace. Saturating his students with a theology of nurture, he set the stage for a powerful orthodox upsurge. If religious education formed the backbone of the aggressive new Calvinism, revivalism was its lifeblood. Dwight interspersed rational apologetics with emotional exhortations. The revivals which resulted in the Yale student body inaugurated the Second Great Awakening.

CHAPTER VI

Nurture and Revivalism

Dwight's lectures on Christian practice not only indoc-
trinated young Americans in a set of conservative values.
It also gave them confidence that their loyalty to the Puritan way would make them virtuous and happy. But more
important, prospective ministers, under Dwight's tutelage,
learned how to orchestrate revivals. Their instructor gave
them an activist theology which bridged the Edwardian
chasm between human means and divine grace. In his
system, a simple, faithful commitment was the foundation
of piety. De-emphasizing the burdensome doctrines of
predestination and moral inability, Dwight deliberately
sought to inspire his listeners with confidence in a God
who dispenses grace in a rational, uniform way. Faith
was nothing more than "trust or confidence exercised
toward the moral character of God, and particularly of
the Saviour." The returning sinner had only to believe in
his heart that a paternal God governs the universe for the
most benevolent purposes.[1]

Dwight criticized Jonathan Edwards for his statement that Paul had spoken of justification *"in the sight of God,"* while James had seen it *"in the sight of men only."* Dwight found no discrepancy in the positions of the two Apostles. The importance of faith lay, for him, in its effect on the believer's overt behavior. *"The faith of the Gospel cannot exist without good works."*[2] Faith was crucial because it rendered the individual willing to *act* virtuously. Hence justification through faith was not vital because of its legal necessity, but because it empowered man to obey the law of God. And the evangelical system was true because it was most useful in renovating moral character.

Regeneration of the heart is the central doctrine of evangelical Christianity. In discussing this event, Dwight again humanized the arbitrary God of Consistent Calvinism. In his lengthy analysis of regeneration, its agent, nature, antecedents, attendants, and consequences, he detailed an orderly process clearly discernible to every Christian. But while he described the observable interaction between God and man, he stopped short of any metaphysical inquiry into the mind of the Redeemer. The "nature of the cause itself," Dwight commented, is either "to subtile [sic] or too entirely hidden from our view . . . to be perceived as to become the materials of real and *useful* knowledge." Judged practically, such speculation only detracts from the evangelical cause by producing needless "controversies . . . within the Christian Church." A confirmed nominalist, Dwight acknowledged the sagacity of the medieval schoolmen, but noted the uselessness of their forgotten inquiries "at the present time."[3] This assessment was an indirect criticism of New Divinity metaphysicals. Where Edwardians began with doctrine, and bent all observable phenomena to conform with it,

Dwight emphasized a more flexible, inductive method. His tendency to work from effect back to cause modified a system deduced from the dogma of absolute sovereignty. Scriptural accounts and his own observations led Dwight to conclude, for example, that God's grace is not irresistable. By granting man the power to resist the Holy Spirit, he impinged on divine sovereignty. The effect was to provide further rationale for evangelical exertion, for if man can resist the Spirit, he can certainly labor in its interest.[4]

Dwight accepted the Consistent Calvinist notion of "instantaneous regeneration," since it harmonized with revival preaching. But such conversion was not for him an all-consuming fire of the soul ignited by the indwelling Spirit. Rather, it was merely the point in time when holiness begins. In contrast to the miraculous nature of Edwardian regeneration, he asserted that nothing extraordinary takes place in the first acts of virtue. "All that makes them extraordinary is, that they are first."[5] Nineteenth-century evangelicals gradually shifted from the idea that conversions are surprising works of God to a new belief that they are natural results of the "correct use of means."[6] In so doing, they followed directly on the heels of Timothy Dwight, who first revised the old supernaturalism by viewing regeneration as a regular and generally indirect process.

Like Hopkins, Dwight held regeneration to be in itself imperceptible. But he specifically repudiated the idea that sinners grow worse under conviction, as well as the doctrine that natural man is incapable of striving effectively for salvation. In his system regeneration was often imperceptible because previous training had rendered the convert an habitual practitioner of Christian duty. He reasoned that individuals who receive religious education and thus seek to obey divine law, undergo far less "deep and distressing convictions" than do their more wayward brethren. While regeneration brought a more radical perception of sin and holiness, it was an almost natural result of continuous adherence to scriptural precept. Dwight formally rejected the Old Calvinists' belief that conversions are gradually accomplished because it so deemphasized experimental piety. But his own reliance on nurture was virtually akin to their seventeenth century concept of preparation for salvation. His belief that natural man can be "conscientious, amiable, and exemplary" in his behavior was anathema to Consistent Calvinists, who saw all unregenerate activity as wholly depraved.[7]

In delineating the convicted sinner's strivings for grace, Dwight ranged even further from the New Divinity and perilously close to Arminianism. In complete disagreement with the Hopkinsians, he argued: "Perhaps no one who persisted in his efforts to gain eternal life was ever finally deserted by the Spirit of grace." Convicted sinners, feeling their "danger of ruin," proceed to inquire "what they shall do to be saved." Recall that the Hopkinsian editors of the *Massachusetts Missionary Magazine* responded to this inquiry with the statement that all unregenerate strivings are worthless and abominable in God's sight. But Dwight disagreed emphatically. Not metaphysical disquisition, but "the controlling anguish" of the sinner's heart decides whether or not he "shall be directed to pray" for grace. If sinners cannot pray for a new heart, he continued, who can? Saints have no need of one. Furthermore, "the mere wish to be saved from suffering is neither sinful, nor holy. . . ." There is nothing "hateful to God in this wish." Sinners are not less, but more likely to receive the grace of a compassionate God. Dwight cited his own observation as well as Scripture to prove that ". . . regeneration regularly follows such prayers. . . ."[8]

This affirmation of unregenerate attempts to procure salvation was closer to Old Calvinism and Arminianism than to the New Divinity. Dwight retained a distinctly Edwardian conception of the nature and effects of the conversion experience. His overall approach to religion was evangelical; hence his disdain for systems which subordinated pure Reformation doctrine to the cultivation of Christian ethics. But ironically, his attempts to revive experimental religion led him to accentuate human resources to such an extent that his theology had much in common with the liberal opposition. His peculiar accomplishment was to blend the rationalism and reliance on means which characterized the moralistic systems with the evangelical purpose of the New Divinity.

It is illuminating to explore the teachings of well-known Old Calvinists and Arminians to see how close Dwight was to the moralism he so detested. The trait which most markedly distinguished these ministers from the New Divinity was their reliance on means, or secondary agencies of grace. William Hart, an Old Calvinist, believed religious education the most significant factor in restoring the soul. He conceived of this nurture as dutiful attendance to all the "instituted means of gaining knowledge and faith of the . . . Gospel."[9] Moses Hemmenway, also an Old Calvinist minister, engaged Samuel Hopkins in prolonged debate. His argument stressed the means of grace as part of a "regular subordination of causes and effects" operative in the natural order, and "in the government of the intelligent and moral world."[10]

While anti-revivalist, Hemmenway often took more strictly Calvinist positions than Dwight. He argued, for example, that a sinner "should not be encouraged to strive for eternal life, from an expectation he shall hereby receive God's compassion."[11] Dwight spoke of God's pity on the striving sinner. But more important, both Dwight and Hemmenway expressed confidence that those who strive assiduously for grace will likely be rewarded. Said Dwight, "In my apprehension it is never true that the attempts of the man concerned towards the attainment of salvation, make no difference as to that event. . . .nor is there any satisfactory reason to believe that those who make them with persevering earnestness and zeal, ultimately fail."[12] Hemmenway softened his contention that the "most serious and earnest endeavors" of the unregenerate "are sinful . . ." by declaring his faith in the sanctifying power of means: ". . . who is there that was deneyed [sic] a blessing if he continued seeking for it in God's appointed way? . . ."[13]

From this position, it was only a short step to Arminianism. Jonathan Mayhew was probably the most famous Arminian of eighteenth century America. A stalwart opponent of Consistent Calvinism, he preached a series of sermons which provoked a storm of New Divinity rebuttal. Not unlike Dwight or Hemmenway, he argued that those who strive diligently will not remain unsanctified. But in making his case, he went so far as to assert that God has made a promise of salvation to the unregenerate who sincerely use the means. Like Dwight, he emphasized that Christ died for all mankind. From the premise of the General Atonement, he reasoned, "surely all who really desire and strive to obtain eternal life shall obtain it."[14] This deduction would follow naturally from Dwight's contention that ". . . the kingdom of God . . . is a kingdom of means regularly connected with their ends."[15] But while Dwight and Hemmenway both held this view, their fears of explicitly advancing justification through works caused them to veer away from the notion that God has made promises to the unregenerate. Mayhew, however, saw no contradiction between such promises and free grace. He maintained that striving in itself is not a virtuous act, and hence those who strive do not render themselves deserving of grace.[16]

Dwight avoided attacking his New Divinity allies directly. Yet his views of Consistent Calvinism tended to coincide with Mayhew's. Both men rejected the notion that means were only for prior converts. Mayhew criticized Hopkinsians for throwing "needless discouragement in the way of those who strive for salvation," and even preventing "others from striving." He denounced the doctrine that "all endeavors of the unregenerate . . . aggravate their guilt, and so their damnation" as representing "the ever good and glorious God in the most odious light possible."[17] Dwight dismissed this piece of Hopkinsian logic as pure speculation, since it is "beyond the power of man to measure degrees of depravity." He saw "no reason why this question should be introduced into theological discourse, since its [only tendency was] to perplex and distress."[18]

Dwight was troubled by these ill effects of Consistent Calvinism. He wanted to provide new incentives to traditional piety without conceding too much to the Arminians and thus sacrificing the religion of the heart for a cold moralism. In order to revitalize evangelical Calvinism, he portrayed God as a paternal Being who has commissioned effectual means to reclaim his errant children. God is not only Creator, Lawgiver, and Judge, but also "a Father and an everlasting Friend. . . ." When He regenerates an individual, God adopts him as a child. Although the convert has been part of the "Divine Family" since baptism, he now ceases his rebellion and estrangement. As a wise and benevolent parent, the Almighty Father instructs

his family in the "Spirit of Truth," reproving and cor-
recting each child when he errs.[19]

This paternal relationship of God to His human family
corresponded to Dwight's treatment of his students. Taylor, Beecher, and Dwight's eulogists attest to his close
personal supervision of the youths in his charge. Dwight's
career encompassed ever widening circles of paternalism.
His family experience had prepared him for Greenfield,
where he had further developed his skills in fatherly guidance. Yale was the culmination of his paternalistic role.
Not only did he treat his students as sons, but he also
looked upon the Connecticut citizenry in much the same
manner. To his mind, all just and orderly government
followed the paternal pattern. It was this aspect of the
Standing Order which so appealed to him. Congregational ministers and magistrates ostensibly functioned
as fathers of the Commonwealth. As president of the highest institution of learning, Dwight was the acknowledged
leader and spokesman for the ecclesiastical establishment.
Hence, he tended to regard himself as something of a chief
father in Connecticut. Paternalism informed all the religious and social view he so freely expounded to his students and to the public-at-large.

The conscientious father seeks to instill virtue in his
children. To motivate the young men of Yale toward evangelical Christianity, Dwight used two basic approaches.
Like an Old Testament patriarch, he set forth the Law of
God, scrupulously applying it to human affairs. And in
his role of loving evangelist, he preached the Gospel message, working to produce convictions of sin and the holy
affections of conversion. Relentlessly, he exhorted his
students to make Christian exertions. His exhaustive
analysis of the means of grace was formulated to convince

them that unregenerate strivings bear fruit, and to describe the way in which each ordinance functions to yield felicitous piety.

The ministerial office of preaching the Gospel was the most important instrument of grace. Dwight stressed that only an evangelical ministry could turn men from carnal to spiritual preoccupations.[20] He rejected metaphysical preaching because it lacked evangelical utility. Since the only purpose of the minister is to lead sinners to Christ, he must preach a simple, powerful Gospel devoid of all "technical or scientific language." Subtle distinctions are never clear to the average person, who responds far more readily to "the obvious investigations of common sense." Concrete reasoning in the style of Christ, Dwight asserted, is the most useful way to enlighten the mind.[21]

Dwight was nothing like a philosophical pragmatist, since he believed in a God-given set of clearly discernible absolutes. But he was pragmatic in his judgment of every institution, every mode of behavior by what he took to be its practical effect. The minister, in Dwight's assessment, is the agent of Christ, and he must be about his Savior's business. He is therefore not only capable of rousing his congregation to spiritual concern, but he is duty bound "to use all means in his power" to do so.

The practical bent and anti-intellectual tendencies of Dwight's revivalistic use of means presaged the development of nineteenth-century evangelical religion. Charles G. Finney, the great evangelist of the Antebellum era, also believed that ministers should be educated for action. Theory must have its foundation in practice, and practice is determined largely by common sense. Finney's revivalism reflected a continuing American dialogue between theoreticians and practitioners and epitomized the oft-repeated attempt to fuse thought with action.[22] Dwight began the process of amalgamation with his utilitarian emphasis on means. But increasing activism carried a tendency toward complete disregard of the intellect and the exaltation of a crude reliance on mere technique.[23] In reaction against New Divinity scholasticism, Dwight endeavored to simplify theology so that the average person could grasp its meaning. With evangelical intentions, he also enhanced the methods of persuasion. Finney had a similar object in mind when he further simplified divinity and elaborated "New Measures" to produce conversions. This trend continued among revivalists and culminated, with Billy Sunday, in the obliteration of all theology in favor of a sensational, melodramatic performance to bring about emotional catharsis.

Dwight, however, was careful to include the entire content of Reformed theology in his system. He did not wish to sacrifice any portion of "the faith once delivered to the saints," but to portray each doctrine and duty in an evangelical light. With this aim in mind, he not only lectured on the correct style of preaching, but he also delivered emotional, pietistic sermons. "The Youth of Nain" and "The Harvest Past" were two such discourses which stirred revivals on more than one occasion. Lyman Beecher recalled the latter sermon's effect in bringing on his own religious awakening.

> When I heard him preach on "The harvest is past, the summer is ended, and we are not saved," a whole avalanche rolled down on my mind. I went home weeping every step.[24]

In "The Youth of Nain," Dwight drew on the image of Christ restoring the dead boy to life to represent the awakening of young sinners before him to new lives of holiness. As Finney later would do, he spoke personally to his congregation. He thoroughly appreciated the importance of such familiarity, as he told his senior class that "a preacher should make it a commanding rule to address the audience directly. Every preacher should be well versed in Biography."[25] Having schooled his students in evangelical doctrine, he had prepared them to writhe in conviction when he warned of the dire consequences of their frivolous behavior. Completely in tune with their feelings, he knew when he had sufficiently dangled the youths over the fiery pit, so that they were ready to grasp at their means of deliverance. He asked them to suppose Christ were present. Would you then continue to "loll in stupid inattention as if benumbed with the torpor of an opiate; and sleep the sleep of death?" Having asked the rhetorical question, he climactically exclaimed that the Savior is now and always present. Christ is forever raising multitudes from the dead and has done so more than once "in this seminary."[26] First delivered in 1802, this sermon ignited a revival of unprecedented proportions in the Yale student body.[27]

Dwight's other most notable revival sermon, "The Harvest Past," was composed of similar material. He admonished the young men that every year they remained impenitent added to their guilt and further hardened their hearts, making it more difficult to break down and repent. This statement contrasted with the Hopkinsian notion that unregenerate strivings are futile. Dwight held that sinners can and must repent immediately if they desire salvation. He described the overwhelming remorse of the unregenerate soul coming before the bar of Final Judgment. In what would later become standard evangelical procedure, he offered his hearers the choice between the horrors of endless punishment, and the perfect joy of salvation. The young sinners had only to repent and receive Christ, and they would be commencing the journey to heaven.[28] Because this sermon had the desired effect, Dwight preached it on more than one occasion. An anonymous contemporary claimed: "At least four or five extensive revivals of religion were supposed to commence in consequence of its delivery."[29]

Probably with lugubrious New Divinity preachers in mind, Dwight cautioned against "vehemence" in "disclosing the doom of the impenitent." He confessed that some ministers in dwelling on this subject aroused his own feelings of "horror and disgust." "The words of a preacher," he said, "should be those of a guilty man to guilty men . . . of a man, who humbly hopes, that he has found pardon for himself, and is most affectionately anxious that his hearers may find the same blessings also."[30]

Dwight expressed such warm concern, often excluding a confident reliance that God's Spirit illuminated his preaching. In "The Youth of Nain," he invoked Christ's promise to attend any gathering in His name to proclaim the Savior's presence in the Yale Chapel. His reliance on personal experience in place of metaphysical deduction served to strengthen his self-assurance. The pietism of his revivalistic sermons was active, rather than quietistic. With his faith in means, he played down the subjective passivity of the Edwardians and made observable behavior a major indicator of piety. While maintaining the indwelling Spirit as the principle of holiness, he asserted that God rewards or punishes individuals according to their "*character* and *conduct*." Hence without apparent injury to his Calvinism, he could state that all men will be rewarded exactly "according to their works."[31] The nominalist idea that man has only limited capacity to see into the mind of God enabled Dwight to enjoy the most productive aspects of both the evangelical and Arminian schemes. He preached for experimental conversion, but judged the effects of his preaching by what he considered the only reliable gauge of holiness, external conduct. By thus restoring the old Puritan belief that behavior can indicate one's spiritual state, and coupling it with the fervor of revival preaching, he was able to relieve much of the doubt and distress of prospective Christians and generate new life in the orthodox faith. He could also give evangelical significance to the inculcation of moral duty. While the revival sermon was the prime stimulant to repentance and faith, many other means were useful in producing Christian conduct. And if conversions were usually imperceptible, individuals who knew the morals of Scripture and loved to practice them could rest reasonably assured of grace.

Dwight never, of course, discountenanced subjective piety. Revival sermons were a most effective means of imparting evangelical faith to the individual. Intensive self-examination and private prayer were also important avenues to personal holiness. But Dwight liked to accentuate the significance of social prayer. Never losing sight of the Puritan national covenant, he explained that: "Public prayer above all things, preserves alive a sense of National dependence on God." It was the way to procure divine blessings. The happy and prosperous state of New England was the result of the prayerful character of its inhabitants and clear proof that virtuous people are recipients of the Lord's bounty.[32] Throughout his career, especially in times of crisis, Dwight would castigate his countrymen for having broken their covenant. Prophetically, he would warn of God's impending wrath if backslidden multitudes failed to repent of their sins and supplicate His mercy.

The social means of grace made up Dwight's Christian environment. In keeping with his accustomed emphasis on nurture, he included in his theology a number of sermons on the supreme value of a religious education. Despite his avowed belief in instantaneous conversion, he could not keep from affirming the gracious content of scriptural instruction given with "steadiness and uniformity." Such indoctrination, begun early in life, renders Christian behavior habitual, and "habits constitute the man. . . ."[33] For evidence that religious education can turn the mind from sin to virtue, Dwight cited the spiritual backgrounds of revival converts, most of whom came from God-fearing parents.[34]

Because spiritual guidance was so essential an instrument of grace, Dwight was careful to elucidate the most fruitful manner of instruction. Observation of his metaphysical colleagues had taught him that "religion should never be exhibited in a . . . gloomy, discouraging light." Perhaps he had Emmons and Hopkins in mind when he commented, there is more to religion than "self mortification." Such "useless teaching" provokes not the child's faith and happiness, but his "hate and dread" of orthodoxy.[35] As in the case of Horace Mann, revulsion might cause him to reject Calvinism and seek comfort in a Unitarian church. To Dwight, Unitarianism was irreligion and flight from orthodoxy was an evil he concentrated his greatest energies to prevent. Hence, he tried to make the old Puritan faith attractive, remarking that Christian nurture should be a "solemn," but also a "pleasing" experience.

As a rational Christian and upholder of an orderly religious establishment, Dwight recoiled at the anarchic impulse of Antinomianism. Notwithstanding the feelings of piety engendered in the experience of conversion, it was necessary to balance the Gospel with the law. The new convert had motives to obey the law, but he needed to understand fully the conduct God re-

quires of him in order to commence virtuous action.
Dwight preached at length on each divine commandment, stressing its utility in securing human happiness.
Voluntary obedience to divine moral government
springs not from dread, but from a combination of fear
and love. Such feelings are similar to those which a
child has for a stern but benevolent parent. Dwight
took pains to distinguish his concept of voluntary submission to the will of a loving Father from Hopkinsian
resignation. Opposing his rational theology to the
arbitrary scheme of Consistent Calvinism, he held
"that willingness to suffer perdition is no part of Christian resignation." Dwight parted company with the
New Divinity in his humanitarian belief that God's
glory always coincides with man's happiness. He reasoned that because Christians seek "the greatest
apparent good," they cannot resign themselves to
perdition, for the damned "hate and oppose the glory
of God throughout eternity."[36]

Submission to God's paternal government was
Dwight's model for godly relationships of children to
parents, students to teachers, and subjects to rulers.
As apologist for the Puritan tradition he never wavered
from his belief that subordination to paternalistic
authority is the divinely sanctioned way to subdue the
passions and insure the rule of pious reason. Advancing a stewardship theory which came in direct conflict with democracy, he declared that God has given
human governors custodianship of His Moral Law.
In the home, school, and state, those persons who
assume the paternal role have the duty to nurture their
subordinates in the scriptural rules of conduct. Their
moral guardianship corresponds to that of a minister

over his congregation. Each temporal authority has particular moral responsibilities assigned to his office.

In copious detail, Dwight expounded a theology of paternal guidance and popular subordination. With strongly conservative implications, he stressed the need for thorough childhood training in reverential obedience to authority. Virtuous parents carry out the will of God by restraining their naturally rebellious children. With strict but affectionate discipline, they fulfill a divine commission by channeling young energies into Christian practice. The ruler-subject relationship was but another pattern of God's moral government analogous to that of parent and child. Magistrates are bound to be virtuous, and their people are constrained to obedience. The most effectual government in the state, as well as in the home, is based on persuasion. A ruler who governs in accordance with the Moral Law will have no need to resort to force. His people, knowing him to be just, will revere him and place full confidence in his leadership. In return for their submission, they may expect "safety, peace, good order, and universal happiness."[37]

Though he spoke in general terms when relating these views to the Yale students as part of their course in theology, his specific meaning was clear. Often in public discourse, as well as in the press, he defended the beneficence of Connecticut's rulers and the godly system which elevated them to prominence. In 1809, for example, he delivered a funeral oration for Governor Jonathan Trumbull. The sermon stressed Trumbull's practical conservatism. In an era of popular upheaval, the Puritan governor had resisted both visionary ideas and the passions of romanticism to steer a "prudent," "moderate" course in Connecticut politics. His firm adherence to the "Manners, and Institutions, of his native State," and ". . . to the Religious System of [his] ancestors" made him a wise guardian. As exponent of Federalist-Congregationalism, Trumbull had governed in the best interests of the people and hence had deserved their unqualified obedience.[38] Of course, Dwight was well aware that a growing number of Connecticut citizens objected to one party rule. Consequently, he gave much attention to indoctrinating youth in the virtues of the established order.

Democracy was plainly a violation of God's prescribed government because it set subjects over rulers. The inevitable result, as in France, was social catastrophe. But if the Standing Order commanded submission, ungodly institutions did not. Subjects were not only bound to obey virtuous rulers, but also to revolt against despotic ones. For all his conservatism, Dwight had participated in the American Revolution, and thus he felt the need to justify resistance to tyranny. From utilitarian premises, he argued that the evils of uprising are less than those caused by despotism. Despotic rule undermines usefulness in the people by corrupting the national morals. "Take away usefulness from man; and there is nothing left, which is good; but everything which is bad."[39] The subject who throws off the yoke of a despot is much the same as the child who runs from a sinful parent. Dwight maintained the right of every person to be governed by useful Christians. And where authorities are corrupt or tyrannical, subjects are obliged to replace them with godly men.

Nowhere is Dwight's theology more utilitarian than in his discussion of morals. He transformed Christ's commandments to love God and one's neighbor into a series of practical lessons. Love to God meant paternalistic family and community arrangements. Love to mankind was translated into sermons on the utility of

good habits and the calamitous effects of vice. Dwight
defined virtue as "the love of doing good." His description of evangelical morality was much more
worldly than Hopkinsian "disinterested benevolence."
His detailed analysis of Christian duty was, in fact,
a novel departure for a revivalist. New Divinity men,
in their exaltation of subjective experience, assumed
that moral behavior would naturally flow from conversion. Consequently they relegated the inculcation
of Christian morals to an almost incidental place in
their systems. Dwight's inclusion of elaborate instructions was the product of his much greater reliance on
human religious efforts. If God regenerates man's soul
by secondary means, He must also influence moral
action in a similar way. Direct inspiration smacked too
much of Antinomian enthusiasm. Finding it unrewarding to dwell on supernatural agency, Dwight preferred
to stress the concrete acts individuals can perform to
secure personal and social happiness. If he was successful in persuading his students to his conception of
virtue, he assumed that the Holy Spirit had enlivened
his preaching and restored their souls.

Dwight always discussed sin, as he did virtue, in
terms of its social background and consequences.
Often he drew his material from contemporary events.
When Aaron Burr shot the Federalist leader Alexander
Hamilton, Dwight preached a public sermon on duelling. Subsequently he incorporated this subject into
his lectures on theology. His argument bore the familiar utilitarian imprint.[40] Duelling is not simply a
violation of the Sixth Commandment, but a socially
patterned vice. In places where it is practiced children
are educated in habits of blood vengeance. They learn
a false notion of honor, which consists in passionate
displays of "wrath and revenge."[41]

Evangelical Protestantism grew up as a middle class religion. In the nineteenth century, its moralistic side, the work ethic, became a rationale for intensive economic development. Those personal characteristics which abetted the national mania for production and material success became virtues. Industry is the classic example. Etymologically, it evolved from a behavioral attribute to the concrete result of that attribute. The virtue gave rise to the factory. Vice, on the other hand, consisted of practices which detracted from productivity. A glaring example was intemperance. A achetypal yankee, Benjamin Franklin has stressed sobriety as one of the essentials for wealth and wisdom. Timothy Dwight, an enterprising man himself, also became an early spokesman for the productive morality. His traditionalism did not extend into the economic realm. As a New England Federalist, he favored the Hamiltonian concept of business aristocracy. Consequently, his more worldly sermons accentuated the value of industry, thrift, and temperance, and the baneful results of drunkenness, sloth, and frivolity. These were not tangential subjects to Dwight, as they were not to increasing numbers of evangelicals. In his theology, he went so far as to condemn intemperance as a form of self-destruction, and hence another violation of the Sixth Commandment. The drunkard is a menace to Dwight's ideal society because his intoxication deprives him of "reason" and "self control." Incapable of conducting business, he brings poverty and disgrace to himself and his family.[42]

The antidote to all such passionate, disorderly behavior was attendance to the means of grace. Observance of the Sabbath, for example, fortifies the individual against all vicious influence. During the Lord's Day, "amendment of the soul, and victory over sin and temptation, are to be planned, resolved on, and achieved."[43] The benevolent movements of the antebellum years, for which Dwight laid much of the groundwork, fused Sabbatarianism with a crusade for temperance. In the theology of Dwight and the emerging evangelical orthodoxy of the nineteenth century, the means of grace were the most potent agency for social control.

In his incessant denunciation of indolence and idle levity, Dwight was encouraging his students to pursue materially productive, middle class lives. Continuously, he reiterated the theme that Christian practice is conducive to a thriving contentment, while vice has the opposite effect. If Dwight reinterpreted "disinterested benevolence" as "voluntary usefulness," he also tended, much more than Edwardians, to view "doing good" as the pursuit of enlightened self-interest. While making the usual exhortations to Christian charity and tender concern for one's fellow beings, he often regarded such morality in mundane terms. Moving in Connecticut's business circles, he developed a pronounced tendency to adjust virtue to the commercial way of life.[44] He condemned avarice because it hardens the heart, destroys the capacity for pleasure, and "the motives to repentance, faith, and obedience." But he heartily approved of serious engagement in one's calling, and he regarded comfortable living as the resultant blessing of God. The work ethic was the path to voluntary usefulness, while idleness and hedonism were root causes of social failure, indigence, and spiritual degeneracy. In place of licentious diversions like theatre-going and lounging about taverns, Dwight recommended hard work as well as practical religious educaton.[45]

Dwight's moral ideals stemmed largely from Puritanism, but by his time secular writers like Franklin and Crevecoeur had largely removed them from their theological matrix. A recent scholar describes the New England mind of the eighteenth century as a continuum, with Edwardian piety at one end and Franklinian moralism at the other.[46] In the early national period, the old Puritan regions were moving rapidly in the latter direction. Dwight's theology represents a transitional fusion of Edwards and Franklin. He sought to retain orthodox viability by merging the emotional appeal of revivalism with the self-interest of utilitarian moralism. In his revised theology, conversion consisted essentially of the individual's commitment to learn and obey scriptural precepts. The Dwight revival was always a rational, educational experience, as well as a pietistic arousal of the "religious affections." Where the New Divinity had drawn inspiration from the principle of God's glory and absolute sovereignty, Dwight's moderate evangelical Calvinism ushered from a rising humanitarian spirit. He too based his system on one major principle, that of utility in producing human happiness.

PART III
The New Orthodoxy

CHAPTER VII

Infidels, Democrats, and Prophecy

In making Reformed theology relevant to contemporary ideas and issues, Dwight utilized two complementary perspectives. The first, which dominated his teaching, was the conception of an intelligible universe of cause and effect. Man is a rational being, capable of learning the operations of God's natural and moral government, and modelling his behavior in accordance with the Creator's benevolent designs. But underlying Dwight's rational Christianity was the prophetic, or apocalyptic view of history. This interpretation informed his reactions to specific events. The orthodox champion did not abandon rational method in his more millennial writings. Indeed, he took pains to show that scriptural prophecy, like the Law and Gospel, can be validated by experience. But his propensity to judge particular individuals, factions, and nations as good or evil participants in the cosmic drama gave his explanations a tendentious, polemical tone. His inclina-

tion to defend the Standing Order by attributing
satanic intentions to its critics and consigning them
to the fires of oblivion, greatly compromised his enlightened outlook.

As defender of the faith, Dwight oscillated between
rational apologetics and impassioned prophecy, depending on the situation. At times when liberal religion
and democracy seemed most threatening, the point
of view in *The Triumph of Infidelity* came to the fore.
But Protestant millennialism was an optimistic faith,
and while Dwight expressed consternation in the
throes of battle, he confidently believed that God's
orthodox warriors would ultimately exterminate the
disruptive legions of the antichrist. The idea of an
imminent millennium gave impetus to Dwight's militant evangelical persuasion. To his mind, both violent
confrontation and revivalistic success were signs of
the coming reign of Christ. Even during orthodoxy's
darkest moments, Dwight never succumbed to despon-
dency, for war and upheaval were the inevitable pre-
cursors of Christian victory. Satan was most active
when the forces of Christ were gathering strength, and
the resurgent spread of the Protestant Gospel was a
clear indication that this situation existed. Eventually
Dwight grew disillusioned about his country's peculiar
role in world redemption, as disestablishmentarians
and democrats gained power, but he did not despair
of his faith's ultimate success. Always the evangelical
activist, he merely reconceived his millennial army in
less nationalistic formation. He and his associates
looked to a worldwide union of evangelical Calvinists
to propagate the Gospel and subdue Infidel conspirators in every locality.

When Dwight took over the presidency of Yale, his immediate aim was to counter the influence of deism and skepticism over the student body. Because reason was the watchword of Infidel writers, Dwight used the method of supernatural rationalism to refute their ideas and defend revelation. Fully convinced that the *philosophes* had precipitated the French Revolution, and worried about the growth of democratic sentiment in America, he felt the need for decisive action to prevent a similar upheaval in his own country.

Pro-French sentiment in Connecticut coincided with the nascent movement of liberals and dissenters against the Standing Order. In a letter to General Ebenezer Huntington, chairman of the aristocratic Society of Cincinnati,[1] Dwight expressed fear for the future of his godly commonwealth, should these sowers of discord succeed in their ill-conceived plot to turn out the virtuous rulers of "the present Council." With an eye on French developments, Dwight, like his fellow New Englander John Adams, believed legislative authority was best divided between an upper and lower house. But the tendency to aristocratic oligarchy in the higher body disturbed him far less than it did Adams. Where the second President's belief in human corruptibility gave him a desire to restrain and balance all political power, the paternalistic Dwight was most afraid of mob rule. In the democratic attacks on the Council, he detected a plan to establish a unicameral legislature, similar to that of revolutionary France. Hence the proliferation of French-inspired political societies in the "land of steady habits" had to be checked by the friends of virtue, order, and stability. If democratic clubs were allowed to flourish, anarchy, "of all despotisms the most dreaded," would result. Dwight noted the prevalence of "steady and well-disposed inhabitants" who were naturally hostile to democracy. But he feared their lack of vigilance.[2]

Dwight's initial forays against infidelity were an attempt to arouse the generally conservative populace to full awareness of their beneficent society's precarious situation. Two lengthy sermons which became especially well known were entitled *The Nature and Danger of Infidel Philosophy*. These discourses, preached to the public as well as the Yale students, were quickly published and widely distributed. The *Connecticut Courant* aided their circulation by printing excerpts. In his customary utilitarian fashion, Dwight attempted to show the disastrous consequences of popular adherence to skeptical ideas. To the orthodox mind, ontological beliefs, not social mores, were the basis of civilization. Infidel philosophy, by alienating man from God, also separates him from the institutional means of social virtue and removes all restraint from vice.[3]

Dwight's technique was to condense the complex reasoning of English deists and skeptics to simple shibboleths, easily refutable. Here is a typical statement:

> Lord Herbert declares that the indulgence of LUST and anger is not more to be blamed, than the thirst of a fever, or the drowsiness of the Lethargy. In this single sentence, by a sweeping stroke, the guilt of gluttony, sloth, drunkenness, lewdness, wrath, contention, and revenge, is entirely blotted out.[4]

Dwight disliked Lord Herbert of Cherbury because as one of the first deists, he had influenced the later more critical schools of infidelity. From the above assessment, it might appear that the English philosopher advocated violent resistance to all social restraint. But

Sir Leslie Stephen notes that Lord Herbert affirmed the "existence of God, the duty of worshipping him, the importance of piety and virtue as the chief parts of this duty, the propriety of repentance, and the existence of a future state of rewards and punishments."[5] His great crime, which so inflamed Dwight, was the belief that man can discover moral principles without the aid of revelation.

In making his case against the British Infidels, Dwight pursued a path well trodden by previous apologists. The Cambridge Platonists and Samuel Clarke, for example, had labored to rebut Hobbesian moral relativism. Dwight added little in his comments on Hobbes' notion that morality is vested in the powers of sovereign and civil law. He concluded that "all the horrid evils of despotism; and an entire annihilation of right and wrong" would result from the practice of such a system.[6] Dwight's purpose was not so much intellectual training as moral indoctrination. Cathechizing his students, he hoped they would acquiesce in orthodoxy as a matter of habit. A later professor of natural philosophy at Yale who had graduated in the class of 1813 recalled that in Dwight's "method of instruction . . . Leading questions were asked, which only had to be affirmed or denied . . . ."[7]

In his attack on Infidel philosophy, Dwight did not merely point out its moral shortcomings. He portrayed thinkers who neglect or disparage Scripture as deliberate villains, cynically leading their gullible followers away from "Truth." For orthodox Protestants, revelation is the only foundation of morality. It was possible therefore, to regard even the mildest departures from Scripture as deliberate acts of malice. A moderate deist like Lord Herbert and an avowed skeptic like Hume were both great evildoers, because they were both willful

adherents to error. Their beliefs violated common
sense, which always harmonized with revelation. But
most heinous were the practical consequences of their
fallacious reasoning. Dwight spent much time con-
trasting the felicity of Christian societies with the misery
of those which had not lived by God's revealed word.
In this way, he worked to place orthodoxy on an empirical basis.

The purpose of any set of ethical principles, as
Dwight saw it, "must be to amend the heart and reform
the conduct." One of his most frequent means of demonstrating the unique truth of Christianity was to
show that it performs these services, while other systems fail. From the orthodox premise that truth is
absolute and immutable, he was able to condemn
philosophy because of its "continually changing character." Amid such diversity of opinion, he asked his
students, "whom are you to follow, and what are you
to believe?" Devoid of the authority of a Supreme Lawgiver, philosophy can never prescribe uncontroverted
rules for man to follow, nor can it provide expiation
for human sin.[8]

Consistent with his overall method, Dwight attacked
philosophy for its lack of utility. Both the ancient
heathen and modern Infidels had failed, without the
aid of God, to devise a system which improved man's
behavior. So eager was Dwight to debunk reliance on
uninspired reason that he stated categorically: "The
whole history of the heathen world furnishes not a single
reason to believe, that its teachings ever reformed one
individual, either among the teachers, or among the
disciples."[9] But Dwight considered modern philosophy
far more insidious and corrosive than ancient systems of
ethics. Classical writers had not, after all, enjoyed access to
Scripture. But contemporary philosophers, who should

know better, voluntarily abandon God and set in His place a false and malicious cult of reason. Hence, they violate their own rational powers of perception and judgment.[10] Dwight admitted that philosophy is useful and important in its proper sphere. But he cautioned that men must always recognize the limits of their reason, and never use it to devise religious doctrines. Such intrusion within the divine province can only have catastrophic results. The influence of philosophers who ridicule scriptural revelation and replace it with licentious creeds of their own, has brought unprecedented immorality to the modern world. In their denial of man's innate depravity and need of redemption, philosophers had opened the door to chaos. Dwight was particularly disturbed by the new heresy of human perfectibility. Like all beliefs which contradict Scripture, this notion was evil because its practice would destroy society.

In a series of brief articles which he contributed to a Federalist-Congregational newspaper in 1801,[11] Dwight imagined grim results if philosopher William Godwin were to put his theories into practice. His literary strategy was to place Godwin in a fictitious setting appropriately called the Land of Nod. Dwight's reference to the banishment of Cain was obvious, but his more immediate aim was to use the term in its colloquial sense, i.e., the land of dreams. In fact, he referred to the articles as an account of his own dreams. Thereby, he gave himself greater leeway with his subject matter. Philosophical dreamers like Godwin are thrust into Nod and taken to the "City of Perfectibility." As "detached" observer Dwight too is conducted to this city, where Infidels "are irresistably forced *to try their philosophical doctrines by facts calculated to shew* [sic] *their true nature.*"

Godwin stands no chance of success in this imagined application of his ideas. For pupils the philosopher has a despicable mob, whose vicious behavior is the inevitable consequence of natural depravity. In keeping with his belief in educational motivation, Dwight reasoned that these persons are particularly unruly because their continuous exposure to Infidel schemes has deprived them of "common sense." The false premise of innate goodness and perfectibility leads Godwin to regard government and religion as needless shackles. His hope is that a free society of common property and labor will permit man's natural excellence to unfold. But such liberty only gives rise to unrestrained selfishness and animosity. The refusal of slothful individuals to work brings them into conflict with industrious farmers, who naturally resent having to labor for the benefit of idlers. The system of common property also encourages a shiftless element to plunder the homes of more well-to-do citizens.

To Dwight's mind, heaven was the only place where true perfectibility can exist. In his theological lectures, he described a progressive growth in knowledge which occurs during the eternal life of the redeemed. Temporal existence, however, is a state of trial, and mortal beings, whose minds are clouded by error and corruption, are incapable of such understanding. In Christian environments, however, they are restrained from indulging their appetites and are instructed in the wisdom of Scripture. God redirects human energies toward useful objects by imparting holiness to believers. The gradual permeation of Christian enlightenment, which will culminate in the millennium, is a foretaste of heavenly perfection, but on this side of the grave, even converts remain prone to erroneous judgment.[12] The Gospel alone mitigates this tendency by preparing the faithful for ultimate perfection.

Preaching incessantly on the evils of Infidel philosophy and the excellence of Scripture, Dwight renewed orthodoxy on the Yale campus. Not that the Puritan faith had ever actually been extinguished. But if Lyman Beecher's somewhat biased account was true, the students had been attracted to French free-thinking at the time of Dwight's arrival.[13] The adolescents at Yale were probably never serious skeptics. In all likelihood, a few youthful rebels had been asserting their identity by assaulting provincial sacred cows. Boys adopting names like Rousseau and D'Alembert appears to the modern historian more as adolescent prankishness than full-scale revolt. These collegians were about the same age as today's high school students, with backgrounds far more parochial. Their minds were undeveloped and impressionable. A commanding figure like Dwight had little trouble returning them to the orthodox fold. It testifies to their lack of real desire to throw off sanctioned authority that so many ultimately accepted Dwight's paternal guidance. In denouncing infidelity, Dwight gave a forensic display far in advance of any would-be young challenger. If the students were not immediately won over, they were certainly awed by their new master's oratory.

Dwight's campaign against infidelity at Yale served as the opening round of his crusade for orthodoxy. Years of scrupulous nurture and a number of well-timed evangelical sermons followed. The result, beginning in 1802, was a full-scale revival of traditional piety on campus.

It was crucially important to reclaim the Puritan college as a training base for New England orthodoxy.

But Yale was only one theater of evangelical operation. The growing influence of the anti-Christ in America as well as Europe necessitated a broad-scale offensive to redeem not only New England, but the nation and the world.

Formerly Dwight had expressed confidence that a godly America would lead mankind to redemption. But by the end of the century, he had come to see the need for a rearguard action. Revolutionary France had planted divisive seeds in American soil, rearing up the party of Jeffersonian Democrats. The provocative maneuverings of the envoy Genet, the XYZ Affair, and the ensuing undeclared naval war with France during the Adams Administration had alarmed conservative Protestants throughout the United States. In 1798, the General Assembly of the Presbyterian Church issued a stern warning to Americans. The document alluded to "formidable innovations and convulsions in Europe" which threatened to undermine a godly America. In the Puritan manner, it exhorted a covenanted nation to heed its ecclesiastical "watchmen," cease backsliding, and return to ancestral piety. If liberal trends were allowed to continue, an angry God would execute chastening judgments.[14] President Adams, a firm believer in divine Providence, proclaimed a day of fasting, humiliation, and prayer.

Jedidiah Morse, a Massachusetts minister who was Dwight's closest associate, responded immediately with his own call to arms.[15] The president of Yale waited until the twenty-second anniversary of American independence to deliver a similar admonition. The discourses of Morse, Dwight, and other Congregational ministers had much in common with seventeenth century Puritan jeremiads. They warned of God's impending wrath if his children continue in their sinful ways. But they also contained a new element which gave them an unusually apocalyptic tone.

In 1797, John Robison, a reputable Scottish mathematician published a book bearing the ominous title, *Proofs of a Conspiracy against all Religions and Governments of Europe, carried on in the secret Meetings of Freemasons, Illuminati, and Reading Societies.* Within a year, the work had arrived in America, and the New England orthodox community had voraciously consumed its contents. Robison provided the rationale for a conspiratorial explanation of the French Revolution widely held by conservative Protestants. Relying largely on hearsay, the British scholar traced the origin of the upheaval to a subversive plot of the Illuminati, an obscure sect of Bavarian freemasons.

The Illuminati had been a small but vocal organization of propagandists for the German Enlightenment.[16] Because the Counter Reformation had been especially successful in Southern Germany, members of the Illuminati espoused a militant anti-clericalism. The Jesuits had gained control of Bavarian public education, securing official censorship of all publications contradicting Catholic dogma. The Illuminati therefore arose as a secret order, formed to replace ecclesiastical tyranny with enlightened reason and tolerance. Like freemasonry, with which it associated, the German order combined a liberal program with occult ritualism. It thrived during the 1780s, when Baron Adolf Knigge worked out a plan for spreading its doctrine within other masonic orders. But inflammatory pamphlets, written for the most part by the founder, Adam Weishaupt, aroused the Jesuits, who in turn persuaded government authorities to suppress the sect. Though

suppression was effective, Bavarian officialdom retained a paranoid fear of the Illuminati, passing pro-
hibitory edicts long after the order's demise.

During the final decade of the eighteenth century,
when liberal ideas were spreading rapidly throughout
Germany, many Protestants and Catholics falsely
assumed the resurgence of Illuminism. Vernon Stauffer,
a modern historian of the Illuminati Controversy, has
recorded widespread fear among "simple-minded and
credulous elements in the Protestant world that a vast
combination of forces was at work, all hostile to the
Christian religion and all striving to supplant faith by
reason."[17] Actually, the conspiratorial world view
was also common among educated Protestants. The
New England orthodox clergy were all accomplished
scholars by the standards of their time; and John
Robison was an esteemed savant, an associate of
James Watt and other prominent British intellectuals.[18]
Yet, the Scottish thinker wrecklessly alleged that "illuminated" masonic lodges in France had effectively
conspired to overthrow all established government
and religion. One such fraternity was the Jacobin Club,
which played a violent role in the French Revolution.

One reason why intelligent men, conversant in Newtonian physics and empirical philosophy, could so
readily accept this theory on such scanty evidence, is
because they glibly connected biblical prophecy with
the fate of contemporary nations. Many prominent British
and American leaders perceived the French Revolution as
an anti-Christian plot. From the time of the Great Awakening, millennial nationalism became an increasingly
prominent aspect of American Protestant belief. It colored
the ideology of the Revolution, and has since been drawn
upon to interpret conflicts such as the French Revolution, the War of 1812, the Civil War, World War I, and
even the Cold War.[19]

Orthodox New Englanders quite naturally viewed the quarter-century conflagration which grew out of the French Revolution as part of the cosmic struggle. As pro-French dissidents assailed Puritan institutions, conservatives resorted to scriptural prophecy to defend their interests. Robison's book confirmed prevailing suspicions and buttressed arguments already being expounded. It enabled ecclesiastics like Dwight to pin all the signs of orthodox decline and disturbing social ferment on an international conspiracy. If such diabolical assault on established institutions could be proven to exist, then it would not be difficult to stir a conservative majority of New Englanders to militant defensive reaction. Such was the aim of Timothy Dwight when he preached on *The Duty of Americans in the Present Crisis.*

In this prophetic outcry, Dwight blended millennial cosmology with both local and international politics. Robison had provided the orthodox clergy with invaluable material for impugning the motives of Jeffersonian defectors from the Standing Order. Dwight began with his own interpretation of Revelation, applying it to contemporary events. The Apocalypse divides history into seven intervals, during each of which an angel pours out a vial of God's wrath over the earth. The period between each vial is to witness specific providential developments. Prophecy depicts these occurrences symbolically and thus allows for varying specious interpretations. Dwight found it useful to place his own era within the bounds of the sixth vial. During that time, "unclean spirits" were to arise, and "by their doctrines and labours, openly, professedly, and in an unusual manner, contend against God, and . . . strive to unite mankind in this opposition."[20]

The emissaries of hell were to be set loose in the dominions of the "Romish hierarchy" with the mission of effecting "a mighty preparation for the ruin of the anti-Christian empire." As a Protestant, Dwight could not with consistency defend the virtues of the French priesthood. But the fact that Infidels opposed the Catholic Church presented a formidable problem. In this sermon, Dwight sidestepped the matter, merely acknowledging that "unclean spirits" would logically arise in Catholic domains. He preferred to concentrate on the prospect of anti-Christian infiltration within godly Protestant communities. Three years later, however, Dwight would feel the need to answer the objection that "Infidels are direct enemies and opposers of the Hierarchy and . . . that their persecution has fallen principally on the Catholics, and not on Protestants."[21] Besides confirming a clear and present danger to United States institutions, Dwight would find it necessary to make some positive reference to the Catholic priesthood because a French prelate, the Abbé Augustin Barruel had published a comprehensive new work on the Infidel conspiracy. Therefore, Dwight would argue that despite the evils of the "Hierarchy," many French Catholics, by "yielding their lives in preference to denying the Saviour and abjuring Christianity, proved themselves to be men of Piety." Such a man was the Abbé, whose research supported Robison, and whose veracity had been certified by the Bishop of London.[22]

Barruel's four volume account was particularly serviceable because it supported opinions which Dwight had long espoused. Not only did the priest attribute conspiratorial designs to Illuminism, but he also related the German movement to a vast anti-Christian plot which included Encyclopedists as well as Jacobins. He made reference to "Voltaire the Chief, D'Alembert, the most subtle agent, Frederick [the

Great] the protector and often adviser, Diderot the forlorn hope," and Rousseau, who had "filled the minds of people with a passion for Liberty and Equality."[23] Thus did a French Catholic provide seemingly irrefutable documentation for beliefs Dwight had held since he had written *The Triumph of Infidelity*. Certainly then the Catholic Church must contain some good Christians.

In his 1798 discourse, Dwight was already regarding Illuminism and Encyclopedism as part of the same overall conspiracy. The Academy of French philosophers had set out to overturn Christianity by a "general diffusion of irreligion and atheism."[24] This work of subversion which had so effectively ruined France was now spreading across the ocean. Dwight believed American malcontents, who were forming secret democratic societies to destroy established institutions, were likely members of the Illuminati. In June of 1797, in a letter to Morse, he related the findings of an inquiry he had made on the subject. A Connecticut "Freemason of distinction" had informed him that peculiar rites practiced in some lodges were "decisive proof of illuminatism in America." Dwight characterized the domestic Illuminati as opponents of government, religion, and vested property interests, who seek to overthrow peace, order, and morality.[25] For his part, Morse thoroughly agreed that Illuminism had spread to America. A few months prior to receiving Dwight's letter he had in fact publicized this view in an impassioned sermon. "I have now in my possession," he proclaimed,

> complete and indubitable proof that such societies do exist, and have for many years existed in the United States. I have, my brethren, an official, authenticated list of the names, ages, place of nativity, professions, & of the officers

and members of a Society of Illuminati . . . consisting of
one hundred members, instituted in Virginia by the Grand
Orient of France. . . .

He also cited a second document attesting to the existence
of "fourteen others, scattered we know not where over the
United States."[26]

While fully convinced that the threat was real, Morse
and Dwight used Illuminism to scare their countrymen
into reaction against democracy. Extreme conservatives
have often since confronted social change by conducting
crusades against internal subversion. The conspiracy
theory of history, compatible with a particular application
of Protestant millenialism, has frequently stirred
Americans to paranoic fear of the enemy within. A century
and a half after Morse alarmed his parishioners, Senator
Joseph McCarthy held before a West Virginia audience
a list of Communists in the State Department. In his
notorious hunt for these twentieth-century Illuminati, he
succeeded in frightening the nation into an outburst of
hysterical intolerance.

In seeking to incite the people of Connecticut to action
against democratic subversives, Dwight proclaimed the
duty of believers to separate from their enemies before the
judgments of the seventh vial commence. He declared
mankind to be on the brink of the final period of history,
when Christian soldiers would subdue God's enemies.
What then was the infamous plan of American democrats? "Is it that we may change our holy worship into a
Jacobin phrenzy? . . ." "Shall our sons become the disciples of Voltaire . . . or our daughters the concubines
of the Illuminati?" Dwight urged godly citizens to obey
and support their existing government and to avoid all
contact with their democratic neighbors. Only unswerving
loyalty to a conservative Federalist Administration and

its supporters of the Standing Order would prevent America from going the way of France. Employing arguments typical of intrenched interests under fire, Dwight added, "the officers of government are possessed of better information than private persons can be; . . . if *they* had the same information, they would probably coincide with the opinions of their rulers." He related criticism of those in power to an Infidel plot hatched in Europe and exported to America. Detailing a catalogue of miseries perpetuated by the alleged conspirators, he warned of plans to set a free people against their government.[27]

The tendency of the orthodox New England clergy to regard dissent in conspiratorial terms accelerated to a point of hysteria as the Jeffersonian opposition made political gains. Federalist-Congregational publicists viewed these new libertarians as American Jacobins. Dwight's younger brother Theodore, a lawyer and politician, also served as editor of the stridently Federalist *Connecticut Courant*. In an anti-democratic diatribe, he openly equated Jeffersonian leaders with the Illuminati. While admitting his ignorance of the society's American membership, he did not hesitate to suggest that the ideas of Jefferson, Gallatin, and "their American associates" made them likely "proselytes."[28] The feeling was common among New England Federalists that a victory for Jefferson's party would dissolve American Christian institutions in a reenactment of the French debacle. Prior to the election campaign of 1800, however, Timothy Dwight, a less open partisan than his brash sibling, remained confident that Americans, and particularly the people of Connecticut, would extinguish the fire before it consumed their house. Writing his friend, Senator James Hillhouse, Treasurer of Yale College, Dwight referred to "the languor of the friends of government." But with an undercurrent of optimism, he asserted that these

"trials" and "afflictions" were a providential means of
strengthening Federalist resolve. "New England," he
judged, "is certainly greatly amended; and I hope irre-
vocably."[29] These were his more private thoughts on
June 20, 1798, two weeks before he preached *The Duty
of Americans in the Present Crisis.* Hence it is likely that
Dwight purposely exaggerated the precariousness of the
American situation in that sermon to arouse conservative
sentiment. For this purpose, the Robison and Barruel
accounts were particularly useful. Even though knowledgeable sources doubted Robison's accuracy, orthodox
stalwarts like Dwight and Morse refused to admit to their
audiences or themselves that the Infidel conspiracy might
not be so all-encompassing. Seeking testimonials in support of Robison, Morse had written a German geographer,
Christopher Ebeling. The scholar's response was severely
critical, noting that few Europeans placed any stock in
the Robison thesis. But the Illuminati conspiracy was far
too powerful a weapon in the anti-democratic arsenal to
be scrapped. In a letter to Morse, Dwight therefore dismissed Ebeling's comments as unreliable since the German was not a Calvinist, and "too much of an equality
man to judge concerning the subject as we do."[30]

By 1800, the growing appeal of Jefferson and his party
augured a dismal future to the minds of Federalists. Dwight
became even more attached to the conspiracy theory as
events made him less hopeful about the destiny of his
country. But to him, the presence of "subversives" meant
that loyal Christians must gird themselves for battle. Of
the older Federalists, he was probably singular in realizing that upholders of the Standing Order must organize
their own party machine if they were to retain control. In
early 1800, he wrote to Hillhouse on this matter. Ac-

knowledging the "immense" political "industry" of the
democrats, he warned that if Federalist leaders in Congress failed "to imitate these active men," they would
surely suffer in the forthcoming election.[31]

As a clergyman, Dwight felt that his own involvement
in political maneuvering would be inconsistent with
propriety. But he found nothing wrong with exercising
his full powers of persuasion to convince the people of
New England that ancestral ways were the ways of God,
and incumbent office holders the guardian of virtue. On
January 7, 1801, following the Republican national victory, but during the deadlock between Jefferson and
Aaron Burr, Dwight preached a sermon in which he
linked major events of the past century to those prophe-
sied in the Apocalypse. The War for Independence had
been a triumph for the American Zion. With its divinely
inspired Constitution, the United States had looked forward to a glorious future. But almost as soon as the bonds
of colonialism had been broken, new storm clouds had
begun to gather. Surreptitiously, Infidel agents, who had
been gaining ground throughout the century, disgorged
their poisons on the young nation. Dwight reiterated the
orthodox explanation of infidelity, attributing it to the
love of sin and hatred of truth. He then plunged into
conspiracy theory, tracing the gradual process of French
corruption, revolution, and influence in America. Well-
intentioned American patriots had been fatally misled
by Frenchmen whom they had "viewed merely as *human
beings, embarked deeply in the glorious cause of liberty. . . .*" But New England Christians had soon perceived that the new rulers of France were licentious
Infidels harboring "base and villainous designs" against
American property. Although the nation as a whole had
recently fallen prey to scheming foreign influence, God-
fearing New England "at least, [had] escaped not only

tributary bondage, but the infinitely more dreadful bondage of infidelity, corruption, and moral ruin."[32]

To ease the minds of traditionalists, who suffered anxiety and disorientation as a result of the rapid changes occurring in their midst, Dwight referred to scriptural prophecy. He sought to console his fellow Puritans by recalling "that all these evils have been foretold by omniscience, and that they cannot extend beyond the Divine permission." The antichrist, whose days are numbered, included all modern Infidels as well as the Pope. Dwight reminded his listeners that nothing could prevent the eventual coming of God's Kingdom, but he also cautioned them to avoid participation in present evils. With Jeffersonians making progress in his home state, he feared they might influence those who had been loyal to the establishment.

Many supporters of Jefferson's party also considered themselves good Christians. They bitterly resented Dwight's equation of their liberal politics with irreligion. But for Dwight, the one true faith was inseparably bound up with the Standing Order. And only if the people resisted the incursions of men he conceived to be plotters and scheming office-seekers, could a godly prosperity continue. He considered all political dissenters unwelcome intruders within the walls of Zion; if they could not be reformed they were to be shunned. Intolerance was a virtue to the evangelical true believer. Dwight advised all who wished to retain a beneficient society to spurn association even with democratic members of their own families.[34]

In this sermon, Dwight was turning away from his earlier vision of a national millennium, toward a more provincial perspective. His faith in world renewal remained undiminished, but the growth of democracy in America had caused him to view the millennium more as a New England Zionist than an American Nationalist. In his *Travels,* which he dictated during the Jefferson and Madison Administrations, he tended to see the process of global evangelization stemming largely from New England.

Great Britain, with whom New England had close commercial and religious ties, was also a vital missionary center. During the War of 1812, which inspired heated opposition from New England Federalism, Dwight would lament the division between the two Protestant nations. He would warn that such enmity was detrimental to their combined evangelistic efforts. Laying the blame for this deplorable situation on the "cunning" politics of Jefferson and the insincerity of Madison, Dwight would divorce himself from American national policy and define himself as "a federalist and a *New Englander.*" While laboring to refute British claims of superiority to the United States, he would stress the natural friendship which ought to exist between the two countries, based on "common origins, language, manners, law, and religion." Reserving his greatest wrath for Jeffersonian Republicans, he would depict them as a power hungry cabal, unprincipled and unpatriotic. Wise Federalist rulers would never have gone to war with Great Britain, but would have joined her in "defending what was left of the liberty and safety of the human race; the Protestant religion; and the remains of Civilization; from the jaws of the *Corsican Cyclop.*"[35]

In the summer of 1812, shortly after war had been declared, a Protestant America spent two days, a month apart, in national fast. These occasions provided Dwight with his last major opportunity to make use of his prophetic interpretation of history. He preached lengthy sermons in the morning and afternoon of each fast day.

All four discourses were based on the same scriptural text, Isaiah 21:11, "Watchman, what of the Night? . . ." Dwight explained that the prophet Isaiah had been "a watchman, appointed by God for the nations of the earth," and that the night had been ". . . the prophet's *watch*, or season of watching." The people of Israel "ask eagerly and anxiously [for Isaiah's prophecy], because they are deeply alarmed by the miserable end of the surrounding nations concerning the fate of their own [sic]." The scriptural passage proceeds: "Morning comes, and also night." Dwight's explication drew the common connections of morning or light with prosperity, and night or darkness with adversity. Peace would come from Israel's return to religion, and further calamities from abandonment of God. "Our own cause," explained Dwight, "as well as that of the rest of mankind, is now in agitation." He reiterated the prophecy of seven vials, referring to the period of international warfare that would precede entry into the seventh, the vial of Armageddon and the millennium. Once again, he reviewed the conflict of Protestant Christians with the "Romish hierarchy" and the Infidel conspiracy. Torturing facts to fit his theory, he declared that Infidels and Jesuits were diverse aspects of the same plot against religion. In complete contradiction of reality, he even went so far as to place Weishaupt in collusion with the Jesuits. France had been the arena where Infidels had joined with Jesuits to overthrow God. Because numerous Frenchmen, like Barruel and other émigrés had opposed the Revolution, Dwight was careful to mention "that there are good people, and real Christians, within the pale of the Romish Church. . . ." Otherwise he would not have been able to describe the grim plight of hapless refugees fleeing the "slavery" and "oppression" of revolutionary France.[36]

The new war, Dwight feared, would divide the Protestant countries, England and the United States, and would bring America into unholy alliance with France. Any such association with this notorious instrument of sin would be fatal to the prosperity of the republic. Contact with France had already sapped the national morality, and if continued, it would lead America to partake of French blasphemy, idolatry, and persecution. When an entire nation gives itself over to depravity, God, in His righteous indignation, destroys it, as He smote Sodom and Gomorrah. As modern day watchman, Dwight warned his countrymen to repent and turn away from their present immoral course, or be thus destroyed.[37]

Dwight maintained that "the Protestant churches are the people of God, now in this world." As such, the Creator had addressed the prophecies of Isaiah and the Apocalypse peculiarly to them. America's natural ally was not France, but England, the country with whom she had wrongfully gone to war. All the Roman Catholic countries, in these tumultuous days of the sixth vial, were undergoing divine retribution. With an ethnocentrism which was rapidly becoming a characteristic American attitude, Dwight pronounced the mission of Anglo-Saxon people to carry the true religion of God throughout the world. How tragic it would be for a nation formerly endowed with piety and unprecedented happiness, to forego its blessings by allying with God's avowed enemies.[38]

Over a decade of successful evangelical activity, begun largely by Dwight, had reinforced his faith that God would deliver his chosen people from evil. Internal and external conflict had been inevitable, for according to Revelation, these were to be times of adversity. The sins which many Americans had committed in succumbing to foreign influence had provoked God to apply the rod of correction.

"The chastisement may be long continued," observed Dwight, "for our sins have deserved much more than this. We may be cast down; but we shall not, I think, be destroyed."[39]

During the Jeffersonian era, a number of conservative New Englanders, following the activist moderate Calvinism of Timothy Dwight, had begun an aggressive movement to preserve their faith and the social order it sanctified. In his concluding Fast Sermon, Dwight called for "determined resistance . . . to all the immoralities, which have been . . . deforming, and disgracing, our land." Specifically, he advocated "one great and general, and many subordinate, Societies, for the suppression of idleness, gaming, drunkenness, profaneness, and sabbath breaking."[40] In fact, such a program of reform was already getting under way as Dwight's followers began to put his ideas into practice. To counter the influence of liberal democracy and religious pluralism, Dwight, Morse and other orthodox ministers had set a powerful evangelical movement in motion. Even though he relied on diverse techniques of persuasion, Dwight still fought to preserve a coercive establishment. His battle for the Standing Order would end in failure, but new religious agencies would take over the function of social control. Dwight's aggressive, practical approach would inspire a younger generation of conservative evangelicals to establish a vast network of voluntary moral societies.[41] While operating in a pluralistic context, these organizations would continue to instill generally conservative social values in the minds of Americans. But prior to the advent of this "benevolent" movement, a long controversy occurred between Connecticut's orthodox and democratic parties. It was

this political embroilment which ultimately forced conservative evangelicals to make formal adjustments to
democracy in order to retain a viable means of diffusing
their traditional ideas.

CHAPTER VIII

The Politics of Religion

The struggle of Connecticut's Standing Order with Jeffersonians and dissenters went on intermittently for some two decades. Political and religious conflict merged in a system which thoroughly integrated the two areas of activity. The orthodox adamently believed that the faith of the Reformation would stand or fall with the existent governing structure. During the period immediately before and after the election of 1800, political warfare was particularly intense. Established leaders, recognizing an unprecedented threat to their preeminence, responded with a series of defensive attacks on the opposition. Dwight was the dominant ecclesiastical apologist for the Standing Order, while younger men like his brother Theodore and David Daggett conducted the lay campaign. As editor of the *Connecticut Courant,* Theodore Dwight saw to it that his newspaper functioned as a vigorous conservative organ. In addition to numerous articles defending established policies and impugning the motives of their critics, the *Courant* often printed quasi-political excerpts from the sermons of Dwight and likeminded clergymen. By and large, its editorial policy corresponded to the social, political, and religious ideas of the Yale president.

In 1797, a year of growing friction between the Adams Administration and revolutionary France, the Federalist newspaper was laden with anti-French propaganda. Followers of Jefferson were denounced as tools of the Revolution, bent on subjecting an independent America to the will of France. On July 2, 1798, an advertisement of Robison's book appeared, and from June to October of 1799, a series of commentaries paraphrased the Barruel thesis. The *Courant* explicitly linked Jeffersonians with Illuminati and French revolutionaries, alternately referring to them as "democrats" and "Jacobins." The usual argument was that because Jeffersonians challenge the Standing Order, they must hate "everything sacred." Christians must therefore resist democracy as they would atheism or anarchy.[1]

The *Courant* frequently made use of Protestant conspiracy theory in its anti-democratic articles. These tirades were often more abrasive than Dwight's most fervent prophetic sermons. Of course, they were all unsigned. In the spring of 1800, while Republicans were preparing for the election campaign, a Federalist partisan made a frantic appeal to the public. Decrying a Jacobin plot, he incited Americans to extremism in defense of their maligned institutions. "In this high treason against society," raged the writer, "there can be no degrees of guilt. . . ."

> Even lukewarmness is a high crime and misdemeanor, as it leads to more fatal consequences. Then let us hear no more, at such times, of amiability and gentleness—of candour, liberality, and moderation—of conciliating, mild and generous feeling. Such qualities are now not

virtues, but vices. . . . Whoever refuses to join in vigor-
ously repelling the attack is either a coward or a traitor.[2]

This totalitarian statement was the outgrowth of a
frightened religious chauvinism. So convinced were
many New England Federalists that theirs was the party
of God, that they could see none but the most deplorable
motives in the opposition. With people in league with
the devil, no compromise was possible.

To the conservative evangelical, Jefferson represented
the arch-conspirator against a sanctified order. During
the election campaign of 1800, the *Courant* denounced
his followers as "murderers" and "atheists." A writer who
identified himself as "Burleigh" speculated that Jefferson
intended to destroy religion, expropriate property, and
repeal the laws against murder, rape, and robbery.[3]

Burleigh inferred from Jefferson's belief in complete
religious freedom that he must be an atheist. Orthodox
Federalists detested the Virginian largely because of his
radical tolerationism. Expressed most articulately by
President Dwight, their belief was that Trinitarian Protestantism was the only basis of order. Toleration of unscriptural religions would sanction immorality and
destroy the social fabric. A more rational partisan than
Burleigh (possibly Dwight) made this point in seeking
to dissuade the electorate from supporting Jefferson. While
admitting the candidate's distinguished accomplishments,
the writer nevertheless held that a President who dis-
believes in the literal truth of Scripture and who refrains
from worshipping with any denomination, would undercut the religious foundations of American happiness. To
the orthodox mind, religion was the chief agency of social
control. Since belief in the divinity of Christ was the only
source of righteousness, the Puritan moralist felt justified
in declaring: "The question is not what he will do, but

what he is. Is he an infidel? Then you cannot elect him without betraying our Lord."[4] He proposed that Jefferson alleviate Christian fears by signing his name to the Apostle's Creed. Of course, such a test act would have violated the Constitution. But orthodox New Englanders remained for some time at odds with that document's strong demarcation between church and state. The wane of religious establishments alarmed Dwight and many other conservative Christians. To them it seemed that Americans were deliberately casting aside God's rulership. National tribulation would certainly follow such betrayal of the faith.[5]

Federalist newspaper writers agreed fully with the social Christianity of Timothy Dwight. As articles in the *Courant* were anonymous or signed with pseudonyms, it is difficult to determine who wrote them. But it is known that Dwight contributed a number of pieces both in Connecticut and Massachusetts. His personal correspondence, and "Biographical Hints" by his son Benjamin, document his authorship of articles in *The New England Palladium,* a stridently Federalist periodical. Benjamin also refers to his father's anonymous criticism in the *Courant* of existing troubles in his home state. He identifies few specific writings, but perusal of the content and mode of reasoning in certain essays reveals them as likely products of Dwight's mind.

The *Courant* and the *Palladium* shared the same editorial policy. Many pieces which Dwight contributed to the *Palladium* gained wider circulation through republication in the Connecticut paper. Prior to 1801, the *Palladium* had been a maritime and commercial journal for the Boston community. But after Jefferson's election, Jedidiah Morse and his friend Timothy Dwight saw the need for immediate action if Puritan Federalism was to be saved. Financial help from prominent Bay State conservatives enabled the two clergymen to acquire control of a functioning newspaper and convert it to an anti-Jeffersonian organ. Writing to Alexander Hamilton, George Cabot, leader of the arch-Federalist Essex County Junto, explained the purpose of the new publication and alluded to Dwight's involvement:

> Dr. Dwight is here stirring us up to oppose the demon of Jacobinism. A newspaper to be entitled the "New-England Anti-Jacobin," is to be published at Boston and circulated, as extensively as possible, especially through New England.[6]

Both Morse and Dwight liked to regard their project as a nonpartisan effort to retain a sanctified order. Dwight expressed this opinion in a letter to his collaborator on December 21, 1800. He wrote primarily to acquaint Morse with one of his Yale disciples, Warren Dutton, whom he was sending to edit the new paper. First, he mentioned the support of Connecticut's Federalist leaders—Chauncy Goodrich, David Daggett, and Lieutenant Governor John Cotton Smith—for a "non-partisan" newspaper to fight Jacobinism and irreligion. "I wish by candlelight," he continued, "just to introduce Mr. Dutton to you. Were it not to serve him and the public, I should part with him with very modified feelings. . . ." Dwight was pleased that orthodox Federalists were beginning to make exertions. "Our people," he observed, "appear to be more spirited and if possible more firm than before the late election. I think N. England will be saved from ruin."[7] The quiet appropriation of an established concern, which already had wide circulation, was a far more politic maneuver than embarkation on a new and avowedly partisan venture. Morse had published a broadside on December 5, which, while outlining new and distinctly

Federalist goals for the paper, yet claimed that it would be nonpartisan. Both he and Dwight maintained that their campaign to preserve New England virtue transcended party lines.

Theodore Dwight, however, saw little point in trying to exhume a decomposing Puritan uniformity. Though his brother was the first orthodox minister to recommend promotionalism, the *Courant* editor went beyond him in coming to terms with the emerging American party system. Commenting to Morse about his advertisement, the younger Dwight questioned the utility of a non-partisan pose for the *Palladium.* Theodore was interested not only in preserving the New England status quo, but in spreading the word that Federalists alone were the friends of law, order, and a moral America. He promised Morse as much support as might be necessary "to counteract and destroy the operation of Jacobinism." A popular form of conservative agitation was to publish abridgements of Robison's and Barruel's works. In this endeavor, Theodore offered his aid to Morse, and the two Federalist periodicals, the *Courant* and the *Palladium,* began an extensive exchange of materials.[8]

Despite pretensions of political objectivity, the *Palladium,* during Dutton's brief tenure of editorship,[9] was full of invective against the Jeffersonians. Nevertheless, scathing Federalist polemics bore such innocuous headlines as "To honest men of All Parties."[10] The usual approach was to portray the Jeffersonians (always labelled democrats or Jacobins) as demagogues, who appeal to mob "passions, prejudices, and feelings," while Federalists "address the public understanding. . . ."[11] The *Palladium* represented middle-class gentility. Small propertied interests, "farmers," and "mechanics," having a material stake in the community, were considered its backbone. The propertyless poor, or "rabble," were considered dangerous instruments for demagogic manipulation.

The elder Dwight expressed this opinion in his *Palladium* essays. An early contribution, entitled "Farmer Johnson's Political Catechism," appeared in a format suited to his accustomed purpose of indoctrination. Dwight's social ideals had not changed since his sturdy yeoman had exalted middle class competence in *Greenfield Hill:*

> Q. What do you mean by the general right of suffrage?
> A. I mean the right of suffrage extended generally, but not universally; a right enjoyed by all men, who hold a good character, and a reasonable share of property.
> Q. What do you mean by a reasonable share of property?
> A. Such a share as proves the owner to possess industry, frugality, and universally good management sufficient to shew that he may be safely trusted with the right of voting.[12]

Dwight believed men in "middling circumstances" to be the best guardians of virtuous stability. A general diffusion of property and wealth would strengthen social conservatism and dampen the appeal of radical ideas.

The first installment of "Farmer Johnson" extolled the Protestant work ethic and delineated means for insuring universal industry. Dwight saw the right to hold property as the greatest inducement to industry and frugality. Where men are permitted to acquire wealth, they will not only work hard and become prosperous and happy, but they will also fight to "preserve the blessings which they enjoy. . . ." In short, a society of independent farmers and craftsmen is a bulwark of tradition.

Succeeding homilies of "Farmer Johnson" reiterate the social religion which Dwight expounded in his theological lectures, his *Travels,* and sermons like *The True Means of Establishing Public Happiness.* Again he set forth the mainstay of his faith, the institutions of religious education and established public worship supplying "motives" to the social well being. Though he described religion as "a wholly voluntary concern," he also maintained that "governments have a right, and are bound, to provide means and opportunities of knowing what religion is, and of becoming religious, for all the people." In other words, religion is the only path to happiness, and legislative support is the best means of promoting religion.[13]

In his concluding "dialogue," "The Duty of Supporting New England Institutions," Dwight suggested a program for enlightening the entire citizenry to the beneficence of the Standing Order. New Englanders should be taught that they have "enjoyed more happiness than any country ever enjoyed; and such a system of happiness demands all the support which its inhabitants can give." If venerable institutions are not prized and defended, happiness will cease; and once lost, it can never be regained. "History furnished no instance in which a Nation, which had once lost these pillars of its happiness ever recovered them." All innovation is disastrous, for only prevailing forms of government and religion have proven their utility. Responding to the current of change, Dwight warned against "untried" institutions precipitously "adopted in times of confusion. . . ."

Dwight's specific recommendations for securing loyalty to established political and religious practices were highly authoritarian. "Wise men," he suggested, should systematize "the glorious inheritance" of New England into a set of precepts. Every member of the "rising generation" should receive thorough training in these traditions, and ". . . a known and decided attachment to them ought to be an indispensable qualification for every public office." Public officials should be required to take oaths of allegiance to the Standing Order. Clergymen, grand jurors, and judges should cooperate to insure its perpetuation;

and each minister should give an annual sermon adulating
the Puritan way. Dwight also recommended that school-
masters steep their pupils in the history of New England,
recounting the glorious blessings of Providence to a God-
fearing people. Unflinching devotion to the status quo
must permeate society. To guard against innovation, as-
semblies should convene periodically in each town, wherein the inhabitants pledge solemnly to "preserve and defend
these Institutions and . . . consider every man who attempts to weaken or destroy them, as an enemy of New-
England happiness: for such he plainly is."[14]

While Dwight wrote such conservative pieces as "Farmer
Johnson" anonymously, his wide range of activities in the
Federalist-Congregational cause were well known throughout New England. As head of Connecticut's chief seminary
of higher learning, and one of the foremost in the country,
he occupied a highly influential position. During his
presidency, the Congregationally-run college functioned
as focal point for dissemination of Puritan and anti-
democratic ideas. With his paternal, activist temper,
Dwight sought to mold young minds into miniature replicas of his own. One forum of indoctrination was the
senior forensics class. Its ostensible purpose was to train
students in the skills of debate. But sessions consisted
largely of high-toned presidential judgments on the great
issues of the day. In 1813, for example, Dwight made
"decisions" in favor of legal support of the clergy; religious tests for civil officers; the encouragement of manufactures in the United States. He condemned theaters as
immoral and "party spirit" as a divisive tool of Illuminati
conspirators. Dwight did not teach his students how to
argue either side of a controversial question, but how to
defend the ideology of Federalist Congregationalism.[15]
Yale served him as a nursery of political religion and la-
boratory for the new evangelical militancy. Benjamin

Silliman, whom Dwight later installed as Professor of Natural Philosophy, was an undergraduate in 1797. In his diary of that year he recorded such incidents as his attendance at a recitation "where the President . . . gave the democratic societies a severe and deserved trimming."[16]

Connecticut's Jeffersonians were far from oblivious to Dwight's Federalist instruction. The *American Mercury*, their leading organ of opinion, recorded numerous incidents of partisan Federalism at Yale. In 1804, a number of Republicans had convened for the purpose of devising a more democratic state constitution. The *Mercury* reported that a group of Yale students invaded the meeting and read an inflammatory anti-Christian address which they alleged to have been a Republican document. The Jeffersonian newspaper dismissed it as a forgery and assailed Dwight's Yale as a "complete repository of political poisons." If religion is in danger, continued the article, it is not due to the machinations of democrats, but to those of "pious federal professors."[17]

A previous article had criticized Dwight for promulgating hatred of the Jefferson Administration among Yale students. Such a stranglehold did Congregational Federalism have on the college, claimed another Republican writer, that Josiah Meigs, a Jeffersonian, had been driven out of his professorship. Dwight had dismissed Meigs from his chair in mathematics and natural philosophy, replacing him with Jeremiah Day, a man of more orthodox sentiments.[18]

Dwight was the most visible among a large number of orthodox ministers who defended the Standing Order and excoriated its democratic critics. From 1800 until 1807, the *Mercury* and other Republican newspapers continuously denounced the Congregational "political clergy." Con-

trary to publicized orthodox opinion, the great majority
of Jeffersonians were in fact Trinitarian Protestants. In
Connecticut, their key difference with orthodoxy was not
in the area of doctrine, but the relationship of church to
state. As non-members of the establishment, they objected
to Congregational privilege and sought to bring about a
more genuinely pluralistic society. Orthodox Federalists
were well aware that Republican objections to their
leadership were more political than doctrinal. But it was
effective to play on the fears of the Congregational public
by categorizing all opponents of the Standing Order as
freethinkers, infidels, and atheists.[19] Deeply resentful of
such smear tactics, Jeffersonian Protestants fought back
with many of the same weapons. They often found scriptural prophecy serviceable for their own war of words
against the orthodox. Casting their objections to Congregational ecclesiasticism in the language of John Adams'
Dissertation on the Canon and Feudal Law, they utilized
his Reformation conception of state religion as an anti-
Christian persecuting power. The democratic interpretation of the Apocalypse simply shifted the Standing
Order from God's to Satan's vanguard. Protestant escha-
tology posited a "Romish hierarchy" united with secular
rulers for the purpose of popular delusion and self-
aggrandizement. Artfully, the Republicans applied this
notion to Connecticut's church-state mechanism.[20]

In September of 1800, a series appeared in the *Mercury*
which cited collusion between Federalist clergymen and
politicians to insure the perpetuation of their oligarchical
dominion. To Jeffersonians, the ministerial influence
which Dwight lauded in his *Travels* was no salutary condition. They found participation of the established clergy
in the electoral process particularly objectionable, as it
served to bias public opinion, giving unfair advantage to
the Federalists. A *Mercury* article criticized the practice of

allowing Congregational ministers to place the name of each officeseeker in nomination. "The personal influence which this *nominator* may have over the minds of many will be considerable, and the people must act precipitatively, without time for information or reflection."[21] The *Courant*, convinced that democratic politicians were conspiring against religion and good order, merely confirmed Jeffersonian suspicions. An article of some months earlier had clearly exposed the anti-democratic nature of Federalist maneuvering. The author proudly revealed the frustration of "a deep-laid plot." "Every Jacobin was left out of the Nomination; and a set of men were voted in who have been tried and are firm and honest-men who love the state, and its old manners and customs. . . ."[22]

Congregational Federalists moved rapidly toward xenophobic nativism, as intruders threatened the status of the Puritan gentry. The Courant writer continued defensively: "Let other states, if they please be governed by Irishmen, Frenchmen, and Jacobins—we will adhere to the principles which have supported us, and made us happy. . . ." Thirteen years later, Dwight, in one of his "decisions," elaborated the nativist viewpoint. Fearing the intrusion of radical foreign ideas, he recommended strenuous scrutiny of disembarking immigrants. "Some foreigners," he said, "mistake liberty for licentiousness and expect to act as they please."[23] Years of crusading against French-inspired democracy led him to judge European immigrants as frequently degenerate, vicious, and prone to mob violence. In the future, nativism would continue to be the reaction of American classes feeling their status threatened by multitudes of newly arrived immigrants.

Actually, most Jeffersonians were not immigrants; neither were they particularly affected by foreign ideas. On the contrary, their movement was wholly indigenous.

In challenging the paternalism of the Standing Order, Connecticut democrats were seeking to broaden the base of social leadership. Recalling the libertarian ideas of 1776, their desires were typically American. Throughout the history of the United States, diverse ethnic, religious, and economic elements have suffered discrimination at the hands of intrenched interests. Periodically, such groups have banded together in social or political bodies to achieve control over their own affairs and to clear away obstacles in the path to success.[24] Like the labor organizations or black movements of later times, Jeffersonians were fighting to enter a power structure which had hitherto excluded them. When Federalists accused them of Jacobin designs against the free exercise of religion, they became infuriated. Their counterattack implied a similarity between the Standing Order and feudal Catholicism. As one Republican put it: Ecclesiastical and lay politicians who arrogate to themselves the exclusive title of *"friends of religion and government* [seek to impose] . . . an union of Church and State—an union which the experience of all countries has proved to be *incompatible with civil and religious liberty."*[25]

While Federalist clergymen defended a paternalistic system, they did not think of the Standing Order as "an union of church and state." Dwight, their most esteemed spokesman, often claimed that full liberty of dissent existed in Connecticut. Congregational control of missionary activities, the school system, and government did not, to his mind endanger freedom. For he conceived religious liberty to mean only that all sects be allowed to exist. They need not be on an equal footing. He did not consider it demeaning to Baptists and Episcopalians to deposit certificates of dissent with Congregational judges in order that they might support their own denominations, rather than the established church. Nor did he deem it discriminatory that only Congregational ministers were allowed to participate in the election procedure.

The Democratic-Republican Party, however, which was composed largely of Baptists and Separatists, interpreted religious freedom in an unqualified sense. Noted clergymen of the disestablishment movement, like John Leland and Isaac Backus, supported Jefferson and wrote anti-ecclesiastical pieces for the Republican press. Based in opposition to the privileged status of New England Congregationalists, Republican anticlericalism grew in intensity as Puritan apologists waged their conservative campaign. For every orthodox tirade against "Jacobinism," there was a Republican attack on Federalist "priestcraft." Frustrated by the oligarchical nature of Connecticut politics and religion, and enraged by self-righteous condemnations of their morality, Republican writers also resorted to a conspiratorial view of their adversaries. The most frequent ecclesiastical target was none other than Timothy Dwight, whom they dubbed "Pope" of Connecticut.

Because Dwight's Yale presidency gave him a preeminent position in the ecclesiastical structure, and because he was so prolific in his defense of the Standing Order, his assailants regarded him as the most powerful man in Connecticut. In 1801, a Republican journalist published a sardonic attack on the college president and the ecclesiasticism for which he stood. The article is notable, however, not only for its acrimony, but for its awareness of Dwight's methods and the scope of his activities. While full of hyperbole, it epitomizes the democratic response to the machinations of the orthodox clergy. The immediate cause of the writer's pique was Dwight's publication of a sermon "in *all* the newspapers in the state"[26] favoring legislative appropriations for missionary work in Connecticut's back country. Seeking public

funds for extension of the Standing Order under the guise
of support for religion in general, provoked the ire of
Republicans. But this writer was more offended by
Dwight's pursuit of "the effulgence of fame. . . ." He
regarded the conservative clergyman as a power hungry
aristocrat.

> . . . in the ecclesiastical carcase of Connecticut, the
> President of Yale is the grand pabulum, and fountainhead
> of political and religious orthodoxy, from which thru'
> associations, and consociations to smaller vehicles &
> minuter channels, flow the dignified results of wisdom,
> and the cautious intrigues of party. . . .

With caustic irony, the writer went on to describe Dwight's
collaboration with Morse and other Massachusetts
divines on the Palladium ". . . to overthrow the works
of darkness and demoralization. . . ." To view Dwight
as a papal figure was not entirely satisfactory, since it
connoted a lordly detachment from immediate political
concerns. The activism of the orthodox commander-in-
chief called for a militant image of the Counter-Reformation.

> Blush ye madly ambitious tools of French fanaticism, and
> be ashamed of your base ingratitude—have ye not abused
> the Reverend Divine incessantly? While he hath been la-
> boring for your welfare—have ye not stigmatized him as
> Pope, when his humility and moderation exceed . . . the
> venerable Loyola? . . . let your repentance be speedy,
> that the steady habits of Connecticut may be preserved in-
> violate, as splendid testimonies of the virtues and zeals of
> our venerable clergy.

For some five years, Republican writers waged a counter-
assault on the orthodox clergy, reserving most of their

venom for "Pope Dwight." He was the symbol of an aristocratic regime which they deplored. Exaggerating his
formal powers, they strenuously tried to discredit the man
and his conservative ideas. In reality, Dwight refrained
from engaging directly in political manipulation. His
brother Theodore was a far more adroit politician. But
Dwight personified the influence which the orthodox
clergy exercised over state politics and the popular mind.
In his *Travels*, he gave an account of the salutary effects
of "ministerial influence." Jeffersonians felt compelled
to focus on Dwight because of his prestigious position and
his formidable authority over the youth of Connecticut. A
battery of young militant conservatives would severely
hamper Republican goals of democratization.

One particularly devastating piece of anti-Dwight
literature bore the embarassing title, "The Triumph of
Infidelity Resuscitated." The brunt of the acrimonious
poem, which Dwight had composed before commencing
his public career, now came back to plague him. In the
first number of its expose, the *Mercury* revealed its icono-
clastic aim of setting ". . . the Doctor in contrast with
himself, and help[ing] the world to a more complete view
of the *man*." The articles sought to expose inconsistency,
hypocrisy, and arrogance in the Federalist clergyman. For
example, Dwight had prayed for the downfall of "popery"
in his poem, but more recently, he had welcomed its return to France. Moreover, his present scheme of unifying
church and state was in contrast to the earlier poetic attack
on priestliness. As versifier, he had also arrogantly styled
the New Divinity and himself as living apostles of Christ,
vilifying all who differed with them.[27]

One Republican expressed the crux of his party's
controversy with Dwight, not in the usual sarcastic tone,
but in words of honest concern. After referring to Dwight's
abusive sermons and the anti-Jeffersonian speeches de-

livered at Yale commencements, this writer dispassion-
ately stated the heart of his case. He denied that Republicans were out to "weaken [Dwight's] authority," or disparage his ability. "But if federalists [sic] will first set him
up as a pattern of all excellence, and will insist that because he is so very excellent, the children of Republicans
shall be taught to despise the principles of their fathers,
we will reserve the right to question this excellence. . . ."[28]

On the heels of this indictment came a series of articles
exposing Dwight's manner of teaching Federalism. The
author attested to the president's "patronizing care" in
nurturing youngsters in the politics of the Standing
Order. Dwight's personal supervision of the senior class
was an especially effective means of influence. At Yale,
Republicans were denied a hearing, and students were
overawed by a barrage of partisan propaganda. Consequently, many graduates emerged with "deeply rooted
prejudices."

With the Standing Order controlling Connecticut
government and religion until 1818, the minority party
was acutely sensitive to an educational process dominated
by Federalists. Since the orthodox clergy were a vocal and
authoritative element in Connecticut society, Republicans
regarded them as the front line of the "federal phalanx."
Angered by partisan election sermons, they condemned
such preaching as part of a plot to unify church and state.
For additional evidence of Federalist-Congregational
oppression, they cited discrimination against Republican
ministers. A *Mercury* article claimed that Reverend Isaac
Jones of New Haven had lost his license to preach because
he supported Jefferson. It went on to accuse Federalist
preachers of refusing to exchange pulpits with Republicans. Another anticlerical piece cited a Federalist minister who had, in a Thanksgiving Day sermon, vilified
Jefferson as "a debaucher, an infidel, [and] a liar." Scores

of other commentaries assailed the electioneering of Connecticut's "political clergy." To counter Federalist claims that Jeffersonians opposed religion, the Republican press asserted that Congregational political preachers were the true cause of infidelity, having abandoned religion for politics.[29]

Federalist writers responded promptly to Republican anticlericalism. In the late spring of 1801, shortly after he had been compared with Loyola, Dwight published a four-part defense of the orthodox clergy in the *Palladium*. Parts two and three were reprinted in the *Courant*. Addressing himself "To the Farmers and Mechanics of New England," his purpose was to win the public back "to religion and to ministers of the gospel."[30] Fearing that "a change in the feelings of [New Englanders would] . . . materially change the state of society," he felt called upon to refute anticlerical arguments.

Dealing first with the assertion that the clergy were too powerful, he described the formal activities of Congregational ministers. In this way, he ignored the question of informal and familial ties between clergymen and legislators,[31] as well as the issue of Congregationalism's privileged status. His main point was that parishes exercised full control over their ministers through their rights of appointment and dismissal and the power of the purse. Dwight refrained from discussing consociational authority to censure deviant Congregational ministers, ostracize them, or try them for heresy.

The Federalist educator stood on firmest ground in considering the political rights of clergymen. Rather than denying the existence of clerical politics, he faced the matter squarely, asserting the minister's freedom to express interest "in the political concerns of his country." Since politics contain "the whole mass of public morals, it is the duty of ministers to "meddle." They are enjoined by Christ ". . . to teach and inculcate public morals as well . . . as private; the duties of citizens, subjects, and rulers, as much as those of men." As in his theological instruction, Dwight stressed that public morals cannot be separate from private. Nations, as well as individuals, are subject to the laws of God.[32]

His arguments, however, contained an element of self-righteousness. He not only defended the clergy's right to speak out on political issues, but he also held that Connecticut (Federalist) parishioners support their (Federalist) ministers because the "clergymen have judged right on all great political subjects." Such claims of infallibility may have been a factor in earning Dwight the title of "Pope." He also defended the Federalist clergy by wallowing in ad hominen conjecture to impugn the integrity of Republican critics. Referring to their "loose morals, principles, and lives," he characterized them as incompetent busybodies "who frequent public places, taverns, and corners of streets." In other words, Federalist ministers not only had a right to preach on political subjects, but also a monopoly on virtue and sound judgment. For anyone who publicly disagreed with them became ipso facto an immoral schemer.[33]

Both the *Palladium* and the *Courant* printed numerous likeminded defenses of the orthodoxy clergy. In early 1801, an essay appearing in both papers praised the ecclesiastical establishment as the major cause of happiness in New England. Dwight may well have been the author, for the style and content resembled his apologetics. New England's virtue was contrasted with the sad state of affairs in places which lacked such an establishment. Also present was Dwight's familiar hope that Puritan "institutions and manners be introduced into every part of the union." Four years later, a series appeared in the *Courant* over the signature "O" elaborating many of the same ideas. Opponents

of the Standing Order were portrayed as "cunning," a
favorite epithet of Dwight. A dominant theme of the "O"
articles and conservative rhetoric in general was ancestor
worship. In describing "the noble structure . . . reared
by our ancestors" as an "impious union of church and
state" the "cunning *miners* " were upsetting its foundation. The point here is that only Infidels can make such
an assertion, for religious liberty exists in Connecticut.
Requiring citizens to support religion is not only consistent with freedom, but the primary cause of it.[34]

By 1807, the tiresome controversy was subsiding.
Jefferson had been in office for nearly two terms, and yet
churches were still flourishing, and French-style revolution had not occurred. With the wind thus removed from
their sails, the orthodox clergy ceased their public dis-
paragement of American "Jacobinism." As a result, Republican writers toned down their anticlericalism. A
Mercury article of March 19 treated clerical politics as a
dying phenomenon, noting that persons who had engaged
in it had found it unprofitable.[35]

Political warfare naturally continued between New
England Federalists and Jeffersonians. The War of 1812
brought renewed controversy and prophetic warnings
from Dwight and other Anglophile ministers. The Hartford Convention, assembled to formulate measures for
opposing the war, spurred a new wave of Republican vi-
tuperation. Pro-Administration newspapers questioned
the patriotism of Theodore Dwight, the Convention's
secretary, and the other arch-Federalist participants.
But ecclesiasticism did not again become a political issue
until after the War, when the Connecticut movement for
disestablishment picked up enough support to pose a
real threat. By that time, however, Dwight was too old
and his health too poor to lead a new defensive campaign.
Leadership of the Standing Order had passed to younger

politicians and clergymen, such as Dwight's energetic disciple, Lyman Beecher.

The battle against Jeffersonian democracy comprised only the negative and purely defensive aspect of Dwight's evangelical crusade. As the Standing Order lost prestige and declined in coercive authority, orthodox partisans began to rely more heavily on voluntary associations as instruments of persuasion. With his evangelical activism and religious education, Dwight hoped to restore loyalty to the Standing Order. But the Federalist Party was dying, and with it support of religious establishments. On the other hand, a new revivalistic movement, which Dwight did so much to set in motion, was sweeping through New England. This positive side of the orthodox crusade succeeded in preserving and vastly extending orthodox Protestantism. In addition, it perpetuated traditional Puritan morals and cosmology. As an expiring establishment relinquished its power to maintain social control, the voluntary agencies and militant revivalism of the Second Great Awakening moved into the void.

CHAPTER IX

The Contrived Awakening

As indicated by Dwight's early writings, New England Calvinists were already becoming alarmed at the accelerating pace of social change in the 1780s. When the Greenfield minister joined Connecticut's General Association in 1788, he was promptly selected along with one other minister, to "draught an exhortation" on the subject of religious backsliding. The address was to be read publicly "in the various Congregations through the state."[1] Connecticut's orthodox clergy at this time made initial moves toward counteracting the spread of liberalism. New Divinity men, who still dominated orthodox circles of both Connecticut and ecclesiastically decentralized Massachusetts, had long been attracted to missionary work. While extensive reliance on means was at odds with Consistent Calvinist theology, missions had clear scriptural sanction. It was the duty of Christians to spread the Word; but whether or not conversions ensued was purely a divine matter.

The Connecticut Missionary Society remained in a formative stage for some five to six years. The project of diffusing the New England faith within darker American regions gained increasing support from orthodox legislators and ministers during the mid-nineties, when liberalism and infidelity began to undermine the old order. Not until 1798, the peak year of orthodox alarm over the "Illuminati Conspiracy," did the plan of sending Congregational missionaries to new settlements really go into effect. Though some proselytizing work had been undertaken previously, 1798 saw the establishment of the official Missionary Society.[2] It is worthy of note that Benjamin Trumbull and the younger Edwards became trustees of the new institution, while Timothy Dwight did not. During the late eighteenth century, these two staunch New Divinity ministers were among the most active participants in Connecticut's ecclesiastical affairs.[3]

Despite the Republican assertion that Dwight was the prime mover in Connecticut clerical politics, it is clear that at least in the early years of Federalist-Jeffersonian controversy, his more flexible brand of evangelical religion had yet to become the ecclesiastical modus operandi. Edwardian intellectuals were firmly in control, and it took the ominous political situation of 1798 to spur them to action. They moved slowly in the area of promotional measures, but their conservative goals paralleled Dwight's. They were also, of course, millennialists, convinced of their mission to uphold Zion. In a 1798 meeting, with Dwight absent, the General Association declared their conservative millennial intentions. The ministers recorded in their minutes a selection from the Missionary Society's new constitution. It evinced a hope that "the time is near, in which God will spread his truth thro' the whole earth. . . ." The document also set forth a strongly social purpose avowing that: ". . . the order and stability of Civil Government are the most effectually advanced by the Diffusion of religion and moral sentiments."[4]

With the flow of population into outlying areas, Connecticut orthodoxy feared that lack of firm ecclesiastical control in these places might lead to a proliferation of heresy and infidelity. Concurring with the notion of a dissolute frontier which Dwight later described in his *Travels*, a conservative General Association set out to bring order out of chaos. The prospect of surrounding communities falling prey to liberalism was more than disconcerting to the Congregational clergy.

The conservative purpose of the new Missionary Society did not long elude the sensitive eyes of the Jeffersonian press. Republican writers denounced the new proselytizing effort as a priestly conspiracy. Because ecclesiastical controls in Connecticut were long established, the Missionary Society concentrated its work in states like Vermont, which lacked a Standing Order. Perceiving a plan to diffuse authoritarian ecclesiasticism, the *Mercury* criticized "Connecticut puritans" for their "luminous display of arrogance. . . ." The liberal newspaper regarded such missions as an insult to the equally "enlightened" inhabitants of other states. A later article condemned the Missionary Society as ". . . a very keystone to the grand Arch of Church and State Union." The author argued that establishment policy was to increase the power of a particular orthodox order" at the expense of all other denominations. The success of such a program would destroy the "equilibrium of religious sects" upheld by the United States Constitution.[5]

The Hopkinsian Massachusetts Missionary Society was formed in 1799, a year after its Connecticut counterpart. Although it was less ecclesiastically oriented, due to the Congregational independence of Bay State orthodoxy, its formation had similar overtones. Nathanael

Emmons, a firm Federalist, preached an abrasive sermon against the international Infidel conspiracy during the same year in which he founded the missionary organization.[6] It is significant also that the Franklin minister earned his laurels primarily as a defender of the faith.[7] The magazine of the Massachusetts Society was never overtly political or even social in content. Strict Calvinists stressed the personal, metaphysical, and supernatural aspects of religion. Explicit connection of piety with social issues would have been too moralistic for their ethereal tastes. But underlying their experimental piety was a prophetic interpretation of history which had distinct social implications. An individual might be either on the Lord's or the devil's side, depending on his religious, social, and political principles.

The Connecticut Missionary Society also published an evangelical magazine. This periodical, however, was not so sectarian as the Massachusetts publication. The Connecticut establishment encompassed varying shades of orthodoxy, from metaphysical New Divinity to Old Calvinism. Among these Congregational ministers was an emerging group of moderately Calvinist evangelicals best represented by the Yale graduates of 1769, Timothy Dwight and Nathan Strong. While they defined themselves as New Divinity men, they were, as we have seen, primarily concerned with evangelical action, rather than metaphysical disquisition. The editorial board was originally composed of fifteen members, to which three other clergymen, including Dwight, were shortly added. Since the magazine commenced publication in 1800, the metaphysically inclined Edwards the younger was never an editor. In 1799, he had been appointed president of Union College in Schenectady, New York, and two years later he died. The board consisted of thirteen New Divinity men, three Old Calvinists, and two ministers whose positions are indiscernible to the historian. However, among the Consistent Calvinist majority, eight clergymen were effective evangelicals, while five were more scholastic types.[8] This cross-section of New England Calvinism produced a periodical containing a somewhat broader approach to religious experience than the Hopkinsian dogmatizing of the *Massachusetts Missionary Magazine*.

New England orthodoxy was moving gradually toward a practical evangelical activism. A perusal of the *Connecticut Evangelical Magazine* over a seventeen-year period reveals a steady shift away from rigid Calvinism toward the more moderate social religion of Dwight and his immediate followers. Like the other evangelical publications, which proliferated in the early nineteenth century, the Connecticut periodical combined doctrinal commentary with accounts of revivals and missionary work. During its early years of existence, the theological pieces ranged from metaphysical scholasticism to quasi-moralistic evangelical appeals. Simultaneous inclusion of these two modes of thought reflected the diverse composition of the editorial board.

Some articles in the early issues expounded Hopkinsian conceptions of human depravity and divine sovereignty. One bit of "Advice to the Awakened Sinner" reiterated the discouraging belief that his "greatest convictions" and most ardent "religious performances" only render him "more guilty in the sight of God, until his heart is regenerated."[9] But at the same time, another writer emphasized the importance of unregenerate attendance to means. Without prior knowledge of Christian doctrine, he argued, subsequent acquisition of faith would be very difficult.[10]

As members of a centralized association of ministers representing the Standing Order, contributors to the *Connecticut Evangelical Magazine* were actively involved in

the public issues of their state. Unlike Massachusetts and
Rhode Island Consistent Calvinists, they were neither
geographically isolated, nor intellectually indisposed to
participate in politics. The Saybrook system had established a unified ecclesiastical corporation with one
common interest. Direct involvement in public affairs
was therefore more natural and inevitable in consociational Connecticut than in the localized Congregationalism
of the other two states. As an official organ, the *Connecticut Evangelical Magazine* expressed an awareness of
immediate social issues that was absent in the sectarian
periodical of Massachusetts Hopkinsians, who occupied
rural, autonomous parishes. Congregational ministers
of Connecticut were not only engaged in a general defense and propagation of their faith; they were intimately
concerned with formulating specific tactics to subdue
opponents of the Standing Order. Hence, they moved
toward "means," or practical measures, for defense. Gradually the Congregational revival lost its supernaturalistic
aura and began instead as a contrived ministerial effort to
retain traditional forms of control over a splintering society. Of course, the weight of New Divinity theological
baggage restrained ministers at first from plunging head-
long into evangelical promotionalism. But as time went
on and the crisis deepened, they began to lay aside the
strict Calvinist doctrines which were becoming barriers
in the way of conservative evangelization. As early as
1800, a writer detailed the importance of working for
revivals. While he paid respect to Calvinist supernaturalism, his intent was to affirm the utility of human exertion.
He admitted that ". . . regeneration is the work of God,
and the immediate effect of his power. . . ." However, he
said, "it does appear from fact and observation, that it is
ordinarily necessary to regeneration that a sinner should
be awakened to attend to means." Those motivated to do

so are usually the ones who experience conversion. On the other hand, individuals who neglect the prescribed ordinances of religion are not likely to receive saving grace. Recognizing the Arminian implications of his argument, the writer backed down somewhat in his conclusion, restating the Calvinist doctrine that natural means have no necessary connection with regeneration. But he had understood the crucial value of concrete action in the campaign to preserve New England Puritanism.[11]

In 1801, the *Connecticut Evangelical Magazine* opened with an editorial call for "vigorous exertions" at a time when "the Prince of Darkness is more than usually active." Revivalism and missionary work were the Lord's means for "erecting a standard against him." The orthodox clergy interpreted Jefferson's election as a national victory for irreligion. In reaction, they began cautiously at first, to promote their faith. After Dwight joined the editorial board, the magazine began to devote more space to articles advocating Christian nurture. In an "Address to the Inhabitants of New Settlements," Abel Flint, Secretary to the Missionary Society, advised them promptly to institutionalize the means of grace. "Faith," he quoted, "comes by hearing, and hearing by the word of God. . . . By . . . preaching it pleaseth him to save them that believe." Teach religion to your children, he continued; pray with them; ". . . govern them well, teaching them subordination to all good government." Flint concluded by stating that Christian institutions are the basis of orderly, righteous communities. These ideas corresponded to Dwight's rationale for a "religious education."[12]

Fifteen years later, at the height of the Second Great Awakening, the Connecticut General Association commissioned Dwight, Lyman Beecher, and two other ministers "to prepare and publish an address to the emigrants from this State and from New England generally, in the

new settlements." Essentially, the discourse reiterated the
advice of Abel Flint. Ancestor worship and institutional
nurture were its guidelines. Retain the traditional Puritan
way, said the ministers, and you will reap God's bounty.
"The liberal support of divine institutions has made
hundreds of parishes wealthy. It never made *one* poor."
The offer of such worldly inducements was characteristic
of Dwight's moralistic evangelism. His influence was also
evident in other parts of the address. The importance of
virtuous habits was stressed. "The early habits of a people"
were compared with "roads in a new country." Once "the
inhabitants . . . have built their houses and farms by
them," they are "extremely . . . difficult to alter." In
typical Dwight fashion, the discourse evoked an image
of pious little New England style communities all the way
to the Pacific.[13]

But a number of years intervened before the General
Association had thus officially adopted Dwight's expansive approach to religion. During the first decade of the
nineteenth century, the *Connecticut Evangelical Magazine* juxtaposed a millennial and moralistic activism with
reassertions of New Divinity metaphysics. The years
1801-1808 were a transitional period in which a kind of
theological schizophrenia pervaded the pages of the journal. Orthodox apologists wanted desperately to do something new, strenuous, and effective to further their cause.
But whenever they ventured into new areas of persuasion, the spectres of Edwards and Hopkins appeared,
warning them against creeping Arminianism. Hence, on
the one hand, sinners were exhorted to use the means of
grace as the best way to "obtain mercy." But at the same
time they were restrained by writers who clung to exclusive divine agency. In direct opposition to Dwight's self-
assured use of means, one New Divinity stalwart insisted

that God needs no secondary cause to renovate the human heart. Regeneration ". . . is effected . . . in a super-natural manner by the power of God immediately."[14]

Other writers, however, who emphasized Christian training, appreciated the power of human influence in advancing orthodoxy. Consequently, they favored a pro-gram of religious education to combat apostasy from the old doctrines. More practical minds among the clergy gave increasing attention to "the reasonableness of immediate repentance." Strongly implying that sinners are capable of pursuing holiness, they advocated early conversion as the key to a joyous, Christian life. Those who returned to God in youth would also be "instrumental in awaken-ing and converting the souls of [others]." With this idea in mind, Dwight was immersing his Yale students in the principles of Federalist-Congregationalism.[15]

By 1808, a utilitarian religion of immediate repentance and Christian nurture had become the dominant motif of the *Connecticut Evangelical Magazine*. A decade of orthodox crusading against liberalism had paid dividends in a general awakening. Deism and skepticism had sub-sided, but the orthodox saw anti-Christian conspiracy persisting in various clever disguises. Unitarianism was engulfing Boston; dissenters were campaigning for dis-establishment in Connecticut; and Republicans still con-trolled the nation. Of course, the vast majority of non-Congregational denominations were firmly Trinitarian. Indeed, Baptism and Methodism were intensely evangeli-cal faiths led by revivalistic ministries. With the cooling of the political warfare which pervaded New England in the early years of Jefferson's Administration, the Calvin-ist clergy began to perceive a more dangerous adversary

in Unitarianism. Because the Unitarians were largely
Federalist, the new controversy took on a less political
tone.

Denial of Christ's divinity occurred predominantly in
Massachusetts parishes. Consociational authority effectively guarded against such heresy in Connecticut. Although Congregationalists were beginning to see the need
for a unified Trinitarian front, Connecticut orthodoxy
was slower to move in this direction than the more embattled Puritan churches of Massachusetts. The General
Association, enjoying far more power than the decentralized establishment of Massachusetts, could afford a
greater parochialism. Connecticut's first movement into
promotional religion was purely a Standing Order effort
to buttress its own position. However, such Congregational ecclesiasticism would generate the institutional
Christianity of the Second Great Awakening. Increased
missionary work and the formation of moral societies
occurred originally to shore up ecclesiastical controls.

Nevertheless, even Connecticut's Congregationalists,
reacted against Unitarianism by moving toward cooperation with other denominations. In 1808, the Missionary
Society made noteworthy changes in its publication. De-
emphasizing metaphysics, the editors turned away from
strict Calvinism toward a more general elucidation of
Reformed doctrine. To defend the faith effectively, a
degree of unacknowledged Arminianization had become
necessary, since Edwardian supernaturalism tended to
discourage Christian exertions. A more moralistic approach to religion, expressing the sinner's ability to
strive and "do good" was a boon to the evangelical cause.
The revised magazine approached the theology of Timothy Dwight. Conversions retained their foremost importance, but they were to occur through regular use of
natural means, and not through the exclusive preroga-

tive of an inscrutable God. Dwight's moderate Calvinist
position was far more flexible than metaphysical New
Divinity. It could be made amenable to the views of a
wide range of evangelical Protestants. The editors of the
refurbished periodical, newly christened the *Connecticut
Evangelical Magazine and Religious Intelligencer*, made
clear the objection to "merely controversial or deeply
metaphysical" subjects. The rejected "polemic discus-
sions" which might alienate any of the "faithful followers
of our divine Redeemer."[16] Five years later, the editors
made a clear profession of Protestant Trinitarian catholicity. "We firmly believe," they stated, "that the Presbyterian, the Episcopal, the Baptist, and the Methodist may
be travelling in the road to life, although in some things
they think differently. . . ."[17] Here in summary was the
new spirit of evangelical union, directed primarily against
the Unitarians. Of course, Connecticut Congregationalists may well have been motivated in their charitable
feeling toward dissenters by the growing movement for
disestablishment. It is likely that the editors were implying
that the Standing Order had the best interests of all Trinitarian Protestants at heart and deserved interdenominational support as a bulwark against Unitarianism.

The *Connecticut Evangelical Magazine*'s development
of a less sectarian viewpoint followed the lead of another
periodical, the *Panoplist*. A group of moderate Calvinists
in Massachusetts, under the direction of Jedidiah Morse,
began publication of this religious magazine in 1805. Two
years earlier, orthodoxy had lost an important stronghold
when Henry Ware, a liberal, was appointed Hollis Professor of Divinity at Harvard. Ware succeeded David
Tappan, a moderate, who had cooperated with Dwight,
and Morse in defending traditional Puritanism. Historians have often alluded to the Ware appointment as
the opening round of the Unitarian controversy. In the

first decade of the nineteenth century, liberals did not
refer to themselves as Unitarians. But Arianism and
Socinianism had been growing among them since the
time of Jonathan Mayhew.[18] Moreover, the Old Calvinist and liberal clergy had long opposed revivalism. They
played down the crucial evangelical process of conversion, preferring instead to preach on moral subjects.[19]

The new controversy between Calvinists and liberals
was a further development of the New Light-Arminian
debate, which followed the first Great Awakening. But
while the liberal party was moving toward Unitarianism,
the Calvinists were gradually Arminianizing their evangelical faith. Moderates like Dwight and Morse, who first
commanded orthodox forces in the Second Great Awakening, were closer, in some important respects, to Mayhew,
the eighteenth century liberal, than to Edwards, their
own spiritual ancestor. Though a Calvinistic belief in
depravity and regeneration formed the basis of their faith,
they combined these doctrines with a quasi-Arminian
emphasis on unregenerate striving. By dispensing with
Consistent Calvinist supernaturalism and expressing an
Arminian confidence in human exertion, they were able
to activate a powerful evangelical movement.

The *Panoplist* was the first great organ for this party of
evangelical synthesizers. It was a practical publication,
which deliberately subordinated metaphysics to the task
of procuring conversions. In so doing, it followed the
lead of President Dwight. As a theologian peculiarly sensitive to the threat of change, Dwight had been a prophet
of the new movement. While at Greenfield, he had begun
to react against liberalism by constructing a more utilitarian theology. A united Connecticut establishment
would remain in power until shortly after his death.
Therefore, with heresy not nearly so evident in Connecticut
as in Massachusetts, the General Association could afford

to move gradually in adopting Dwight's instrumentalist approach. Dwight was a powerful figure in the Connecticut establishment, but many of his early colleagues were too encumbered by their Edwardian heritage to countenance many new measures for defense of the faith. Dwight's greatest influence was on his students, many of whom would put his activist theology into successful practice during the first twenty years of the nineteenth century. While the General Association in Connecticut was gradually accepting Dwight's enhancement of means, Massachusetts Calvinists, with liberalism storming the ramparts, felt a more urgent need for swift and decisive action. As focal point of the Unitarian controversy, the Boston area became a seedbed for a resourceful evangelical orthodoxy which coincided with the methods of Timothy Dwight. Together with Morse, Dwight assumed command of the new evangelical activists in Massachusetts. The movement moderated Calvinist doctrine in the interest of rapid evangelization. Corresponding frequently, Dwight and Morse mapped out plans for their campaign. In 1810, Dwight sent Jeremiah Evarts, a lay disciple and militant evangelical, to work directly with Morse as editor of the *Panoplist*.

But Massachusetts was also the home of Emmons and his Hopkinsian circle. These sectarians refused at first to join the new moderates in united action against Unitarianism. Consequently, the *Panoplist* began without the aid of Consistent Calvinists, who preferred to support their own publication. This situation freed the moderates from metaphysical influence and enabled them to pursue a more practical, catholic evangelism. Unlike the *Connecticut Evangelical Magazine,* the *Panoplist* was a moderate Calvinist enterprise from its inception. If Dwight was the prophet of the new evangelism, the new journal, to which he contributed frequently, became its chief popularizer.[20]

In a preface to its first number, Morse announced the
Panoplist's goal of uniting evangelical Christians against
"the enemies of truth." Narrow sectarianism and doctrinal
hairsplitting were to be shunned. Evangelical denominations were asked to abjure internecine disputes as counter-
productive in the mighty task of converting the world to
pristine Reformed religion.[21]

Like Dwight, the *Panoplist* fused religion with social
conservatism. Also like him, its other contributors
realized that only confident reliance on means would
produce revivals of religion, thus breaking the spell of
"fashionable" moralism. New England's Second Great
Awakening had its beginnings in Dwight's Yale campaign
against liberalism and infidelity. His prophetic warnings,
rational arguments, and emotional sermons like "The
Harvest Past" had inaugurated a new revivalism. The
Panoplist reflected the growth of a moderate wing of
Calvinist evangelicals, who resorted to similar methods
of persuasion. Following in Dwight's path, they greatly
expanded the scope of the new Awakening. In writing
their sermons and tracts, they scrupulously avoided the
pitfalls of Consistent Calvinism. The *Panoplist* printed
exhortations to repent and believe in Christ side by side
with implicitly anti-Hopkinsian statements accentuating
the positive, heartening aspects of orthodoxy. A series on
experimental religion sought to distill the vitality of conversion from the depressing metaphysical context of
Consistent Calvinism. The author claimed that experimental Christianity had been "grossly misunderstood and
misrepresented." Consciously avoiding reference to the
sinner's inability, he described holiness as a glowing
affection for "the transcendant loveliness of the adorable
creator." Invoking a paternal divine image similar to that
of Dwight's theology, he remarked that God "permits us
not only to reverence him as a Father, but to love him as
a friend." This humane piece was a clear sign that evan-

gelical Calvinists were ceasing their preoccupation with omnipotence and wrath. They were developing a warm, sentimental religion, which stressed a protective Father and a loving Savior.[22]

One of the most explicitly anti-New Divinity tracts which the *Panoplist* printed was a posthumous work by David Tappan. The late Hollis Professor was a formative influence on evangelical moderates. His position approximated that of Dwight. "The most lamentable errors and mischiefs," Tappan remarked, "have arisen from a disproportionate or exclusive zeal for certain parts of Christianity, detached from the system at large."[23] Those ministers who "confine their heads and hearts within a small circle of favorite speculations . . . condemn as an ignorant or unconverted heretic every Christian brother or preacher, who steps over this circle." Tappan indicted these doctrinal extremists for laying far too heavy emphasis on "the depravity of man" and the "satisfaction of Christ." In criticizing Hopkinsians, he was careful, however, to distinguish evangelical Christianity from the merely *"moral or practical"* systems of the liberals. Conversion was for him, as for Dwight, the only sound basis of morality. His utilitarian arguments for evangelical faith and repentence were virtually identical to those of his New Haven colleague. The theological positions of Tappan and Dwight epitomized the emerging spirit of a moderate evangelical Calvinism.

The *Panoplist* represented a general orthodox shift in the direction of Dwight's humanized Calvinism. An essay on regeneration with nominalist overtones exemplifies this trend. Quoting from Watts, a popular British evangelical, the writer held that it is impossible to distinguish the workings of the Holy Spirit "in a sensible manner from the motion of [our] own souls." Though regeneration is God's work, sinners should never despair of their chances for salvation. The Creator has perfect knowledge of man's precarious state and the worldly temptations to which Christians are exposed. Humble prayer and "watchful endeavors" will surely save them "from the hour of temptation. . . ."[24] Such evangelical pieces drew from Calvinist doctrines the same heartening conclusions of Dwight's theology. They depicted a God who kindly motivates sinners to love him. In contrast, Hopkinsian writings accentuated an Absolute Sovereign's righteous condemnation of helpless mortals.

As the *Connecticut Evangelical Magazine* gravitated toward a similar point of view, it also published more encouraging materials. In 1808, a writer described God's justice not in the awful tones of Consistent Calvinism, but the compassionate language of the new moderate school. Possibly Dwight was the contributor; but regardless of who wrote the article, it illustrates the prevailing direction of New England theology. The writer portrayed God as a "just and good" Father, who takes no delight in punishing his unfaithful children. In the interest of winning souls, moderate Calvinists were adjusting to the humanitarian currents of the era. This evangelical underscored his departure from the old supernaturalism by stressing the need of clergymen to balance the justice of God with the Cross of Christ. In the new revivalism, evangelical persuasion was becoming master, and taming metaphysics to its service. The tract concludes with an exhortation to "retire into your closet, and ask your conscience, what reason there is that you should not immediately repent."[25]

Much of this study has focused on the social foundation of controversy and change in New England religion. The new evangelical moderates, under the direction of Dwight and Morse, were particularly attuned to the social aspects of faith. Their counter-reformation was a calculated response to the rise of liberal pluralism. As they supplanted the metaphysicals, moderates revised orthodoxy in order to cope with immediate issues. Confident expansion of the means of grace was an effective way to gain converts and thereby overcome the challenge to orthodoxy. Merging theory with practice, the moderates rendered piety more easily obtainable than did the Consistent Calvinists. They developed a series of measures to aid in procuring the change of heart. Revival sermons, free of metaphysical conundrums, and brimming with calls to repentance, were the most powerful force in the new Awakening. Another agency of conversion was the renewed emphasis on Christian nurture. An 1809 article in the *Connecticut Evangelical Magazine* held that godly parents usually bring up godly children; whereas "ignorant and ungodly parents" neglect to instruct their offspring "in the principles of religion and morality."[26]

The *Panoplist* of the following year began a series on human depravity which stressed not its metaphysical origins, but its effects on daily life. Relying heavily on moralistic illustrations, these articles were indistinguishable in content from the theological lectures on depravity which Dwight delivered at Yale. War, duelling, neglect of the Sabbath, and religious persecution were typical subjects for consideration. The author argued that such evil practices occurred most often in places bereft of Christian institutions. These essays were written to support the doctrine of innate depravity with empirical evidence. But in offering examples of depraved social behavior, the author indicted specific institutional practices for purveying sin. The universality of war, for example, was a direct consequence of exposing individuals from an early age to depraved notions of martial glory. Hence natural depravity became the nurture of depravity. The child was not born with a fondness for organized

violence; an impious environment taught him to love it.
Moderates reaffirmed the idea that human beings have
inherently evil tendencies. But unlike Consistent Calvinists, they believed that social institutions, depending on
their Christian or un-Christian nature, could wean individuals from sin, or reinforce the innate propensity to
depravity.[27]

The *Panoplist* moderates followed Dwight's early lead
in postulating a God who imparts grace through secondary agencies, or natural religious ordinances. This point
of view led them, as it had Dwight, to stress the importance of religious education. The editors called for expanded instruction in the principles of "true religion"
to guard against the doctrinal meanderings of "moral-
izing divines" and "turbulent sectaries." Despite their
avowed desire to unify the evangelical denominations,
New England Congregationalists retained an aversion to
the "enthusiasm" of frontier religion. Dwight expressed
disdain for backwoods exhorters in his *Travels*. Also, it
is important to remember that moderate Calvinists were
members of established churches in Massachusetts and
Connecticut. As such, they remained committed to the
perpetuation of ecclesiastical control. Hence, their evangelical program entailed the formation of an "educated
ministry," which would secure public adherence to traditional orthodoxy.[28]

When Harvard fell to Unitarianism, Massachusetts Calvinists, with their backs to the wall, set about establishing
their own "theological institution." Connecticut's religious education remained safely in orthodox hands. At
Yale, Dwight was scrupulously explaining and defending
theology. His friend Morse took the initiative in founding
a similar fulcrum of orthodoxy in Massachusetts. By 1808,

Morse had become preoccupied with a plan to unite Hopkinsians and moderates in order to wage a more effective
war on Unitarianism. The *Massachusetts Missionary Magazine* was running into financial trouble due to its failure
to attract an extensive readership.[29] As a result, the Consistent Calvinists were becoming more disposed to unite
with Morse's group. The flourishing liberal movement
caused Hopkinsians to reassess their parochial attitude.

Morse's goal was to secure cooperation of the Hopkinsians in the founding of a new seminary and get them to
combine their own flagging publication with the *Panoplist*. To approach the Emmons group, Morse enlisted
the aid of Leonard Woods, a minister of strict Calvinist
opinions who also endorsed the concept of evangelical
union.[30] Because he was a close friend of Emmons,
Spring, and other Consistent Calvinist notables, Woods
was able to persuade them that they could join the
moderates without risk of compromising their principles.
For his part, Morse was more interested in unifying Massachusetts orthodoxy than in eradicating Hopkinsian
influence from the proposed theological institution.
Dwight agreed that Trinitarian union must be of first
priority. In an 1805 letter to Morse, he expressed disap-
pointment in both the Arminian union with the Unitarians and the split between moderates and Hopkinsians.
He noted "very serious sensations" in Connecticut over
the Harvard apostasy, and wished Morse well in reuniting
Calvinist factions to defend the Trinity.[31]

Eliphalet Pearson, a self-exiled professor from Harvard,[32]
became an important Morse ally in establishing the new
seminary. Pearson was president of the Phillips Academy
Andover Board of Trustees, a moderate Calvinist corporation of which Morse was a member. The two moderates,
working through the diplomacy of Woods, persuaded the
Hopkinsians to abort plans for their own seminary in the

remote town of West Newbury and join with moderates to
found one in the established academic community of
Andover.[33]

Morse appeased Hopkinsian purists on the matter of
incorporating some of their doctrines into the creed of the
new school. Such concessions did not bother him because
he was primarily concerned with evangelical action. Some
Hopkinsians, moreover, were adept at subordinating
doctrine to evangelical appeal in the pulpit. Morse further placated them by securing the appointment of Leonard Woods as Andover's first Professor of Theology.
Woods was actually a compromise figure, standing mid-
way between the orthodox camps. Morse had previously
appointed him co-editor of the *Panoplist.* "He knew,"
recalled Woods, "that in a moderate sense I was a Hopkinsian, but on account of this moderate sense he had
chosen me."[34] By 1808, Morse had successfully reunified
Massachusetts orthodoxy at Andover and in the *Panoplist.*
The Massachusetts Missionary Society and its magazine
had been thoroughly absorbed into the moderate movement.

As Professor of Sacred Literature at Andover, Morse
obtained the selection of his moderate associate, Eliphalet
Pearson. Since Pearson was a layman, he needed ordination to join the new faculty. The founders combined
this procedure with the ceremonies which opened the
divinity school. They chose the president of Yale to deliver
the ordination sermon. Dwight's discourse was a compound of evangelical appeal, ecclesiasticism, and millennial prophecy. He mentioned the desperate need for
"respectable" ministers "of one accord, and of one mind"
to propagate orthodoxy. A good minister, he said, should
preach the undefiled Christian doctrines which would be
taught at Andover. And he should preach them in such a

way as to stir his congregation to vital piety. For the clergy
are the "chief instruments in the hand of God" to accomplish the salvation of man. During the present awesome
period of history, evangelical religion is destined to
scourge the "Romish hierarchy" and convert the world
to Christ. Dwight hoped Andover graduates would devote
their fullest energies to this mission.[35]

Despite the Hopkinsian influence at Andover, the
school followed the moderate line of Trinitarian union.
It became an early embodiment of the new orthodox activism. An article appearing in the *Panoplist* shortly before
Andover opened its doors outlined the purpose of the
seminary. The writer, commissioned by Morse and the
other moderates involved, was Eliphalet Pearson. His
arguments captured the temper of the movement. In
praising Christian union, Pearson was not referring to
the tolerant ecumenism of an Ezra Stiles, but a broadly-
based, militant Trinitarianism. His point of view was
closely akin to that of Dwight. Knowledge was not important for its own sake; it was important only inasmuch
as it laid a foundation for orthodox piety. The new seminary would be formed to counterattack those "who, by
philosophy and cunning craftiness, wherewith they lie
in wait to deceive, are secretly and assiduously under-
mining the fabric of Christianity." Diabolical conspiracy
remained an impetus as Pearson called for "a vigorous
band of young men, already trained for this holy war,
armed with the whole armour of God, and ready for the
attack." The spirit of the new evangelical movement
continued to be defensive, as Pearson stated that it is
wholly false to assume "that it is of little consequence,
what a man believes, if his life be good. . . ." For one
to be truly moral ". . . it is of the greatest consequence
that his creed be correct." Andover's purpose was to train

a militant cadre of orthodox ministers whose mission was to close "the floodgates of error" and reestablish public adherence to a single body of "evangelical truth."[36]

Pearson's forceful statement suggests that he was ready to assume a key position in the anti-liberal crusade begun by Dwight and Morse. But the former Harvard professor quickly lost his stomach for battle. He was too much the intellectual to become an ardent revivalist. With an ingrained moralistic approach to religion, he failed to accommodate himself to Andover's emotional evangelism. Disillusioned, he withdrew from the orthodox training camp in 1809. In his later years he completely abandoned the evangelical counter-reformation, becoming more sympathetic to the Unitarians.[37]

In replacing Pearson, the Andover Trustees reached into more safely orthodox territory. For over a decade, Yale had been the heart of contentious orthodoxy in New England. Dwight was ably producing a number of activist disciples to continue his crusade. One of his most capable and enthusiastic students was the young minister of New Haven's Center Church. Moses Stuart had become such a successful revivalist and defender of the faith, that he was, by 1809, one of the most valuable men in the Connecticut establishment. Consequently, Dwight was not at first willing to part with his gifted lieutenant. Neither was Stuart's congregation, which was enjoying a sustained revival of religion.[38]

Drawing inspiration from Dwight, Stuart had skillfully developed the techniques of evangelical persuasion. He preached emotionally for conversion and steeped the children of his parish in religious education. Of course, he was also a staunch Federalist who stressed Christian nurture as the best means of molding "useful members of society." He publicized his traditional views in such orthodox journals as the *Panoplist*. Neither Stuart, nor

Dwight could long resist the call of Andover. Inevitably both men came to view the move as an important step in strengthening New England orthodoxy. Once installed in his new position, Stuart lost no time in taking up the cudgel against the Unitarians. He made his early reputation as a theological controversialist and a captivating expounder of Calvinist exegetics. With its new Professor of Sacred Literature, Andover became more closely tied to Yale as a center for advancing Dwight's activist theology.[39]

In the merger of Hopkinsians with evangelical moderates, the latter faction dominated. Particularly after Stuart arrived, New Divinity influence was rapidly eclipsed. The promotional, non-metaphysical spirit of the Second Great Awakening came to pervade the *Panoplist and Missionary Magazine United*. During the first year or so of the combined publication, a few Hopkinsian tracts appeared. Morse's magazine had become the outlet for metaphysical Calvinists, many of whom were prolific writers who had previously contributed to their own periodical. One article on the means of grace doggedly clung to the inability of sinners to repent on their own, or for that matter to make any "good use" of ministerial instructions prior to regeneration. Another Hopkinsian piece stressed the infinite evil of sin, and a third, entitled "Self-Abhorrence" portrayed the sinner feeling "justly condemned," because his heart had yet to be revivified.[40] But such lingering bits of Consistent Calvinism were overshadhowed by an increasing commitment to evangelical action.

By 1810, the Awakening was moving into high gear, and the evangelical moderates of Connecticut and Massachusetts had begun to devise new methods to revive orthodoxy. Full scale religious promotionalism now emerged under the auspices of Morse and Dwight's well-trained students, Lyman Beecher and Jeremiah Evarts.

Moral and religious tract societies, a Sabbatarian movement, and an enlarged missionary effort spread the orthodox gospel. Again it was Dwight who had set the theological stage for this kind of action. As early as 1788, he
had recommended a national union of ministers to suppress vice and encourage morality. He spent years
immersing one class after another in a theology of institutional moralism and confident Christian exertion. By
1808, he began to see his labors come to fruition in an
expansive promotional campaign engineered chiefly by
his students.

With the new Awakening well under way, orthodox
publicists began to institutionalize their socially conservative revivalism. In 1809, the first year of the aggressive
union between Yale and Andover, the Connecticut General Association completed its transition from an essentially defensive position to a militant one. Formation of
the state-supported Missionary Society had been the
initial step in this direction. Secretary Flint made yearly
reports to the General Association, usually detailing
the improved state of religion in the missionaries' theater
of operation. This procedure became the prototype for
committees of inquiry into the progress of more local
religion. The first committee report, coming in 1809, was
generally encouraging. It observed that God had begun
to answer the prayers of Christians and the labors of their
ministers. The 1810 report was similarly favorable, re-
cording a "union of sentiment on religious doctrines" in
the Congregational churches, and an "increasing attention to the means of grace." Outpourings of the Spirit
were numerous. Both reports, however, also mentioned
the persistence of "coldness," "stupidity," and impeni-
tence in the midst of the general awakening. Because
evangelical efforts had provoked such a hearty response,
the orthodox clergy's confidence in the value of human

efforts grew. As a result, they formed new institutions to promote religion. In 1809, a society was formed to distribute Bibles to the poor.[41]

The success of early cautious exertions begat subsequent bolder ones. By 1812, the General Association had begun an unprecedented elaboration of means in a program of moralistic evangelism. Lyman Beecher, the complete religious promoter, was the principal architect of this movement. While still a college student, he had taken it upon himself to put the practical theology of his master into action. In 1797, while President Dwight was busy exposing infidelity, Beecher and a number of other students set about the task of eradicating it from the campus. To aid in restoring the ancestral faith, they founded a moral society.[42] Beecher gave full credit to Dwight for reviving religion at Yale, but the peer group pressure exerted by these young conservative activists probably abetted his effort.

Within two years after his first pastoral settlement, Beecher had revived the concept of a moral society.[43] In 1812, the annual report on the state of religion noted a decline in infidelity. But the committee also referred to a general cooling of the Awakening and the prevalence of vice in certain regions. At this time, Beecher became chairman of a new committee to suppress the vice of intemperance. Another minister gave an address which outlined the conservative ideas behind the new temperance campaign. By expunging the evils of "unbelief and sloth," he argued, we will help "to transmit to our children the precious inheritance received from our fathers."[44] Sober parishioners would certainly be more attentive to the moral instructions of their ministers.

A year later, Beecher delivered the first "Report of the Temperance Committee." Public opinion, he said, has been successfully aroused against the use of ardent spirits.

He continued by praising the value of united moral action. With complete confidence, he asserted that "nothing is impossible to faith. . . . When [God's] people begin to awake to a sense of their duty, he will bless their humble endeavors, and exceed their most sanguine hopes." For Beecher and the evangelicals of the Second Great Awakening the new moral societies were the best means to defend cherished New England institutions "against the torrent of iniquity which threatens to sweep [them] away. . . ." During the same year in which Beecher had organized the Temperance Committee, Dwight was calling for the establishment of a whole battery of societies to suppress the different forms of vice. Both the president of Yale and his former student believed that such enterprising Christianity would reform society and hasten defeat of "the great adversary." "Now therefore is the time," said Beecher, "to rally round the institutions of our forefathers, to build up the breaches, to fortify the walls and strengthen the standards."[45]

Spearheaded by Dwight's initial ideas and Beecher's organizational skill, the new evangelical moralism deluged New England, giving rise to a wide variety of voluntary societies. This method of diffusing evangelical conservatism was far more effective than the decaying authority of coercive establishments. Orthodox periodicals, during much of the second decade of the nineteenth century, were full of appeals to united moral action. No scruples against Arminian moralism now prevented religious edifiers from proclaiming the value of means. An 1813 writer for the *Connecticut Evangelical Magazine* made an explicit break with Consistent Calvinism on the subject of unregenerate striving. It is preposterous, he held, to believe, as some do, "that the necessary means of conversion, are to be used by those only, who are already converted. . . ." He added that Hopkinsians are inconsistent, for they too are encouraged when sinners in their congregations attend to means. Furthermore, they have joined in promoting missionary and Bible societies. In the following year, another article appeared which claimed that sinners who use the means "with a temper of love, of penitence, of obedience . . . will reap the blessedness of heaven." Concurring with the institutional theology of Dwight, the writer observed that revival converts are most often those who have observed the Sabbath, avoided vice, studied Scripture, and habitually prayed for divine forgiveness.[46]

At about the same time, Beecher became chairman of a state-supported Moral Society which devoted much of its work to Sabbatarianism.[47] This organization represented a transition between the old and new orthodoxy. As a creation of the establishment, it was a public institution supported by taxation. Liberals and dissenters had long opposed orthodoxy's collective endeavors to "suppress vice" and propagate the Gospel. The "promulgation of Blue Laws"[48] was as offensive to them as the incorporation of the Missionary Society. They saw in both developments an effort by the Standing Order to reassert traditional forms of authoritarian control. In agitating against violation of the Sabbath, the Congregational ministers were expressing anxiety over pluralistic trends which were diminishing their social influence. Sabbatarianism would eventually become an important means of securing outward public conformity. But it would succeed as a voluntary movement, rather than the product of a religious establishment. Orthodox promoters were actually creating a new, voluntaristic conservatism within the old ecclesiastical husk. Once the shell had been sloughed off, the germ of evangelical moralism could rapidly pollinate the nation.

During and immediately after the War of 1812, the

growth of societies to suppress vice outran even revivalism. In 1815, the Connecticut General Association's report on the state of religion observed that while revivals
had decreased somewhat, a number of moral societies
were flourishing. These agencies were effectively com-
batting liberal pluralism. The Report concluded "that
heresy is not in a progressive state; that moral societies
have by bold and decisive measures, done much for the
suppression of vice, particularly Sabbath-breaking."[49]

One of the most popular and well publicized aspects
of the Second Great Awakening was the tremendous increase in missionary work. Bringing on the millennium
entailed conversion of the human race to one faith and
one body of moral truth. But orthodox revivalists, confident of their divine commission, cheerfully shouldered
the arduous task. Jeremiah Evarts, one of Dwight's most
industrious students, was a contemporary of Lyman
Beecher, and of similar activist temper. Like Beecher, he
graduated in 1802 and was deeply affected by the great
Yale revival of that year. As a layman, he was not burdened
with purely theological or ecclesiastical matters, and was
therefore free to devote himself fully to evangelical organizations. While still in New Haven, he joined with others
to found the Connecticut Religious Tract Society.[50] In
1810, the same year in which he became editor of the
Panoplist, he organized the American Board of Commissioners for Foreign Missions. Under his supervision, the
Panoplist became a major outlet for the "religious intelligence" of this new institution. It also served as publicist
for the Massachusetts Bible Society and the American
Bible Society. Both of these associations were largely
products of Evarts' organizational talent.

The *Panoplist* editor typified the spirit of the Second
Great Awakening. From Dwight, he had early received

a lasting hatred of liberalism and infidelity, as well as an overall practical approach to religion. With Evarts in control, the *Panoplist* served as watchman and guide to the millennium. It reported the steady advancement of God's missionary army and interpreted the events of the era in millennial terms. In 1812, Evarts printed a succinct digest of Dwight's Fast Sermons together with moralistic accounts of the progress of militant Christianity. The Infidel conspiracy was faltering and the reign of Christ would soon commence if only the new "benevolent" movement could return the nation to orthodox ideals. A lengthy review of Beecher's sermon, "A Reformation of Morals Practicable and Indispensable," appeared shortly after the abstract of Dwight's prophetic discourses. It was printed in conjunction with the Constitutions of the Massachusetts and Connecticut Moral Societies. The editorial comment praised these organizations as a fulfillment of Beecher's call for "vigorous and united efforts on the part of all the wise and good for the preservation of our moral and religious institutions."[51]

Evangelical activism triumphed in the Evarts publication. An article implored the friends of Christianity to distribute sermons, tracts, newspapers, and magazines to awaken the moral conscience of the public. The writer's major concern was that the "rising generation" learn traditional religious values. He advocated prompt execution of "laws against immorality [and preservation of] the righteous connexion [sic] between sin and shame. . . ."[52] Other *Panoplist* items included persuasive expositions of evangelical doctrine and utilitarian inducements to obey divine law.

A supposed comparison of Calvinism with Arminianism attempted to show that the former system is more hopeful and encouraging. Never realizing how much they had Arminianized their own faith, the new evangelicals argued that the doctrine of election guarantees the salvation of some, while the Arminian scheme does not. Probably unconsciously, they reinterpreted election to mean the manner by which the Holy Spirit operates to save the faithful, rather than the predestined decrees of an omnipotent Sovereign. A compassionate God now granted mercy to those who asked. No impediment stood in the way of salvation, for God had become more the Kindly Humanitarian than the wrathful Judge. The new evangelicals retained the Calvinist emphasis on experimental piety, for the emotional conversion experience was the most powerful aspect of revivalistic orthodoxy. Moral suasion alone could never produce a militant Christianity. But in discussing original sin and the need for regeneration, evangelicals now stressed the glory of salvation and all but forgot "the justice of God in the damnation of sinners." Hellfire preaching continued, but it became part of a calculated, self-reliant plan of the evangelical ministry to lead sinners to Christ (i.e., an integral part of the means of grace). Essays purporting to defend the Puritan faith contained a greater element of worldly moralism than Calvinist supernaturalism.[53]

Evangelicals of the Second Great Awakening objected to Arminianism not because it granted too much power to the striving sinner, but because it de-emphasized conversion. If they opposed moral suasion *per se,* they would have been highly inconsistent, for the major thrust of their new evangelism was moralistic. They thoroughly absorbed the utilitarian social theology of Timothy Dwight. If the old Reformation doctrines set in a positive light were useful to their cause, so too was the exhortation to "do good." In 1817, a *Panoplist* editorial "Address to the Public" exulted in the proliferation of revivals. It attributed the Awakening not to a surprising and miraculous work of God, but to the united and purposeful exertions of evangelical Christians—Christians who had applied "the science of doing good. . . ." The "Address" continued with an exhortation to all believers to mind their neighbors' business and thus become guardians of the public morality. In the manner of Timothy Dwight, it recommended the diffusion of religious education so that the entire nation would absorb the orthodox way of life. Combined evangelical labors would surely "change the face of the world . . . in a moderate time."[54]

With the conclusion of the conflicts which had embroiled Europe and America for a generation, New England evangelical conservatives felt more confident than ever that the millennial corner had been turned. If human exertions had accomplished so much in times of adversity, the return of peace promised unexampled progress toward world redemption. Now America and Great Britain were free to cooperate in spreading godliness to ignorant peoples. A few years after the war, both the *Panoplist* and the *Connecticut Evangelical Magazine,* having participated in a successful containment of liberal free-thinking, dissolved themselves and gave way to two new publications exclusively devoted to advancing the Protestant world missionary movement. In 1816, the Connecticut periodical was succeeded by a promotional journal called the *Religious Intelligencer,* while four years later the *Panoplist* was replaced by the *Missionary Herald,* an official publication of the American Board of Commissioners for Foreign Missions.

During the *Religious Intelligencer's* first year of existence, Dwight contributed a series of articles entitled "Observations on the Present State of Religion in the World."[55] Writing at the climax of his life, the old orthodox commander exuded optimism. In effect, he was giving his blessing to trends which paralleled his own conception of theology. On the one hand, the religion of the heart had vanquished cold moralism; and on the other,

ministers had seen the value of balancing religious doctrines with duties. Dwight lauded the success of recent
promotional ventures, citing the British and Foreign
Bible Society as a model for similar American organizations. Paying particular attention to the thriving missionary movement, he praised the liberality with which zealous
Christians were voluntarily financing evangelization.
Dwight never logically deduced from this occurrence that
religious establishments were no longer necessary for
social control. Ironically, it had been his practical enhancement of means which provided the theological
rationale for the new voluntaryism. But even Beecher,
the most adept originator of promotional religion, did
not recognize its revolutionary implications until disestablishment finally occurred in Connecticut, a short
time after Dwight's death. At first, Beecher despaired over
the cruel fate of the "Church of God." But suddenly it
dawned on him that the establishment had been a vestigial
organ. The voluntary societies of the new benevolent
movement were a far more flexible way to preserve a
traditional faith and morality in a country of regional
and sectarian diversity.[56]

Dwight and Morse had begun the movement toward a
national voluntary evangelism by seeking to minimize
lines of cleavage among Trinitarians. In the final remarks
of his "Observations," Dwight praised the emerging
catholic spirit. Unity of evangelical Christians in basic
doctrine and practice was a clear sign of the approaching
millennium. Dwight realized that interdenominational
cooperation was the most effective way to national religious uniformity. With his inveterate utilitarianism, he
judged large, centralized Bible, tract, and missionary
societies to be far more potent than small, sectarian ones,
whose "plans [would be confined] to narrow bounds
and very limited objects." Another of his suggestions for

improving religion epitomized the practical mentality that had become dominant in America and was converting many evangelicals to religious publicists. Every family, he remarked, can afford to contribute two cents a week to a Bible society. Such a fund would "in all probability save many souls. . . . " In his final statement, Dwight proclaimed: "A new era in the moral concerns of man [has] commenced." A new era had in fact begun in American religion. Orthodoxy, having lost its coercive ecclesiastical powers, had effectively adopted a new voluntaristic method of propagating its conservative ideals. Timothy Dwight had been a strong, capable leader. His theology was thoroughly practical and humane. As spiritual guide, he had acted with compassion and evangelical warmth. His weakness lay in the parochialism which narrowed his outlook and gave him a frequent air of self-righteousness.

CHAPTER X

Bearers of the Standard

When Timothy Dwight died in 1817, New England orthodoxy lost its foremost advocate. Clergymen and lay Federalists eulogized him and mourned the passing of an undaunted champion of the Puritan tradition. Less than a year later the Standing Order crumbled as the Federalist Party succumbed to a coalition of Republicans and dissenters. But the demise of the Connecticut establishment did not spell the end of orthodoxy. In formulating and carrying on his defense, Dwight had inspired a movement which had lasting effects on American Protestantism. The younger evangelical ministry of New England drew on his activist theology to build a set of orthodox institutions which would permeate the nation. The *Panoplist* alluded to Dwight's profound effect on the course of evangelical Protestantism. Its eulogy remarked on "what an amazing chasm" is made by "the death of such a man. . . ." Vast numbers of his students throughout the nation had "good reason to regard him as their spiritual

parent."[1] Jeremiah Evarts, the editor, probably supervised if he did not write this panegyric. He was himself
a prize disciple of President Dwight. It was no coincidence
that Evarts was a key organizer of the nationwide benevolent movement and one of the major luminaries of the
Second Great Awakening.

In a section on "Works Proposed" the *Panoplist*
reviewed the forthcoming first edition of Dwight's
Theology. The article noted that "about a thousand
gentlemen, now scattered through every part of our
country, heard the whole system during their residence
at Yale College." It commended the work as "superior to
any theological system now in possession of the public."
Dwight's *Theology* rapidly became one of the most widely
used systems of divinity in the colleges of the nineteenth
century. Popular in the British Isles as well as the United
States, it went through over twelve editions.[2]

During the period from 1818 to 1820, the *Panoplist*
changed its format from diverse evangelical materials and
polemics against Unitarianism to exclusive promotion
of missions. In its last editorial address before becoming
a publication of the American Board of Commissioners
for Foreign Missions, the dissolving journal acknowledged
its most important contributors. Dwight's stature in the
orthodox community had been so exalted that the editors
did little more than pay homage to the late President of
Yale.

The theology of Timothy Dwight had been cast in
defense of the Standing Order. But its key premises far
exceeded their connection with the expiring establishment. Nineteenth century evangelicals, as they forged a
new American orthodoxy, developed various aspects of
Dwight's inclusive system. Its two major themes were
intensification of means to foment revivals, and reliance
on institutional nurture to gain public loyalty to a distinct world view and body of ethical standards. The

promoted revival became a major source of religious diffusion in a sprawling, decentralized country. Two of Dwight's most capable students, Lyman Beecher and Nathaniel W. Taylor, refined his evangelical method into a powerful vehicle of mass conversion. Beecher's organizational development of means has already been explored. If he and Evarts were the master strategists of the new orthodoxy, Taylor succeeded Dwight as its chief theoretician. Having served as stenographer to the Yale president, Taylor had transcribed both the *Travels* and *Theology*. Probably no one had more intimate knowledge of Dwight's ideas. In 1812, the young evangelical was called to New Haven's Center Church to replace Moses Stuart, whose congregation had reluctantly dismissed him to the Andover professorship. Taylor had qualms about succeeding such a popular minister, but Dwight, with full confidence in his talented protégé, persuaded him to accept.[3]

Taylor was more than a revival preacher. His penetrating mind began early to discern revolutionary implications in Dwight's theology. The revisionist direction of his thought was apparent in an 1817 statement before the General Association. As Secretary of the Domestic Missionary Society, Taylor spoke of the "animating confidence inspired by the known success of every effort which has been made in this great work." With marked self-assurance, he added: "At every step, our expectations have been confirmed, and in the result more than realized." As if to assuage any doubts concerning his orthodoxy in the minds of stricter Calvinists, Taylor attributed the spiritual renewal to divine intervention. "This work is God's," he said. "It is commanded by his authority, it is blessed with his smiles."[4]

Both Beecher and Taylor were working toward a new interpretation which would give unequivocal power to man's religious enterprise. With Dwight's example, they relied increasingly on their own initiatives to enlist the aid of the Holy Spirit. But the originators of the New Haven Theology moved very cautiously, emphasizing action and playing down doctrine, so as not to redivide a shaky, if effective orthodox union.[5]

But eventual schism was inevitable. The combination of Taylor's irrepressible intellect and the ebullient self-reliance of Charles G. Finney ultimately split orthodoxy into theologically liberal and conservative factions. The Old School, drawing support from Hopkinsians and the arch-Calvinist Presbyterians of the Princeton Theological Seminary, continued to view revivals as solely the work of God. Their rigid stand made them deeply suspicious of excessive reliance on means. Asahel Nettleton, a Connecticut itinerant evangelist, adhered to the old supernaturalism. Friend and associate of Beecher and Taylor, this soft-spoken minister condemned the brash new western revivalism personified in Finney.[6]

Charles Grandison Finney was the first great lay evangelist in America.[7] Having grown up in the fluid society of frontier New York, he looked askance at the sober intellectualism of the New England clergy. His method was intensely emotional, practical, and democratic. Clerical dignity and doctrinal exposition were useless formalities to this self-styled soul winner. He employed a dramatic, provocative technique of evangelical persuasion which became known as the "New Measures." To the dismay of polished orthodox clergymen, he seemed to flaunt all established rules of decorum. He engaged in pulpit histrionics; he addressed God personally; and he flagrantly ignored class distinctions, familiarly rebuking every member of his audience as a vile sinner, in need of a radical change of heart. Moreover, he minced no words on the matter of self-help. Entrepreneurial individualism had become a way of life in the rude new settlements. Genteel society and traditional forms of control were absent in these regions of rapid social change. Finney unabashedly preached the ability and duty of every man to renew his own heart.[8]

At first, Beecher and Taylor were as disturbed as Nettleton at Finney's brazen style. Their conservative New England tempers recoiled at this populistic spirit come to invade their evangelical domain. The anarchic spectre of enthusiasm had once again raised itself in the land of steady habits. But as Finney won scores of converts and received invitations to preach in the major cities, it became more difficult to ignore him. His fruitful plain dealing ultimately forced the hands of Beecher and Taylor. While they eschewed Finney's techniques, it became apparent that they diverged little from him in doctrine. They had little choice but to support the evangelist, if they wished to procure national adherence to revivalistic orthodoxy, and at the same time exert a measure of control over the democratic excesses of the frontier movement.[9]

The growing suspicions of strict Calvinists that something was rotten in the orthodox camp were confirmed when Taylor delivered his *Concio ad Clerum* sermon in 1828. Though couched in metaphysical subtlety and buttressed by frequent allusion to revered Calvinist fathers, his new interpretation of moral freedom was a clear break with Consistent Calvinism. Essentially, Taylor proclaimed the doctrine that sinners can use the means of grace to change their own hearts. In his theological discourses, Dwight had often broached the same conclusion, without stating it so openly as his former student. Taylor in fact appended a prefatory comment to his controversial sermon, in which he declared that his views did not constitute "any departure in any article of doctrinal belief, from his revered instructor in theology, the former President of Yale College."[10]

Gradually and reluctantly, Beecher, Taylor, and their followers in the New Haven Theology joined forces with the Finneyites and accepted a schism with doctrinaire Calvinists which had become unavoidable.[11] The lines of cleavage solidified as Princeton became the bastion of Old School orthodoxy, and Beecher and Taylor created a New School seminary in the Yale Divinity School. Beecher had become dissatisfied with Andover because it remained preoccupied with attacking the Unitarians.[12] For the New Haven men, the scope of revivalism extended far beyond the parochial controversies of Massachusetts. By the 1830s, evangelicals had successfully contained Unitarianism within the Boston area, and the West had become the new battleground for orthodoxy.

During the individualistic antebellum era, the promotional orthodoxy of the New School became the dominant American religion. This emotional faith accentuated the love of Christ to humanity and the ability of the individual to choose for himself between the cross of salvation and the fires of perdition. An overwhelming majority of Protestant churches fully accepted the Arminianized revivalism of Finney and the New Haven school. As they carried it westward, each denomination sought to out-evangelize the others. But the interdenominational Bible and tract societies, home missionary movement, and Sunday School Union joined them together in support of a uniform, moralistic gospel.

The organizations of the benevolent movement served as a conservative brake on the antinomian tendencies of revivalism. They continued to use evangelical Protestantism as a means to imbue Americans with respect for sober order and the ingrained work ethic. Their leadership was generally well-born and descended from the Federalist

gentry of Dwight's period. Without the coercive agency
of a Standing Order or the aristocratic pretensions of the
Federalist Party, they yet maintained an unyielding belief
in their mission to enlighten and supervise the morals of
every citizen. Both ministerial and lay spokesmen for these
orthodox institutions expressed deep anxiety over the
course of Jacksonian America. As their forebears had
resisted the libertarianism of Jefferson, they opposed the
social experimentation which was occurring during the
era of the common man. Continuing the fight against
pluralism, they employed their agencies of Christian nurture to disseminate antipathy to Catholicism, socialism,
communitarianism and every other departure from the
Protestant-capitalist consensus. When Irish Catholics
arrived in great numbers during the 1840s and class conflicts began to occur, these descendents of New England
Federalism again publicized their concern for the future
of the republic. Through evangelization, they hoped to
curtail the impetus of the poor, and dissident elements
to restructure society. Much of their work was directed
against Catholicism. Working class Catholics, committed
to populistic democracy, threatened to flood the country
and undermine the hegemony of the eastern gentry. Ministers of the benevolent movement preached against
Jackson's war on privilege and assailed the western
states' repudiation of their debts to financial interests of
the Northeast during the Panic of 1837. In much the same
way that Dwight had once denounced the viciousness
and irresponsibility of farmers in Western Massachusetts
during Shays' Rebellion, these orthodox institutionalists
condemned the new debtors' insubordination. No less
than their ancestor of the Connecticut Standing Order,
they were apostles of a creed which commanded due obedience to sanctioned authority and deference to genteel
leadership. Men of wealth and stature were the bene-

ficiaries of providence, deserving of respect and imitation.[13]

With his copious attention to religious education, Timothy Dwight had sought to instill such conservative ideals in his students at Yale. Many of them continued this practice as managers of the benevolent societies. In Dwight's system, the effectiveness of revivalism depended on its firm association with proper Christian practice. Severed from intensive moral indoctrination, emotional conversion could generate social disorder and wild behavioral aberrations. Dwight saw benevolent societies as valuable moralistic adjuncts to revivalism. But in themselves they could not create a thoroughly religious environment.

Many evangelicals had become so caught up in the dynamics of revivalism that they were all but ignoring the equally important means of nurture. By the 1840s, the influence of Taylor, Finney, and a multitude of other revivalists transformed orthodox preaching into a single-minded quest for conversions. Bitter controversy continued between the Old and New Schools over the tiresome question of divine sovereignty and the doings of the unregenerate. But while the two theological camps differed over the propriety of continuing revivals, they both proceeded as if these spectacular "effusions of the Holy Spirit" were the only means by which God gathers his Church. It was Horace Bushnell, one of Taylor's divinity students, who set out to redress the balance between revivalism and Christian nurture. Bushnell did not differ from the New Haven evangelicals in doctrine; his goal was to modify practice. Like Beecher and Taylor, he stressed human agency, but in so doing, he returned to Dwight's concept of a religious environment. He was reacting against what

he called the "extreme individualism" of his time. It was
erroneous, he believed, to regard each man as a self-
enclosed unit, requiring "a technical experience" to
attain piety. Moreover, it was severely detrimental to
religion for children to learn that they are born enemies
of God. Bushnell concurred with the doctrine of human
depravity, but like Dwight, he felt that parental example
could influence the child toward virtuous living. He
cited Dwight's observation that making religion appear
"odious" to the child may inspire dread and do irrepara-
ble damage to his soul.[14]

As Dwight had emphasized and capitalized on the
impressionableness of youth, Bushnell referred to the
child's "ductile nature." Returning to Dwight's paternalism, he too stressed the power of "influence" and "habit"
as means of grace.[15] Recall Dwight's comment that
persons surrounded by the Christian example of parents
and other figures of authority may become regenerate
without any conscious or visible change in conduct. Bushnell elaborated the concept of religious education in much
the same way as his predecessor. But he went somewhat
further than Dwight, as Taylor had on the procurement
of conversion.

Affected deeply by the conservative romanticism of
Europeans like Coleridge, he made much of the organic
nature of society. Virtue was not necessarily the outcome
of the individual's choice, but the result of the influences
which surrounded him. "All society," said Bushnell, "is
organic—the church, the state, the school, the family...."
These agencies, if imbued with orthodox ideals, could
inspire "religious character," since they were "to some
extent, at least, sovereign over the individual man."[16]
Bushnell, in the same way as Dwight, tried to reassert
the concept of central, authoritative institutions in the
midst of a competitive chaos. He acknowledged European

sources of his organicism, but he also owed much to
Puritan social theory, whose last great expositor had been
Timothy Dwight. Dwight too had looked to a British
institutional conservatism for inspiration. The utilitarianism of William Paley had colored his defense of the
Standing Order. Bushnell, living in the romantic era,
adopted its idealistic philosophy to similarly paternalistic ends. After the Civil War, he became one of the most
popular and influential ministers in the United States.
His institutional nationalism and his belief in America's
millennial destiny held great appeal for Americans of the
latter nineteenth century. Dwight's virtually identical
sentiments had sparked the missionary impulse of the
Second Great Awakening.

Bushnell de-emphasized the conversion experience to
a greater extent than did Dwight, as he jettisoned the
pietism of Edwardian orthodoxy. But in asserting that parents might teach their children to love Christ, and thereby
impart the Spirit to them, he was simply expanding
Dwight's paternalism. There was no need to grow up in
wrath. Christian nurture would expunge sinful tendency
and enable piety to flower gradually. The Taylorites never
came out against Bushnell. Even though they were entirely committed to revivalism, they had drawn upon the
work of the same spiritual ancestor. Bushnell's opponents were the lingering band of strict Calvinists, who
resisted any such invigoration of human power as a
blow to divine sovereignty. In words which could as
easily have come from Dwight, Bushnell countered that:
"The sovereignty of God has always a relation to means,
and we are not authorized to think of it, in any case, as
separated from means."[17]

Responding to the criticism of the Old School, Bushnell
cited not only Dwight, but also Hopkins as an advocate of
Christian nurture.[18] Although he maintained that high

Calvinist supernaturalism had been exploded in a former
interchange between Taylor and Bennett Tyler, Bushnell
found it useful to show that a Consistent Calvinist had
recommended a program of parental nurture. Of course,
Bushnell, who was rebutting among others the same
Bennett Tyler who had assailed his instructor, did not
add that Hopkinsian doctrine also took the dimmest possible view of unregenerate activity. Strict Calvinists always
resisted the idea that religious education was a way to
induce piety.

Between them, Taylor and Bushnell strengthened and
gained popular adherence to the two great elements of
Dwight's theological synthesis. Enhancement of the
means of grace was the center of the Yale President's
system. Taylor further developed this reliance on secondary agency by asserting the sinner's moral ability to
choose God and relinquish depravity. His pupil, relying
wholeheartedly on means, went back to Dwight's Christian paternalism. Both religious perspectives, individual
and social, placed piety within the grasp of anyone who
would help himself.

Moralistic and practical, the new evangelical orthodoxy
buttressed the values of the American majority. It con-
formed to prevailing ideals of individual responsibility,
free competitive enterprise, and rule of the (rightly informed) people. But it never accepted the tolerance of
social diversity essential to libertarian democracy. There
was to be not many, but one American way of life enthu-
siastically endorsed by multitudes of solid middle class
Protestants. The churches encouraged every citizen to be
his brother's keeper and suppress any deviant ethnic, political, or social group. Evangelical Protestantism blessed
the home as inculcator of industry, thrift, temperance and
the Gospel of Wealth. An aggressive, optimistic faith, it
viewed the world as its field of action and the millennium

as its goal. It was thoroughly in tune with the American cult of progress and territorial expansion. With an intolerant, if well-intentioned parochialism, it set out to recast humanity in its own Anglo-Saxon image.

In recent years, evangelicals, particularly young people, affected by the "counter-cultural" movements of the 1960's, have been seeking to extricate orthodox Christianity from its connection with economic and social conservatism. A movement is currently blossoming in evangelical circles which is sensitive to the cultural relativism of twentieth century anthropology. Public figures such as Senators Mark Hatfield of Oregon and Harold Hughes of Iowa express an evangelical point of view which jettisons traditional allegiance to the Protestant work ethic, laissez-faire individualism, and American religious chauvinism. They and other liberals are seeking to join evangelical Christianity with social awareness. A host of books and articles have recently been published in this cause. One of the most important publications of the new social evangelicalism is a periodical entitled *The Other Side*. Its contributors bring Christian conscience to bear on problems such as poverty, civil rights, and the ecological crisis. On the more popular level, revivals of the burgeoning Jesus movement are restoring an almost primitive Christianity, purified of connection with the ethnocentrism of nineteenth century middle class America.

Notes

Chapter I

1. For a concise and illuminating account of this process of change, see Bernard Bailyn, "Political Experience and Enlightenment Ideas in Eighteenth Century America," *American Historical Review*, LXVII (1962), 339-51. For a more detailed analysis, see his *Origins of American Politics* (New York: A. A. Knopf, 1968).

2. See Robert R. Palmer, *Age of Democratic Revolution*, I (Princeton: Princeton University Press, 1959), 213-34.

3. Gaspare J. Saladino, "The Economic Revolution in Late Eighteenth Century Connecticut" (unpublished Doctors dissertation, University of Wisconsin, 1964), chapters 3-6, passim. This study focuses on development in the region of our major concern.

4. Two studies of the contest for power between Federalist-Congregationalism and Jeffersonian dissent are Richard Purcell, *Connecticut in Transition*, ed. by Hugh Brockunier (Middletown, Conn.: Wesleyan University Press, 1963); and Maria L. Greene, *The Development of Religious Liberty in Connecticut* (Boston: Houghton, Mifflin, and Co., 1905), particularly pp. 342-496.

5. A classic study of this process in Massachusetts is Perry Miller, *The New England Mind from Colony to Province* (Boston: Beacon Press, 1961).

6. Perry Miller and Thomas Johnsons, eds., *The Puritan Mind*, I (New York: Harper & Row, 1963), 206-7.

7. See Charles W. Akers, *Called Unto Liberty: A Life of Jonathan Mayhew 1720-1766* (Cambridge, Mass.: Harvard University Press, 1964), pp. 82-89. See also Carl Bridenbaugh, *Mitre and Sceptre* (Oxford: Oxford University Press, 1962), pp. 97-103.

8. Miller and Johnson, eds., *The Puritans*, I, 210-12.

9. See Perry Miller, *Errand Into the Wilderness* (New York: Harper & Row, 1964), pp. 82-92.

10. See Richard I. Bushman, *From Puritan to Yankee: Character and the Social Order in Connecticut 1690-1765* (Cambridge, Mass.: Harvard University Press, 1967), pp. 54-73.

11. Greene, *Religious Liberty*, p. 151.

12. Bushman, *From Puritan to Yankee*, pp. 122-43, 182-95. The author finds a correlation between regions undergoing rapid economic development and the prevalence of revivalism.

13. See Edwin S. Gaustad, *The Great Awakening in New England* (New York: Harper and Brothers, 1957); Alan Heimert, *Religion and the American Mind From the Great Awakening to the Revolution* (Cambridge, Mass.: Harvard University Press, 1966); Herbert Schneider, *The Puritan Mind* (Ann Arbor, Mich.: University of Michigan Press, 1958), pp. 102-55; Stow Persons, *American Minds* (New York: Henry Holt and Co., 1958), pp. 85-97, 102-9.

14. Charles C. Goen, *Revivalism and Separatism in New England, 1740-1800* (New Haven, Conn.: Yale University, 1962), pp. 184-85, 228, 282-84.

15. See Perry Miller, " 'Preparation For Salvation' in Seventeenth Century New England," *Journal of the History of Ideas*, IV (1943), 253-86.

16. For an exhaustive account of the development of Arminianism in Puritan New England, see Conrad Wright, *The Beginnings of Unitarianism in America* (Boston: Beacon Press, 1955).

17. For Heimert's argument, see his *Religion and the American Mind*, particularly pp. 95-157. For two cogent critiques of this thesis, see Sidney E. Mead, "Through and Between the Lines," *Journal of Religion*, XLVIII (July, 1968), 274-88; and Edmund Morgan, *William and Mary Quarterly*, XXIV (1967), 454-59.

18. See Bushman, *From Puritan to Yankee*, pp. 214-20, 228-48.

19. See Edmund Morgan, *The Gentle Puritan: A Life of Ezra Stiles* (New Haven: Yale University Press, 1962), pp. 316-17.

20. Ibid., p. 178.

21. Greene states: "There was no formal coercive power; but the public provision for the minister's support, and the withdrawal of it from recalcitrant members formed a coercive power of no mean efficiency." *Religious Liberty*, p. 152.

22. See J. Robert Livingston Ferm, "Jonathan Edwards the Younger and the Reformed American Tradition" (unpublished Doctor's dissertation, Yale University, 1958), p. 164.

23. William B. Sprague, "Life of Timothy Dwight," *Library of American Biography*, ed. by Jared Sparks, IV (Boston, 1845), 278.

Chapter II

1. For an excellent discussion of American nationalistic millennialism, see Ernest Lee Tuveson, *Redeemer Nation* (Chicago: University of Chicago Press, 1966). The author credits Timothy Dwight with the first comprehensive statement of America's millennial destiny. See pp. 102-36.

2. Heimert, *Religion and the American Mind,* chapter 3.

3. See Alice Baldwin, *The New England Clergy and the American Revolution* (Durham, N.C.: Duke University Press, 1928).

4. Tuveson, *Redeemer Nation*, pp. 129-36, discusses common Edenic and Zionistic conceptions of America.

5. Ibid., p. 131. See also Daniel Boorstin, *The Lost World of Thomas Jefferson* (Boston: Beacon Press, 1960), p. 59.

6. See Leo Marx, *The Machine in the Garden: Technology and the Pastoral Idea in America* (New York: Oxford University Press, 1967), pp. 34-72. The author uses Shakespeare's *Tempest* to illustrate a common Renaissance conception of the New World as Paradise. He goes on to trace the widespread American acceptance of this myth down to the twentieth century.

7. Timothy Dwight, *A Valedictory Address to the Young Gentlemen, who Commenced Bachelors of Arts at Yale College, July 25th, 1776* (New Haven, 1776), pp. 6-7.

8. Ibid., p. 9.

9. Ibid., p. 11.

10. Ibid., pp. 13-14.

11. Heimert, *Religion and the American Mind*, p. 149, notes a dominant "martial image" in eighteenth century millennialist preaching.

12. Dwight, *A Sermon Preached at Stamford in Connecticut upon the General Thanksgiving, December 18, 1777* (Hartford, 1778), pp. 13, 16.

13. Puritans, in their earnest concern with the divine purpose of life, regarded poetry as merely recreational. Hence it was never worthy of serious attention. And like other forms of literature, it had to be plainly written and edifying. See Kenneth B. Murdock, *Literature and Theology in Colonial New England* (Cambridge, Mass.: Harvard University Press, 1949), chapter 5.

14. Dwight, *Greenfield Hill: A Poem in seven parts* (New York, 1794), pp. 6-7.

15. See Leon Harvard, *The Connecticut Wits* (Chicago: University of Chicago Press, 1943), pp. 83-84.

16. Dwight, *America: or a Poem on the Settlement of the British Colonies; Addressed to the Friends of Freedom and their Country* (New Haven, 1780 [?]), p. 5.

17. [Dwight], *Remarks on the Review of Inchiquin's Letters, published in the Quarterly Review, addressed to the Right Honourable George Canning, Esq., By an Inhabitant of New-England* (Boston, 1815). The major theme of this lengthy essay, which Dwight published two years before his death, was the incompetent slander in English reviews of American publications.

18. Dwight was one of a group of Connecticut poets including Joel Barlow, David Humphreys and John Trumbull. Known as the "Connecticut Wits," these writers of the post-revolutionary era were intensely nationalistic. Nevertheless, the style of their American epics was devised from such British figures as Pope and Milton. Coming from genteel, Puritan backgrounds, they were all conservative Federalists. Joel Barlow, however, ultimately became a Francophile and Jeffersonian Democrat. Dwight and the others recoiled at Barlow's apostasy. See Howard, *The Connecticut Wits*, passim.

19. Dwight to Webster, June 6, 1788 (MS in Yale University Library, New Haven).

20. Howard, *Connecticut Wits*, p. 93; Kenneth Silverman, *Timothy Dwight* (New York: Twayne Publishers, 1969), pp. 19-45.

21. Dwight, *A Discourse delivered at New-Haven, Feb. 22,*

1800 on the Character of George Washington, Esq., at the Request of the Citizens (New Haven, 1800), p. 16.

22. Dwight, *The Conquest of Canaan; a poem in Eleven Books* (Hartford, 1785), p. 258.

23. Saladino, "The Economic Revolution," pp. 74-106.

24. See for example, Miller, *The New England Mind from Colony to Province,* chapters 22, 23.

25. Wright, *Beginnings of Unitarianism,* pp. 6-7.

26. Saladino, "The Economic Revolution," p. 370.

27. *The Records of the General Association of Ye Colony of Connecticut* (Hartford, 1888), p. 105.

28. Morgan, *The Gentle Puritan,* pp. 312-16.

29. Morgan, "Ezra Stiles and Timothy Dwight," *Proceedings of the Massachusetts Historical Society,* LXXII (1957-60), 109.

30. See, for example, the memoir of Samuel Hopkins, *Works,* I (Boston, 1852), 92. The writer describes British devastation to the city of Newport during the war. Hopkins' church was badly damaged and his people dispersed. Morgan, *The Gentle Puritan,* pp. 329-33, describes the chaos caused by destructive British forays into Connecticut.

31. See also Purcell, *Connecticut in Transition,* pp. 7-32; Greene, *Religious Liberty,* pp. 410-13; Vernon Stauffer, *The New England Clergy and the Bavarian Illuminati* (New York: Columbia University, 1919), pp. 61-87; Herbert M. Morais, *Deism in Eighteenth Century America* (New York: Columbia University Press, 1934), chapter 1; G. Adolph Koch, *Religion of the American Enlightenment* (New York: Thomas Y. Crowell Co., 1968), pp. 239-84.

32. Lyman Beecher, *Autobiography I,* ed. by Barbara Cross (Cambridge, Mass.: The Belknap Press of Harvard University Press, 1961), p. 27.

33. Dwight, "The Triumph of Infidelity," *The Connecticut Wits,* ed. by V. L. Parrington (New York: Harcourt, Brace, and Co., 1956). For a cogent explication of the poem, see Lewis Leary, "The Author of *The Triumph of Infidelity*," *New England Quarterly,* XX (September, 1947), 377-85.

34. Ibid., p. 256.

35. See Benjamin Dwight, "Biographical Hints and Parts Respecting the Late Rev. Timothy Dwight, D.D., President of Yale College, written in March to July 1817" (MS in Yale University Library, New Haven).

36. Benjamin Silliman, *A Sketch of the Life and Character of President Dwight* (New Haven, 1817), p. 11.

37. Dwight, *Theology Explained and Defended in a Series of Sermons,* I (Middletown, Conn., 1818), xix.

Chapter III

1. Purcell, *Connecticut in Transition,* p. 136.

2. See Edward Augustus Kendall, *Travels through the Northern Parts of the United States,* I (New York, 1809), 37-44. Dwight also described the Connecticut electoral process in his *Travels,* I, 253-72. He argued that the influence of the Congregational ministry was salutary, helping to continue good men in office.

3. Saladino, "The Economic Revolution," pp. 272-81.

4. Opposition to the control of aristocratic bodies in Connecticut was a particular instance of the international democratic insurgency analyzed by Robert R. Palmer, *Age of Democratic Revolution,* I, passim.

5. Dwight, *Virtuous Rulers a National Blessing: A sermon preached at the General Election, May 12, 1791* (Hartford, 1791), p. 28.

6. Purcell, *Connecticut in Transition,* pp. 62-64.

7. Greene, *Religious Liberty,* pp. 389-92, finds the agitation of dissenters responsible for achieving a more equitable distribution of funds in the finally approved law.

8. *The Connecticut Courant,* March 16, 23, 30, 1795.

9. David Hackett Fischer, *The Revolution of American Conservatism* (New York: Harper & Row, 1965), pp. 1-28.

10. See Saul K. Padover, ed., *Thomas Jefferson on Democracy* (New York: D. Appleton-Century, 1939), pp. 30-32.

11. Richard B. Morris, ed., *The Basic Ideas of Alexander Hamilton* (New York: Pocketbooks, Inc., 1957), pp. 268-72, 275-84.

12. Adrienne Koch, ed., *The American Enlightenment* (New York: G. Braziller, 1965), pp. 182, 192, 195-8, 225.

13. Saladino, "The Economic Revolution," pp. 190-203.

14. Koch, ed., *The American Enlightenment,* p. 216.

15. Ibid., pp. 249, 199.

16. Fischer, *The Revolution of American Conservatism,* pp. 29-72.

17. See Hector St. John De Crevecoeur, *Letters from an American Farmer* (New York: New American Library, 1963), pp. 27-159.

18. Dwight, *Greenfield Hill*, 11. 138-40, 154-57, 307-10.

19. Ibid., 11. 711-12, 721-22, 741-44; 5. 87-96, 199, 215-32, 235-40, 247.

20. Ibid., 6. 31, 49-52, 73-8, 84-5, 101-2, 287-92, 339-42, 352, 361-2, 369-70, 435-8, 457-60.

21. William K. Bottorf, *American Poems*, ed. by Elihu Hubbard Smith (Gainesville, Fla.: Scholars' Facsimiles and Reprints, 1966), pp. 79-80.

22. Dwight to Humphreys, December 18, 1799 (MS in Yale University Library, New Haven), emphasis author's.

23. *The New-Haven Gazette and Connecticut Magazine*, April 12, 1787.

24. Ibid., March 1, 1787.

25. *American Museum*, IV (July, 1788), 30-33.

Chapter IV

1. Jonathan Edwards, "Personal Narrative," *Representative Selections*, ed. by Clarence Faust and Thomas H. Johnson (New York: Hill and Wang, Inc., 1935), pp. 57-59.

2. Ibid., p. 354, emphasis author's.

3. Ibid., "Freedom of the Will," pp. 282-92. Edwards considers the voluntary nature of sin in "The Justice of God in the Damnation of Sinners," ibid., p. 115.

4. William Buell Sprague, *Annals of the American Pulpit*, I (New York, 1857), 433-34. William Ellery Channing, *Works* (Boston, 1888), p. 425, who had heard Hopkins, assessed his preaching as labored and uninspiring. However, he acknowledged Hopkin's intellectual ability and influential views on the subject of "universal benevolence." Richard D. Birdsall, "Ezra Stiles Versus the New Divinity Men," *American Quarterly*, XVII (Summer, 1965), attempts to refute the commonly held opinion that Hopkins and other New Divinity preachers were unpopular. But he confuses their influence in the ministry with their pulpit appeal. Birdsall also obscures stylistic difference within the New Divinity and even classes Timothy Dwight with the Edwardians. Contrary to his thesis, the moralism of the Second

Great Awakening was not the product of Consistent Calvinism, but of a new moderate movement led by Dwight.

5. Samuel Hopkins, *Works,* I (Boston, 1852), 23.

6. Ibid., I, 36.

7. Ibid., I, 111.

8. Sprague, *Annals,* I, 433-34.

9. Hopkins, *Works,* I, 263.

10. Ibid., p. 274.

11. See Conrad Cherry, *The Theology of Jonathan Edwards, A Reappraisal* (Garden City, New York: Anchor Books, 1966), pp. 44-55. The author exhaustively analyzes the Calvinism of Edwards, distinguishing it from the total subjectivity of Antinomianism.

12. Sprague, *Annals,* I, 411.

13. Ibid., p. 412.

14. Joseph Bellamy, *Works,* I (Boston, 1853), 156, 564.

15. Ibid., p. 561.

16. Ibid., p. 168.

17. Ibid., p. 564, emphasis mine.

18. Sprague, *Annals,* I, 561-64. Two nineteenth century evangelicals who participated in the Second Great Awakening provided Sprague with this assessment of John Smalley. Calvin Chapin was a revivalist deeply involved in the promotionalist benevolent movement. He played a "prominent part" in the formation of the American Bible Society and was one of the five men who organized the American Board of Commissioners for Foreign Missions. Chapin also collaborated with Lyman Beecher in the 1813 founding of the Connecticut Moral Society. The other minister, Royal Robbins, had been a student of Timothy Dwight. A prolific writer, he devoted himself exclusively to practical, non-controversial subjects. Both of these men were comfortable with evangelical activism and obviously out of sympathy with Consistent Calvinism. See Franklin Bowditch Dexter, *Yale Biographies and Annals* (New York: Henry Holt and Co., 1907), IV, 592-95; VI, 53-58.

19. Ferm, "Edwards the Younger," p. 177.

20. Ibid., pp. 172, 182.

21. One of Connecticut's most ardent New Divinity men was Benjamin Trumbull. Sprague's correspondents recall him as an "exceedingly zealous disputant" who preached abstract doctrine in a "lugubrious" manner. *Annals,* I, 586-89. He was a contemporary of Smalley, and like him, a poor revivalist. An active participant in the Congregational establishment, he was

commissioned to write the official ecclesiastical history of Connecticut. See *Records of the General Association Colony of Connecticut,* particular 1790, '97, '98.

22. Sprague, *Annals,* I, 553.

23. Ibid., II, 88-9.

24. Ibid., 38; Strong's parish enjoyed extensive revivals in 1794, 1798-99, 1808, and 1815. See pp. 34-9 for evaluations of his ministry.

25. See the autobiography which prefaces Nathanael Emmons, *Works,* I, ed. by Jacob Ide (Boston, 1842), xvii.

26. Ibid., p. xxxi.

27. Emmons, *Works,* III (Boston, 1860), 112.

28. Ibid., pp. 105-06.

29. Ibid., pp. 106, 112. Edwards A. Park, Memoir of Nathanael Emmons, *Works,* I, ed. by Jacob Ide (Boston, 1861), 375, 383.

30. Emmons mentions three revivals in his congregation. The only sizeable one, however, was the first, which had spilled over from a neighboring parish. A fourth revival occurred in 1827, shortly after he had relinquished his pulpit to a young colleague. Jacob Ide, the minister of a nearby town, who wrote a memoir to the first edition of Emmons' Works, remembered his friend more as an effective guardian of orthodoxy than as a revival preacher. See *Works,* 1842 ed., xxxviii, lxxviii-ix; Park, *Memoir,* 352.

31. Park, *Memoir,* p. 354.

32. Harriet Beecher Stowe, *Oldtown Folks* (Cambridge, Mass.: Belknap Press of Harvard University Press), p. 403. This work is a fictionalized account of the late eighteenth century transition in the New England theology from Consistent Calvinism to a warmer and more confident evangelical faith. Stowe portrays Emmons as a Calvinistic grotesque, giving him the name of Dr. Stern. She was a personal friend of Congregational theologian Edwards A. Park, and probably gained much of her knowledge of Emmons from him. Park was the most knowledgeable person in the life and theology of Nathanael Emmons. See Charles H. Foster, *The Rungless Ladder: Harriet Beecher Stowe and New England Puritanism* (Durham, N.C.: Duke University Press, 1954), p. 97.

33. Quoted in Raymond B. Culver, *Horace Mann and Religion in the Massachusetts Public Schools* (New Haven: Yale University Press, 1929), pp. 225, 228.

34. See, for example, *Massachusetts Missionary Magazine,*
I (1803), 269-72 and IV (1806-07), 62-63.

35. Ibid., V (1807-08), 223-24.

36. Ibid., II (1804-05), 22, emphasis author's.

37. Ibid., I (1803-04), 23.

38. Beecher, *Autobiography,* I, 119.

39. Dwight to Dr. Ryland, March 16, 1805 (MS in Yale
University Library, New Haven).

Chapter V

1. For a biography of Dwight which concentrates on his
career as a teacher, see Charles E. Cuningham, *Timothy Dwight*
(New York: McMillan Co., 1942).

2. Dwight, *The True Means of Establishing Public Happiness* (New Haven, 1795), pp. 14, 35-37.

3. Dwight, *Travels,* II, 238, 334; III, 64-66; IV, 403, 407.

4. Ibid., I, 336, 338.

5. Ibid., II, 238-40. Dwight regarded New York state as an
appendage of New England, subject to the strong influence of its
institutions. Ibid., III, 266. His observations on the migration
of New Englanders and the spread of their culture into New
York have been corroborated by modern historical scholarship.
See Whitney Cross, *The Burned-Over District* (New York:
Harper & Row, 1950).

6. My discussion of supernatural rationalism draws from
Conrad Wright, *The Liberal Christians* (Boston: Beacon Press,
1970), pp. 1-21.

7. See Cuningham, *Timothy Dwight,* pp. 43-50, for an
explanation of Dwight's eye affliction. In an essay for the Connecticut Academy of Arts and Sciences, of which he was a
founder, Dwight made empirical use of his condition to postu-
late a hypothesis about the relationship of light to the optic
nerve. This piece is a fine example of his familiarity with scientific method. See Dwight, "On Light," *Memoirs of the Connecticut Academy of Arts and Sciences,* I (New Haven, 1816),
387-91.

8. Dwight, *Theology Explained and Defended in a Series
of Sermons,* I (Middletown, Conn., 1818), 4-9.

9. Ibid., p. 17.

10. Ibid., pp. 20, 27-31.

11. Ibid., pp. 38-40.

12. Ibid., p. 52.

13. Ibid., III, 440-51.

14. See Elie Halevy, *The Growth of Philosophic Radicalism* (Boston: Beacon Press, 1955), pp. 22-26, 157-62. A good synopsis of Paley's theology, particularly the argument from design, is in Leslie Stephen, *English Thought in the Eighteenth Century*, I (New York: Harcourt, Brace, and World, 1962), 346-66.

15. See David Lewis Daggett, "Dr. Dwight's Observations on Paley's Moral and Political Philosophy, 1807-8" (MS in Yale University Library, New Haven), passim.

16. Ibid., pp. 10, 18.

17. Dwight, *Theology*, I, 107-22.

18. Ibid., p. 249.

19. Ibid., II, 405-06.

20. Ibid., I, 265.

21. Dwight, in fact, was confident that the American nation would ultimately adopt New England's religious culture. See *Travels*, IV, 525.

22. Dwight, *Theology*, II, 29-30.

23. David Lewis Daggett, "Miscellaneous Notes from Doct. Dwight's Remarks, 1807" (MS in Yale University Library, New Haven), p. 25.

24. Dwight, *Theology*, I, 535.

25. See Lyman Beecher, *A Plea for the West* (New York, 1835), especially pp. 11, 13, 14, 21, 23, 31-33, 37, 39, 41, 45, 47-56, 60-63, 69-70, 71-75, 78-79, 81, 83-86, 90, 114, 121, 125.

26. See Ray Allen Billington, *The Protestant Crusade: 1800-1860* (Chicago: Quadrangle Books, 1964), pp. 43-44, 103, 122-25, 132, 137-8, 168, 346.

27. Dwight, *Theology*, II, 18.

28. Ibid., p. 19.

Chapter VI

1. Dwight, *Theology*, II, 560-61.

2. Ibid., p. 584, emphasis author's.

3. Ibid., III, 39-40, emphasis author's.

4. Ibid., p. 40.

5. Ibid., p. 70.

6. See William G. McLoughlin, *Modern Revivalism: Charles Grandison Finney to Billy Graham* (New York: Ronald Press, 1959), pp. 65-121.

7. *Theology*, III, 86, 88.

8. Ibid., pp. 91, 101, 102.

9. William Hart, *A Discourse Concerning the Nature of Regeneration and the Way Wherein it is Wrought, preached at New Haven, September 13, 1741* (New London, 1742), p. 13. Samuel Moody, another Old Calvinist opponent of the Great Awakening, defended the power of means, or preparation for salvation in an essay attacking Joseph Bellamy's evangelical system. See Moody, *An attempt to Point out the fatal and pernicious Consequences of the Rev. Mr. Joseph Bellamy's Doctrines Respecting Moral Evil* (Boston, 1759), p. 14.

10. Moses Hemmenway, *Seven Sermons on the Obligation and Encouragement of the Unregenerate, to Labor for the Meat which endureth to Everlasting Life* (Boston, 1767), p. 49.

11. Ibid., p. 44.

12. Dwight, *Theology*, I, 254.

13. Hemmenway, *Seven Sermons*, pp. 125-26.

14. Jonathan Mayhew, *Striving to Enter in at the Strait Gate explained and inculcated; and the Connexion of Salvation therewith Proved from the Holy Scriptures* (Boston, 1761), p. 48.

15. Dwight, *Theology*, I, 255.

16. Mayhew, *Striving to Enter*, pp. 19-20.

17. Ibid., pp. 76, 83-84.

18. Dwight, *Theology*, IV, 528.

19. Ibid., III, 182-90, 198-99, 218.

20. Ibid., IV, 481.

21. Ibid., V, 219-20.

22. See Charles G. Finney, *Memoirs* (New York, 1876), pp. 81, 86-93, 156; *Lectures on Revivals of Religion* (Cambridge, Mass.: Belknap Press of Harvard University Press, 1960), pp. 105, 145-6, 194-222, 253-76, 279.

23. A lengthy discussion of this problem is in Richard Hofstadter, *Anti-Intellectualism in American Life* (New York: A. A. Knopf, 1966).

24. Beecher, *Autobiography*, I, 29.

25. Daggett, "Miscellaneous Notes," p. 26.

26. Dwight, "The Youth of Nain," *Sermons*, II (New Haven, 1828), p. 194.

27. A former student of Dwight recalled "The Youth of Nain" as the catalyst for at least five revivals. See Charles Augustus Goodrich, *Incidents in the Life of President Dwight* (New Haven, 1831), pp. 126-37.

28. Dwight, *Sermons*, II, 401-18.

29. Ibid., I, iv.

30. Dwight, *Theology*, V, 161.

31. Ibid., I, 161.

32. Ibid., V, 35-40.

33. Ibid., p. 131.

34. Ibid., pp. 131, 143. On March 24, 1970, James Walsh of Central Connecticut State College read a paper before the Connecticut Historical Society entitled, "A Quantitative Study of the Great Awakening in the First Church of Woodbury." His empirical research has led him to conclude that individuals converted during the revivals were almost exclusively members of religious families. Walsh thus verifies the observations of Timothy Dwight.

35. Ibid., p. 136. True to his teaching, Dwight referred often to the joy of conversion and the eternal happiness of the redeemed. On the whole, his *Theology* had a far more reassuring tone than the New Divinity systems. See, for example, III, 262, 407, 432; V, 452-57, 521-30, 535-48.

36. Ibid., III, 374-82.

37. Ibid., IV, 132, 147.

38. Dwight, *A Discourse Occasioned by the Death of His Excellency Jonathan Trumbull, Esq., Governor of the State of Connecticut, and Delivered at the Request of the General Assembly in the Brick Church in New-Haven* (New Haven, 1809), passim.

39. Dwight, *Theology*, IV, 155-57.

40. See Dwight, *A Sermon on Duelling, Preached in the Chapel of Yale College, New Haven, September 9, 1804, and in the Old Church, New York, 1805* (New York, 1805), p. 14.

41. Dwight, *Theology*, IV, 187.

42. Ibid., p. 220.

43. Ibid., p. 60.

44. For an analysis of the development of the Protestant ethic in the thought of three Americans—Cotton Mather, Benjamin Franklin, and Timothy Dwight—see A. Whitney Griswold, "Three Puritans on Prosperity," *New England Quarterly*, VIII (1934), 475-90.

45. Dwight, *Theology*, IV, 429, 439; *Sermons*, II, 27-28; *Travels*, I, 33, 169-73.

46. See Herbert Schneider, *The Puritan Mind* (Ann Arbor: University of Michigan Press, 1958), p. 256.

Chapter VII

1. G. Adolf Koch, *Religion of the American Enlightenment*, pp. 76, 290n, comments on the Federalist conservatism of the veterans' group.

2. Dwight to Huntington, January 31, 1795 (MS in Yale University Library, New Haven).

3. Dwight, "The Nature and Danger of Infidel Philosophy," *Sermons*, I, 360, 365.

4. Ibid., p. 334.

5. Stephen, *History of English Thought in the Eighteenth Century*, I, 70.

6. Dwight, *Sermons*, I, 336.

7. Denison Olmstead, "Analysis of the Character of President Dwight as a Teacher," *Barnard's American Journal of Education*, 1854, p. 583.

8. See Dwight, *Sermons*, I, "On Revelation," 98, 107; "Infidel Philosophy," 333.

9. Dwight, *Sermons*, I, "On Revelation," 103.

10. Ibid., p. 58.

11. [Dwight], "Morpheus," *Mercury and New England Palladium*, November 24, 27, December 8, 11, 15, 1801, and March 2, 5, 9, 1802.

12. Dwight, *Decisions of Questions Discussed by the Senior Class . . . in 1813 and 1814*, ed. by Theodore Dwight (New York, 1833), p. 332.

13. See supra, chapter 2, n. 32.

14. Quoted in Vernon Stauffer, *The New England Clergy and the Bavarian Illuminati* (New York: Columbia University Press, 1919), p. 100.

15. See James King Morse, *Jedidiah Morse: A Champion of New England Orthodoxy* (New York: Columbia University Press, 1949), pp. 230-39.

16. For the following description of the Illuminati, I am indebted to Vernon Stauffer, *The New England Clergy*, passim.

17. Ibid., p. 190.

18. Ibid., p. 194; see also *Dictionary of National Biography*, XVII (Oxford, Oxford University Press, 1921-22, 1937-38), 57-59.

19. For millennial interpretations of the Civil War and Cold War respectively, see Tuveson, *Redeemer Nation*, pp. 188-208; and McLoughlin, *Modern Revivalism*, pp. 508, 510-11.

20. Dwight, *The Duty of Americans at the Present Crisis* (New Haven, 1798), p. 3.

21. Dwight, *A Discourse on Some Events of the Last Century* (New Haven, 1801), p. 54.

22. Ibid., p. 55.

23. Stauffer, *The New England Clergy*, pp. 218, 221.

24. Dwight, *Duty of Americans*, p. 11.

25. Dwight to Morse, June 29, 1797 (MS in Yale University Library, New Haven).

26. Quoted in Stauffer, *The New England Clergy*, pp. 292-93.

27. Dwight, *Duty of Americans*, pp. 20-21, 23, 24-26, emphasis author's.

28. Stauffer, *The. New England Clergy*, p. 30. Theodore Dwight spoke these words in an oration before Soc. of Cincinnati given on the same day of his brother's *Duty of Americans in the Present Crisis*.

29. Dwight to Hillhouse, June 20, 1798 (MS in Yale University Library, New Haven).

30. Dwight to Morse, December [?], 1797 (MS in Yale University Library, New Haven). In an appendix to his 1801 *Discourse on Some Events of the Last Century*, p. 46, he included a character assassination of Ebeling. He conjectured that the German geographer might himself be an Illuminus or Jacobin. If this was the case, his testimony was "foreclosed and destroyed of course."

31. Dwight to Hillhouse, March 1, 1800 (MS Yale University Library, New Haven).

32. Dwight, *A Discourse on Some Events of the Last Century*, pp. 19, 21, 32-4, emphasis author's.

33. Ibid., pp. 35, 37, 44-5.

34. Ibid., p. 61.

35. [Dwight], *Remarks on the Review of Inchiquin's Letters*, pp. iii, 15-19, 171, emphasis author's.

36. Dwight, *A Discourse in Two Parts Delivered July 23, 1812, on the Public Fast* (New Haven, 1812), pp. 5-7, 21-22, 25-26, 30, 38, emphasis author's.

37. Ibid., p. 52.

38. Dwight, *A Discourse in Two Parts Delivered August 20, 1812, on the National Fast* (New York, 1812), pp. 54, 59.

39. Ibid., pp. 55-56.

40. Ibid., p. 51.

41. For a seminal article on the conservative basis of evangelical reformism in nineteenth century America, see Clifford S. Griffin, "Religious Benevolence as Social Control, 1815-1860," *Antebellum Reform*, ed. by David Brion Davis (New York: Harper & Row, 1967), pp. 81-96. The article originally appeared in *Mississippi Valley Historical Review*, XLIV (December, 1957), 423-44.

Chapter VIII

1. *Connecticut Courant*, March 17, 1800.

2. Ibid., May 26, 1800.

3. Ibid., June 23, 1800.

4. Ibid., September 8, 1800.

5. Ibid., October 6, 1800.

6. Quoted in Robert Edson Lee, "Timothy Dwight and the Boston *Palladium*," *New England Quarterly*, XXXV (June, 1962), 231.

7. Dwight to Morse, December 21, 1800 (MS in Yale University Library, New Haven).

8. Theodore Dwight to Morse, December 12, 1800 (MS in Yale University Library, New Haven).

9. Dutton resigned in 1803 to enter a law practice. See Lee, "Dwight and *Palladium*," p. 237.

10. *The Mercury and New England Palladium*, March 13, 1800.

11. Ibid., January 16, 1801.

12. Ibid., March 31, 1801.

13. Ibid., April 17, May 8, 1801.

14. Ibid., May 8, 1801.

15. See Dwight, *Decisions*, ed. by Theodore Dwight, passim; and Ralph Henry Gabriel, *Religion and Learning at Yale* (New Haven: Yale University Press, 1958), chapter four, passim.

16. Benjamin Silliman, "Diary" (MS" (MS in Yale University Library, New Haven).

17. *American Mercury*, September 13, 1804.

18. Ibid., July 26, 1804, August 1, 1805. See also Franklin B. Dexter, *Student Life at Yale College under the First President Dwight* (Worcester, Mass.: American Antiquarian Society, 1918), pp. 8-9; Gabriel, *Religion and Learning*, p. 55.

19. A *Mercury* article of September 7, 1804, supported Baptist opposition to certificates of dissent and contended that revivals were plentiful among democratic congregations. The point was that evangelical religion was not political, nor was it exclusively the faith of Federalist Congregationalists.

20. Ibid., March 26, 1801.

21. Ibid., September 11, 1800, emphasis author's.

22. *Connecticut Courant*, March 24, 1800.

23. Dwight, *Decisions*, ed. by Theodore Dwight, pp. 15-26.

24. Richard E. Rubenstein, *Rebels in Eden: Mass Political Violence in the United States* (Boston: Little, Brown and Company, 1970), passim, presents a convincing theory that throughout the course of American history, suppressed groups have periodically revolted in order to achieve self-determination, or independence from governing elites.

25. *American Mercury*, September 25, 1800, emphasis author's.

26. Ibid., April 30, 1801.

27. Ibid., February 3, 10, 24; March 10, 1803.

28. Ibid., November 24, 1803.

29. Ibid., August 4, 1803; November 2, 1805; and "To Friends of Christianity," August 4, 1808.

30. Benjamin Dwight identifies this series as his father's in "Biographical Hints."

31. See William A. Robinson, *Jeffersonian Democracy in New England* (New Haven: Yale University Press, 1916), pp. 112-13; Purcell, *Connecticut in Transition*, pp. 129-32.

32. *Connecticut Courant*, June 15, 1801.

33. Ibid., June 5, 1801.

34. Ibid., January 12, 26, 1801; January 23, 1805, emphasis author's.

35. *American Mercury*, March 19, 1807.

Chapter IX

1. *The Records of the General Association of Ye Colony of Connecticut*, p. 127.

2. Ibid., pp. 153, 160, 165.

3. Ibid., pp. 125, 133, 142, 179, 182.

4. Ibid., p. 179.

5. *American Mercury*, July 2, 1801; June 27, 1805.

6. See Stauffer, *The New England Clergy*, p. 302.

7. See Emmons, *Works*, I, ed. by Jacob Ide, lxxxix.

8. For brief accounts of each minister, revealing theological views, approach in the pulpit, public activities, etc., see Sprague, *Annals*, I, 445-47, 560-64, 584-89, 591-94, 662-68, 672-77; II, 2, 4-5, 34-39, 61-66, 273-75; Dexter, *Yale Biographies*, II, 395-97, 412; III, 334-35.

9. *Connecticut Evangelical Magazine*, I (Hartford, 1800), 278; see also a letter on the sovereignty of God, p. 94.

10. Ibid., p. 157.

11. Ibid., p. 288.

12. Ibid., II (1801-02), editorial preface; pp. 114-15.

13. [Dwight], *An Address to the Emigrants From Connecticut and From New England Generally, in the New Settlements of the United States* (Hartford, 1817), pp. 13, 17, emphasis author's.

14. *Connecticut Evangelical Magazine*, IV (1803-04), 409; VI (1805-06), 365; VII (1806-07), 123.

15. Ibid., VI (1805-06), 384-87, 412-14.

16. *Connecticut Magazine and Religious Intelligencer*, I (1808), editorial preface.

17. Ibid., VI (1813), iii.

18. Arianism is the doctrine that Christ is a lesser figure than God the Father, but greater than natural man. Socinianism views Christ as merely a perfect human being. See Conrad Wright, *The Beginnings of Unitarianism*, pp. 4, 201-02, 209, 210, 216-17; chapter 9, passim.

19. Dwight had complained of Old Calvinist moralism in *The Triumph of Infidelity*. The New Divinity position, which he had accepted at this point in his career, was that Old Calvinists were covert Arminians. In later years, however, as Dwight moved closer to the liberal position on regeneration, he became more the Trinitarian catholic than the Edwardian sectarian. See Sprague, *Annals*, I, 565-70, for the New Divinity view of Old Calvinism.

20. Dwight's articles were chiefly in the area of Christian apologetics. They included: "Lectures on the Evidences of Divine Revelation," June to December, 1810, January to March and June to September, 1811, January, March, May, 1812, June

to August, 1813; and an essay, "On the Manner in which Scriptures are to be Understood," summer, 1816. The *Panoplist* editors identified these commentaries as Dwight's in their last address to their "Patrons and Readers," *Panoplist and Missionary Herald,* XVI (1820), iii.

21. *Panoplist,* I (1805-06), iv-v.

22. Ibid., pp. 203, 399.

23. Ibid., II (1806-07), 166.

24. Ibid., pp. 417, 451.

25. "On the Divine Compassion to Sinners," *Connecticut Evangelical Magazine and Religious Intelligence,* I (1808), 25, 28.

26. Ibid., II (1809), 251.

27. *Panoplist and Missionary Magazine United,* VI (1810-11), 357, 553-54.

28. Ibid., p. iv (editorial address); Dwight, *Travels,* II, 238.

29. See Leonard Woods, *History of Andover Theological Seminary* (Boston, 1885), p. 42.

30. Ibid., p. 43. See also p. 612 for a letter from Woods to Morse. Here he expresses his great admiration for Dwight and asks for "a new edition of Dr. Dwight's sermon on infidel philosophy." We may surmise that Woods was largely motivated by the campaign against liberalism.

31. Dwight to Morse, July 6, 1805, in ibid., p. 454.

32. See Sprague, *Annals,* II, 126-31.

33. Woods, *History of Andover,* pp. 77-81.

34. Ibid., p. 106.

35. Dwight, *A Sermon at the Opening of the Theological Institution in Andover; and at the Ordination of Reverend Eliphalet Pearson, LLD. September 28, 1808* (Boston, 1808), pp. 9, 12-14, 20-22, 24-27.

36. Woods, *History of Andover,* pp. 54-55; *Panoplist,* III (1807-08), 312-13, 315-16.

37. Woods, *History of Andover,* p. 146; Sprague, *Annals,* II, 129, 131.

38. See John Herbert Giltner, "Moses Stuart: 1780-1852" (unpublished Doctor's dissertation, Yale University, 1956), pp. 91, 93-94; Woods, *History of Andover,* p. 150.

39. Giltner, "Moses Stuart," pp. 96, 292, Part II, passim; Woods, *History of Andover,* pp. 152-55.

40. *Panoplist and Missionary Magazine United,* V (1809-10), 250-54, 503.

41. *Acts and Proceedings of the General Association of Connecticut* (1809), p. 11; (1810), p. 12.

42. See Gabriel, *Religion and Learning at Yale*, pp. 74-76; see also Silliman, "Diary," January 5, 1797.

43. See Beecher, *Autobiography*, I, 180-93.

44. *Acts and Proceedings* (1812), p. 32.

45. Ibid. (1813), pp. 10-11; Dwight, *A Discourse in Two Parts Delivered August 20, 1812 on the National Fast*, p. 51.

46. *Connecticut Evangelical Magazine and Religious Intelligencer*, VI (1813), 281-91; VII (1814), 54, 88, 90.

47. *Acts and Proceedings* (1814), p. 10.

48. *American Mercury*, April 30.

49. *Acts and Proceedings* (1815), p. 12.

50. See E. C. Tracy, *Memoir of the Life of Jeremiah Evarts, Esq.* (Boston, 1845), pp. 48-49.

51. *Panoplist and Missionary Magazine United*, IX (1813), 32-38, 368.

52. Ibid., p. 506.

53. Ibid., pp. 33-34.

54. Ibid., XIII (1817), 1, 4-6.

55. *Religious Intelligencer*, August 10, 17, 24, 31; September 7, 14, 1816.

56. See Beecher, *Autobiography*, I, 252-53.

Chapter X

1. *Panoplist and Missionary Magazine United*, XIII (1817), 44.

2. Ibid., p. 185. See William Gribben, "The Legacy of Timothy Dwight: A Reappraisal," *The Connecticut Historical Society Bulletin*, XXXVII (April, 1972), 34, 36, 38-9.

3. See Sidney E. Mead, *Nathaniel W. Taylor 1786-1858: A Connecticut Liberal* (Chicago: University of Chicago Press, 1942), p. 58.

4. *Acts and Proceedings* (1817), p. 14.

5. See McLoughlin, *Modern Revivalism*, p. 67.

6. Beecher, *Autobiography*, II, 68-70.

7. He was eventually ordained as a minister in the Presbyterian church. But he had little formal training, having originally been a lawyer.

8. See Finney, *Lectures on Revivals of Religion*, pp. 13-18, 106-08, 198; McLoughlin, *Modern Revivalism*, p. 34.

9. The New Haven theologians ultimately made their peace with Finney at a convention in New Lebanon, Connecticut in 1827. Nettleton, however, remained intractable. See Finney, *Memoirs*, pp. 202-22; Beecher, *Autobiography*, II, 74-80.

10. Nathaniel W. Taylor, "Concio ad Clerum. A Sermon Delivered in the Chapel of Yale College, September 10, 1828," *Theology in America*, ed. by Sydney Ahlstrom (New York: Bobbs Merrill Co., 1967), pp. 239-42, 214.

11. McLoughlin, *Modern Revivalism*, pp. 64-65.

12. Ahlstrom, *Theology in America*, p. 212.

13. Material in the above paragraph on the continuing conservatism of the benevolent movement is from Clifford Griffin, "Religious Benevolence as Social Control, 1815-1860," *Ante-Bellum Reform*, ed. by David B. Davis, pp. 89-96.

14. Horace Bushnell, *Views of Christian Nurture and Subjects Adjacent Thereto* (Hartford, 1847), pp. 20, 6, 12, 75-76.

15. Ibid., p. 14.

16. Ibid., p. 21.

17. Ibid., pp. 43, 25, 34-35.

18. Ibid., pp. 175-76, 89.

Bibliography

I. Primary

A Note on Manuscripts:

Letters cited in this work are all in the manuscript collections of Yale University's Sterling Library. Since 1942, when Charles Cuningham wrote his exhaustively researched biography of Timothy Dwight, Yale has acquired many important materials previously in the hands of Dwight's descendants and other private parties. Such manuscripts as Benjamin Dwight's "Biographical Hints" of his father's life are now in the Dwight Family Papers. This collection, as well as the papers of such families as Morse, Hillhouse, Baldwin, and Daggett, are fertile sources of information on Dwight's ideas, activities, and associations. While in this study Dwight is not the subject of a biography, he is the central figure. As such, all pertinent information on him can be found at Yale. Manuscripts there are catalogued by individual name. Therefore Dwight's letters and related materials are easy to locate in the aforementioned and other collections.

Another excellent source of Dwight correspondence is the appendix to Leonard Woods' *History of Andover Theological Seminary,* cited below.

UNPUBLISHED CONTEMPORARY MANUSCRIPTS:

Daggett, David Lewis. "Dr. Dwight's observations on Paley's Moral and Political Philosophy 1807-8." Yale University Library MS. New Haven.

———. "Miscellaneous Notes from Doct. Dwight's Remarks. Yale College, 1807." Yale University Library MS. New Haven.

Dwight, Benjamin W. "Biographical Hints and Parts respecting the late Rev. Timothy Dwight, D.D., President of Yale College; written in March to July 1817." Yale University Library MS. New Haven.

Silliman, Benjamin. Five Diaries, 1795-6. Yale University Library MSS. New Haven.

———. "Reminiscences, 1792-1862." Yale University MSS. New Haven.

NEWSPAPERS AND MAGAZINES:

American Mercury

American Museum

Connecticut Courant

Connecticut Evangelical Magazine

Connecticut Evangelical Magazine and Religious Intelligencer

Massachusetts Missionary Magazine

Mercury and New England Palladium

Missionary Herald

New-Haven Gazette and Connecticut Magazine

Panoplist

Panoplist and Missionary Herald

Panoplist and Missionary Magazine United

Religious Intelligencer

Printed Works by Timothy Dwight:

A Dissertation on the History, Eloquence, and Poetry of the Bible, Delivered at the Public Commencement at New Haven. New Haven, 1772.

A Valedictory Address to the Young Gentlemen who Commenced Bachelor of Arts at Yale College, July 25, 1776. New Haven, 1776.

A Sermon preached at Stamford in Connecticut upon the General Thanksgiving, December 18, 1777. Hartford, 1778.

America: or a Poem on the Settlement of the British Colonies; Addressed to the Friends of Freedom and their Country. New Haven, 1780.

A Sermon Preached at Northampton on the twenty-eighth of November, 1781 Occassioned by the Capture of the British Army under the Command of Earl Cornwallis. Hartford, 1781.

"Columbia; a Song." *The Boston Magazine,* December, 1783.

The Conquest of Canaan: A Poem, in Eleven Books. Hartford, 1785.

"The Trial of Faith." *New-Haven Gazette and Connecticut Magazine,* September 21, October 12 and 19, 1786, pp. 245-46, 269-70.

"A Historical Account of the Gothic Gospel." *New-Haven Gazette and Connecticut Magazine,* March 1, 1787.

"An Essay on the judgment of history concerning America." *New-Haven Gazette and Connecticut Magazine,* April 12, 1787.

"Address to the Ministers of the Gospel of every Denomination in the United States." *American Museum,* IV (July, 1788), 30-33.

The Triumph of Infidelity: A Poem. 1788.

"The Friend." Nos. 1-6, *American Museum,* V and VI (January, March, May, June, August, and October, 1789), 69-71, 220-22, 445-47, 564-47, 154-56.

"The Seasons Moralized." *American Museum,* V (March, 1789), 302-303.

"A Song: written in 1771." *American Museum,* V (April, 1789), 408-09.

"A Hymn Sung at the Public Exhibition of the Scholars, Belonging to the Academy at Greenfield." *American Museum,* VI (August, 1789), 171-72.

"Epistle from Dr. Dwight to Col. Humphreys. Greenfield, 1785." *The Miscellaneous Works of Colonel Humphreys.* New York, 1790, pp. 102-10.

"The Critics. A Fable." *Gazette of the United States,* July 13, 1791, p. 2.

Virtuous Rulers a National Blessing: A Sermon, preached at the General Election, May 12, 1791. Hartford, 1791.

A Discourse on the Genuineness and Authenticity of the New Testament, Delivered at New-Haven. September 10, 1793. New York, 1794.

Greenfield Hill: A Poem in Seven Parts. New York, 1794.

The True Means of Establishing Public Happiness: A Sermon delivered on the 7th of July, 1795, before the Connecticut Society of Cincinnati, and published at their request. New Haven, 1795.

Extracts from a Thanksgiving Sermon. *Connecticut Courant,* March 16, 23, 30, 1795.

A Discourse Preached at the Funeral of the Reverend Elizur Goodrich, D.D., Pastor of the Church in Durham, and one of the Members of the Corporation of Yale-College, November 25, 1797. New Haven, 1797.

The Nature and Danger of Infidel Philosophy, exhibited in two Discourses, addressed to the Candidates for the Baccalaureate, in Yale College; September 9, 1797. New Haven, 1798.

The Duty of Americans at the present Crisis, Illustrated in a Discourse, Preached on the fourth of July, 1798, at the request of the Citizens of New-Haven. New Haven, 1798.

A Discourse Delivered at New-Haven, February 22, 1800 on the Character of George Washington, Esq., at the Request of the Citizens. New Haven, 1800.

!'An Extract from 'The Retrospect,' " Mercury and New-England Palladium, January 3, 1801.

A Discourse on Some Events of the Last Century, delivered in the Brick Church in New-Haven on Wednesday, January 7, 1801. New Haven, 1801.

"To the Farmers and Mechanics of New-England." Mercury and New-England Palladium, May 12-June 5, cury and New-England Palladium, May 12-June 5, 1801.

"Farmer Johnson's Political Catechism." Mercury and New-England Palladium, March 31, April 3, 14, 17, May 8, 1801.

"Morpheus." Mercury and New-England Palladium, November 24, 27, December 8, 11, 15, 1801 and March 2, 5, 9, 1802.

"Brief Account of the revival of religion now prevailing in Yale College." Connecticut Evangelical Magazine, III (July, 1802), 30-3.

A Sermon on the Death of Mr. Ebenezer Grant Marsh, Senior-Tutor and Professor Elect of Languages and Ecclesiastical History in Yale College, who died November 16, 1803, in the 27th year of his Age. Hartford, 1804.

A Sermon on Duelling, preached in the Chapel of Yale College, New-Haven, September 9, 1804, and in the Old Presbyterian Church, New-York, January 21, 1805. New York, 1805.

A Sermon Preached at the Opening of the Theological Institution in Andover; and at the Ordination of Reverend Eliphalet Pearson, LL.D., September 28, 1808. Boston, 1808.

A Discourse Occasioned by the Death of His Excellency Jonathan Trumbull, Esq., Governor of the State of Connecticut, and Delivered at the Request of the General Assembly in the Brick Church in New-Haven. New Haven, 1809.

The Charitable Blessed. A Sermon Preached in the First Church in New-Haven, August 8, 1810. New Haven, 1810.

A Statistical Account of the Towns and Parishes in the State of Connecticut. New Haven, 1811.

A Discourse in two Parts Delivered July 23, 1812; on the Public Fast in the Chapel of Yale College. New Haven, 1812.

A Discourse in two Parts Delivered August 20, 1812 on the National Fast, in the Chapel of Yale College. New York, 1812.

"Lectures on the Evidences of Divine Revelation." *Panoplist and Missionary Magazine United*, June-December, 1810, January-March and June-September, 1811, January, March, May, 1812, June-August, 1813.

A Sermon in Boston, September 11, 1813, Before the American Board of Commissioners for Foreign Missions at their Fourth Annual Meeting. Boston, 1813.

Remarks on the Review of Inchiquin's Letters, published in the Quarterly Review, addressed to the Right Honourable George Canning, Esq., By an Inhabitant of New-England. Boston, 1815.

"Observations on Language." *Memoirs of the Connecticut Academy of Arts and Sciences*, I (1816), 365-86.

"Observations on Light." *Memoirs of the Connecticut Academy of Arts and Sciences,* I (1816), 387-91.

"Summary account of the Church of Christ in Yale College." *Religious Intelligencer,* June 8, 1816, pp. 30-31.

"Observations on the Present State of Religion in the World." *Religious Intelligencer,* August 10, 17, 24, 31, September 7, 14, 1816.

"On the Manner in which the Scriptures are to be understood." *Panoplist and Missionary Magazine United,* Vol. XII (1816).

An Address to the Emigrants from Connecticut, and From New-England Generally, in the New Settlements in the United States. Hartford, 1817.

Theology Explained and Defended in a Series of Sermons —With a Memoir of the Life of the Author [by Sereno E. Dwight]. 5 volumes. Middletown, 1818.

Travels in New-England and New-York. 4 volumes. New Haven, 1822.

Sermons. 2 volumes. New Haven, 1828.

President Dwight's Decisions of Question, Discussed by the Senior Class in Yale College in 1813 and 1814. Edited by Theodore Dwight. New York, 1833.

PRIMARY PRINTED WORKS:

Beecher, Lyman. *A Plea for the West.* New York, 1835.

Bellamy, Joseph. *Works.* Volumes I and II. Boston, 1853.

Bushnell, Horace. *Views of Christian Nurture and of Subjects Adjacent Thereto.* Hartford, 1847.

Channing, William Ellery. *Works.* Boston: American Unitarian Association, 1888.

Crevecoeur, Hector Saint Jean de. *Letters From an American Farmer.* New York: E. P. Dutton and Company, 1912.

Edwards, Jonatha, the Younger. *Works.* Volume II. Andover, 1842.

Emmons, Nathanael. *Works*. Volume I. Edited by Jacob Ide. Boston, 1842, 1861.

————. *Works*. Volumes I and III. Edited by Edwards A. Park. Boston, 1860.

Finney, Charles Grandison. *Lectures on Revivals of Religion*. Edited by William G. McLoughlin. Cambridge, Mass.: Belknap Press of Harvard University Press, 1960.

Hart, William. *A Discourse Concerning the Nature of Regeneration and the Way Wherein it is Wrought, preached at New-Haven September 13, 1741*. New London, 1742.

————. *A Letter to the Reverend Samuel Hopkins*. New London, 1770.

Hemmenway, Moses. *A Vindication of the Power, Obligation and Encouragement of the unregenerate to attend the Means of Grace*. Boston, 1772.

————. *Seven Sermons on the Obligation and Encouragement of the Unregenerate, to labor for the Meat which endureth to Everlasting life*. Boston, 1767.

Hopkins, Samuel. *Works*. Volumes I, II, and III. Boston, 1852.

Mayhew, Jonathan. *Striving to Enter in at the Strait Gate explained and inculcated; and the connexion of Salvation therewith Proved from the Holy Scriptures*. Boston, 1761.

Moody, Samuel. *An Attempt to point out the fatal and pernicious Consequences of the Rev. Mr. Joseph Bellamy's Doctrines Respecting Moral Evil*. Boston, 1759.

Taylor, Nathaniel W. "Concio ad Clerum. A Sermon Delivered in the Chapel of Yale College, September 18, 1828." *Theology in America*. Edited by Sydney Ahlstrom. New York: Bobbs Merrill Company, 1967, pp. 213-49.

EDITED COLLECTIONS OF PRIMARY WORKS:

Faust, Clarence and Thomas H. Johnson. *Jonathan Edwards: Representative Selections.* New York: Hill and Wang, 1935.

Koch, Adrienne. *The American Enlightenment.* New York: G. Braziller, 1965.

Miller, Perry and Thomas H. Johnson. *The Puritans.* 2 volumes. New York: Harper and Row, 1963.

Morris, Richard. *The Basic Ideas of Alexander Hamilton.* New York: Pocket Books, 1958.

Padover, Saul K. *Thomas Jefferson on Democracy.* New York: D. Appleton Century Company, 1939.

Parrington, Vernon Lewis. *The Connecticut Wits.* New York: Harcourt, Brace, and Company, 1956.

Smith, Elihu Hubbard. *American Poems (1793).* Re-edited by William K. Bottorf. Gainesville, Fla.: Scholars' Facsimiles and Reprints, 1966.

MEMOIRS:

Beecher, Lyman. *Autobiography.* 2 volumes. Edited by Barbara M. Cross. Cambridge, Mass.: Belknap Press of Harvard University Press, 1961.

Finney, Charles Grandison. *Memoirs.* New York, 1876.

Goodrich, S. G. *Recollections of a Lifetime.* New York, 1856.

Park, Edwards A. "A Memoir of Nathanael Emmons; with Sketches of his friends and pupils." *Works.* Edited by Edwards A. Park. Boston, 1860.

Sprague, William Buell. *Annals of the American Pulpit.* Volumes I and II. New York, 1857.

Tracy, E. C. *Memoir of the Life of Jeremiah Evarts.* Boston, 1845.

Woods, Leonard. *History of Andover Theological Seminary.* Boston, 1885.

PROCEEDINGS:

The Records of the General Association of Ye Colony of Connecticut, 1738-1799. Hartford, 1888.

Acts and Proceedings of the General Association of Connecticut. Hartford, 1800-1817.

PUBLISHED SKETCHES OF DWIGHT BY CONTEMPORARIES:

Anon. "Biographical Memoir of the Rev. Timothy Dwight." *Port Folio,* Volume IV, 355-369.

[Goodrich, Charles A.] *Incidents in the Life of President Dwight, Illustrative of his Moral and Religious Character; Designed for young Persons.* New Haven, 1831.

Olmstead, Denison. "Analysis of President Dwight as a teacher." *American Journal of Education,* V (September, 1858).

Silliman, Benjamin. *A Sketch of the Life and Character of President Dwight, delivered as a eulogium in New-Haven, February 12, 1817, before the academic body of Yale College, composed of Senatus, academicus, faculty, and students.* New Haven, 1817.

Spring, Gardiner. *An Oration, pronounced in the evening of the 5th February before the alumni of Yale College, resident in the City of New York, in commemoration of their late President, Timothy Dwight, D.D., LL.D.* New York, 1817.

II. Secondary

Published:

Ahlstrom, Sydney, ed. *Theology in America.* New York: Bobbs Merrill Company, 1967.

Akers, Charles W. *Called Unto Liberty: A Life of Jonathan Mayhew 1720-1766.* Cambridge, Mass.: Harvard University Press, 1964.

Bailyn, Bernard. *Ideological Origins of the American Revolution.* Cambridge, Mass.: Belknap Press of Harvard University Press, 1967.

_____ . *Origins of American Politics.* New York: Alfred A. Knopf, 1968.

_____ . "Political Experience and Enlightenment Ideas in Eighteenth Century America." *American Historical Review,* LXXVII (1962), 339-51.

Baldwin, Alice. *The New England Clergy and the American Revolution.* Durham, N.C.: Duke University Press, 1928.

Billington, Ray Allen. *The Protestant Crusade, 1800-1860, A Study of the Origins of American Nativism.* New York: Macmillan, 1938.

Birdsall, Richard D. "Ezra Stiles Versus the New Divinity Men." *American Quarterly,* XVII (Summer, 1965), 248-57.

_____ . "The Second Great Awakening and the New England Social Order." *Church History,* XXXIX (September, 1970), 345-64.

Boorstin, Daniel. *The Americans: The Colonial Experience.* New York: Alfred A. Knopf, 1958.

_____ . *The Lost World of Thomas Jefferson.* Boston: Beacon Press, 1960.

Bridenbaugh, Carl. *Mitre and Sceptre. Transatlantic Faiths, Ideas, Personalities, and Politics 1689-1775.* Oxford: Oxford University Press, 1962.

Buchanan, Lewis E. "The Ethical Ideas of Timothy Dwight." *Research Studies of the State College of Washington,* XIII (September, 1945), 185-99.

Bushman, Richard L. *From Puritan to Yankee: Character and the Social Order in Connecticut, 1690-1765.* Cambridge, Mass.: Harvard University Press, 1967.

Cherry, Conrad. *The Theology of Jonathan Edwards: A Reappraisal.* Garden City, N.Y.: Anchor Books, 1966.

Cross, Whitney R. *The Burned-Over District*. New York: Harper and Row, 1950.

Culver, Raymond B. *Horace Mann and Religion in the Massachusetts Public Schools*. New Haven: Yale University Press, 1929.

Cuningham, Charles. *Timothy Dwight 1752-1817: A Biography*. New York: Macmillan, 1942.

Davis, David Brion, ed. *Antebellum Reform*. New York: Harper and Row, 1967.

Dexter, Franklin Bowditch. *Student Life at Yale College under the First President Dwight*. Worcester, Mass.: American Antiquarian Society, 1918.

————— . *Yale Biographies and Annals*. Volumes I-VI. New York: Henry Holt and Company, 1907.

Fischer, David Hackett. *The Revolution of American Conservatism*. New York: Harper and Row, 1965.

Fisher, G. P. *Life of Benjamin Silliman*. 2 volumes. New York, 1866.

Foster, Charles H. *The Rungless Ladder: Harriet Beecher Stowe and New England Puritanism*. Durham, N.C.: Duke University Press, 1954.

Foster, Frank Hugh. *A Genetic History of the New England Theology*. Chicago: University of Chicago Press, 1907.

Fox, Dixon Ryan. "Protestant Counter-Reformation in America." *New York History*, XVI (January, 1935), 19-35.

Fromm, Erich. *Escape From Freedom*. New York: Holt, Rinehart, and Winston, 1941.

Gabriel, Ralph Henry. *The Course of American Democratic Thought*. New York: Ronald Press, 1956.

————— . *Religion and Learning at Yale*. New Haven: Yale University Press, 1958.

Gaustad, Edwin S. *The Great Awakening in New England*. New York: Harper and Brothers, 1957.

Gerth, H. H. and C. Wright Mills, eds. *From Max Weber: Essays in Sociology.* New York: Oxford University Press, 1958.

Goen, Charles C. *Revivalism and Separatism in New England, 1740-1800.* New Haven: Yale University Press, 1962.

Greene, Maria Louise. *The Development of Religious Liberty in Connecticut.* Boston: Houghton, Mifflin and Company, 1905.

Gribben, William. "The Legacy of Timothy Dwight: A Reappraisal." *The Connecticut Historical Society Bulletin,* XXXVII (April, 1972), 33-41.

Griswold, A. Whitney. "Three Puritans on Prosperity." *New England Quarterly,* VIII (1934), 475-90.

Halevy, Elie. *The Growth of Philosophic Radicalism.* Boston: Beacon Press, 1955.

Haroutunian, Joseph. *Piety Versus Moralism.* New York: Henry Holt and Company, 1932.

Heimert, Alan. *Religion and the American Mind from the Great Awakening to the Revolution.* Cambridge, Mass.; Harvard University Press, 1966.

Hofstadter, Richard. *Anti-Intellectualism in American Life.* New York: Alfred A. Knopf, 1966.

_____ . *The Paranoid Style in American Politics.* New York: Alfred A. Knopf, 1965.

Howard, Leon. *The Connecticut Wits.* Chicago: University of Chicago Press, 1943.

Jameson, J. Franklin. *The American Revolution Considered as a Social Movement.* Princeton, N.J.: Princeton University Press, 1926.

Jensen, Merrill. "Democracy and the American Revolution." *The Huntington Library Quarterly,* XX (1957), 321-40.

Keller, Charles Roy. *The Second Great Awakening in Connecticut.* New Haven: Yale University Press, 1942.

Kendall, Edward Augustus. *Travels through the Northern Part of the United States.* Volume I. New York,
1809.

Koch, G. Adolph. *Religion of the American Enlightenment.* New York: Thomas Y. Crowell Company,
1968.

Leary, Lewis. "The Author of *The Triumph of Infidelity.*" *New England Quarterly,* XX (September,
1947), 377-85.

Lee, Robert Edson. "Timothy Dwight and the Boston
Palladium." *New England Quarterly,* XXXV
(June, 1962), 229-39.

McLoughlin, William G. "Pietism and the American
Character." *American Quarterly,* XVII (1965),
163-86.

————. *Modern Revivalism: Charles Grandison Finney
to Billy Graham.* New York: Ronald Press, 1959.

Marx, Leo. *The Machine in the Garden. Technology and
the Pastoral Ideal in America.* New York: Oxford
University Press, 1967.

Mead, Sidney Earl. *The Lively Experiment.* New York:
Harper and Row, 1963.

————. *Nathaniel W. Taylor 1786-1858: A Connecticut
Liberal.* Chicago: University of Chicago Press,
1942.

————. "Through and Beyond the Lines." *Journal of
Religion,* XLVIII (July, 1968), 274-88.

Miller, Perry. *Errand into the Wilderness.* New York:
Harper and Row, 1964.

————. " 'Preparation for Salvation' in Seventeenth
Century New England." *Journal of the History
of Ideas,* IV (June, 1943), 253-86.

————. *The New England Mind From Colony to Province.* Boston: Beacon Press, 1961.

Morgan, Edmund S. "Ezra Stiles and Timothy Dwight." *Proceedings of the Massachusetts Historical Society*, LXXII (1957-60), 109.

_____ . *The Gentle Puritan: A Life of Ezra Stiles 1727-1795.* New Haven: Yale University Press, 1962.

_____ . Review of Alan Heimert, *Religion and the American Mind* (Harvard University Press). *William and Mary Quarterly*, XXIV (1967), 454-59.

Morse, James King. *Jedidiah Morse: A Champion of New England Orthodoxy.* New York: Columbia University Press, 1949.

Murdock, Kenneth B. *Literature and Theology in Colonial New England.* Cambridge, Mass.: Harvard University Press, 1949.

Neibuhr, H. Richard. *The Kingdom of God in America.* New York: Harper and Row, 1937.

Palmer, Robert R. *Age of Democratic Revolution.* Volume I. Princeton, N.J.: Princeton University Press, 1959.

Persons, Stow. *American Minds.* New York: Henry Holt and Company, 1958.

Purcell, Richard J. *Connecticut in Transition: 1775-1818. Edited by Hugh Brockunier. Middletown, Conn.: Wesleyan University Press, 1963.*

Ravitz, Abe C. "Timothy Dwight's Decisions." New England Quarterly, XXXI (December, 1958), 514-19.

Robinson, William A. *Jeffersonian Democracy in New England.* New Haven: Yale University Press, 1916.

Rubenstein, Richard E. *Rebels in Eden: Mass Political Violence in the United States.* Boston: Little, Brown and Company, 1970.

Schneider, Herbert. *The Puritan Mind.* Ann Arbor, Mich.: University of Michigan Press, 1958.

Silverman, Kenneth. *Timothy Dwight.* New York: Twayne Publishers, 1969.

Simpson, Alan. *Puritanism in Old and New England.* Chicago: University of Chicago Press, 1955.

Sprague, William Buell. "Life of Timothy Dwight." *Library of American Biography.* Edited by Jared Sparks. Boston, 1845.

Stauffer, Vernon. *The New England Clergy and the Bavarian Illuminati.* New York: Columbia University Press, 1919.

Stephen, Sir Leslie. *English Thought in the Eighteenth Century.* 2 volumes. New York: Harcourt, Brace, and World, 1962.

Stillinger, Jack. "Dwight's *Triumph of Infidelity:* Text and Interpretation." *Studies in Bibliography,* XV (1962), 259-66.

Stowe, Harriet Beecher. *The Minister's Wooing.* New York, 1859.

————. *Oldtown Folks.* Edited by Henry May. Cambridge, Mass.: Belknap Press of Harvard University Press, 1962.

Tolles, Frederick B. "The American Revolution Considered as a Social Movement: A Re-Evaluation." *American Historical Review,* LX (1954), 1-12.

Trinterud, Leonard J. *The Forming of an American Tradition: a Re-examination of Colonial Presbyterianism.* Philadelphia, Pa.: The Westminster Press, 1949.

Tuveson, Ernest Lee. *Redeemer Nation.* Chicago: University of Chicago Press, 1966.

Tyler, Moses Coit. *Three Men of Letters.* New York, 1895.

Welling, James C. *Connecticut Federalism, or Aristocratic Politics in a Social Democracy.* New York, 1890.

Wright, Conrad. *The Beginnings of Unitarianism in America.* Boston: Beacon Press, 1966.

————, ed. *The Liberal Christians.* Boston: Beacon Press, 1970.

Unpublished

Ferm, J. Robert Livingston. "Jonathan Edwards the Younger and the American Reformed Tradition." Unpublished Doctor's dissertation, Yale University, 1958.

Giltner, John Herbert. "Moses Stuart: 1780-1852." Unpublished Doctor's dissertation, Yale University, 1956.

Saladino, Gaspare J. "The Economic Revolution in Late Eighteenth Century Connecticut." Unpublished Doctor's dissertation, University of Wisconsin, 1964.

Walsh, James. "A Quantitative Study of the Great Awakening in the First Church of Woodbury [Connecticut]." A paper read before the Connecticut Historical Association, Hartford, March 24, 1970.

Index